McCLANE'S FIELD GUIDE

TO SALTWATER FISHES

OF NORTH AMERICA

McCLANE'S

Field Guide to

Saltwater Fishes

OF

NORTH AMERICA

EDITED BY

A. J. McClane

A project of The Gamefish Research Association

ILLUSTRATIONS BY
Dr. Frances Watkins
and Richard E. Younger

An Owl Book

Henry Holt and Company
New York

Published by Henry Holt and Company, Inc.,
115 West 18th Street, New York, New York 10011.
Published in Canada by Fitzhenry & Whiteside Limited,
195 Allstate Parkway, Markham, Ontario L3R 4T8.

Library of Congress Cataloging-in-Publication Data
McClane, Albert Jules, 1922–
McClane's Field guide to saltwater fishes of North America
Portions originally published in McClane's standard fishing encyclopedia
and international angling guide (1965) and McClane's new standard fishing
encyclopedia and international angling guide (1974).
Includes index.
1. Marine fishes. 2. Fishes—North America. I. Gamefish Research
Association. II. Title. III. Title: Field guide to saltwater fishes of
North America.
QL625.M32 1978 597'.09207 77-14417
ISBN 0-8050-0733-4 (An Owl book: pbk.)

Henry Holt books are available at special discounts
for bulk purchases for sales promotions, premiums,
fund-raising, or educational use. Special editions
or book excerpts can also be created to specification.

For details contact:

Special Sales Director
Henry Holt and Company, Inc.
115 West 18th Street
New York, New York 10011

Printed in Hong Kong

10 9 8 7

CONTENTS

PREFACE

The source volume of this guidebook, *McClane's New Standard Fishing Encyclopedia* (Holt, Rinehart and Winston, 1974), itself a revised and expanded edition of *McClane's Standard Fishing Encyclopedia* (Holt, Rinehart and Winston, 1965), is a book of 1,156 two-column pages, hardly of a size suitable for field identification. To meet the demand for a handy "tackle box" reference, descriptions of the most important game-, food-, and foragefish found in North American waters have been divided into two small volumes, *McClane's Field Guide to Saltwater Fishes of North America* and *McClane's Field Guide to Freshwater Fishes of North America*. Much of this material has again been revised with respect to new information concerning life histories and the inevitable changes in scientific names. To make fish identification easier, those fish portraits that appeared in black and white in the encyclopedia have been replaced with color.

These field guides are designed for the angler, and while the family arrangement generally follows scientific order, exceptions were made to relate the text to the illustrations or to group species that are similar in appearance for quick comparison. Thus, in the freshwater guide a jawless fish (Class Agnatha), the lamprey, will be found adjacent to the American eel, one of the bony fishes (Class Osteichthyes); to an angler discovering a dead lamprey in the stream, which happens with some frequency, the "eellike" form is primary and the class relationship secondary.

It is not practical to include every freshwater and saltwater species endemic to North America in a tackle-box-size field guide, but all those of angling importance are encompassed. In our continental waters there are about 200 minnows and 136 sculpins, for example, and most of these are of very local distribution. However, many of the "minor" fishes that are of special interest to the angler, and those having an especially wide range, are included. Anadromous species, such as the salmon and shad, are treated as freshwater fish, while certain marine species that enter freshwater or have become established as inland populations, such as the tarpon and snook, appear in both volumes with annotations.

The following authors contributed in part or whole to descriptions of the saltwater fish species: Frederick H. Berry, Dr. John C. Briggs, Frederick Brockman, Dr. Robert H. Gibbs, Henry Lyman, Frank J. Mather III, A. J. McClane, James E. Morrow, H. Geoffrey Moser, Dr. John Rayner, Luis Rivas, and Dr. Donald deSylva.

Special thanks are due to Mr. John Rybovitch of The Gamefish Research Association and Mrs. Wayne Hicklin for their financial support in making the color plates possible. A prorated share of the sales of these guides will be contributed to funding the association's ongoing research projects.

The common and scientific names of fishes used in this guide are those recognized by the American Fisheries Society (*Common and Scientific Names of Fishes from the United States and Canada*: 3rd ed., 1970).

GLOSSARY

ADIPOSE FIN A small, fleshy fin without rays located dorsally on the caudal peduncle. It is typical of the salmonids but occurs on other species.

AMMOCETE The larval stage of a lamprey.

ANADROMOUS Any fish that migrates from the sea into freshwater rivers for the purpose of spawning. Some anadromous species are the salmons, striped bass, alewife, and shad. Fishes that migrate in the reverse direction from freshwater into the sea for their spawning are catadromous.

ANAL FIN The unpaired or single fin on the ventral surface of the body.

ANDATE Attached to, or grown together.

ANTERIOR Toward the front; the opposite of posterior.

AXIL The region behind the pelvic or pectoral fin base.

AXILLARY PROCESS An elongate structure at the base of the pelvic or pectoral fins.

BAND A diagonal or oblique marking on a fish's body.

BAR A vertical marking on a fish's body that has more or less straight sides.

BARBEL A threadlike structure or "whisker" near the mouth.

BASIBRANCHIAL TEETH Very small teeth on the basibranchial plate near the base of the tongue.

BRANCHIOSTEGAL RAYS Slender bones in the gill membrane located below the gill cover at the edge of the gill opening.

CANINE TEETH Long, pointed teeth; they may be straight or curved and are often fanglike.

CARDIFORM TEETH Short, pointed teeth in multiple rows.

CATADROMOUS Any fish that migrates from freshwater to the sea for purposes of spawning, as does the American eel. Catadromous is the opposite of anadromous.

CAUDAL Toward the tail or pertaining to the tail.

CAUDAL FIN The tail or tail fin.

CAUDAL PEDUNCLE That portion of a fish's body immediately preceding the tail, from the base of the anal fin to the base of the caudal fin.

CIRCULUS (pl. circuli) One of a series of concentric ridges that form rings or arcs on the scales of fishes.

CONICAL TEETH Short, pointed teeth.

CTENOID SCALES Scales with pointed projections (teeth or ctenii) on their posterior margin. In some species the ctenii are microscopic; in others they are pronounced and make the fish feel rough to the touch.

CYCLOID SCALES Smooth scales with an evenly curved posterior margin.

DORSAL FIN   The prominent fin on the back. Some species have 2 or more dorsal fins; most cods, for example, have 3 dorsal fins.

EMARGINATE   A tail fin that is concavely curved but not definitely forked (such as the tails of trouts).

FALCATE   A tail fin shaped like a sickle (such as the tails of jacks); it is deeply concave, with the middle rays much shorter than the anterior or posterior rays.

FRENUM   The connecting membrane that holds the upper jaw to the snout.

GANOID SCALES   Hard, diamond-shaped scales that occur on the more primitive bony fishes, such as the gars, and on the upturned lobe of the tail in sturgeons and paddlefish.

GAS BLADDER   A membranous structure occurring under the kidney in most but not all fishes, also known as the swim or air bladder. The gas bladder acts as a flotation organ that adjusts the weight of the fish to equalize water displacement so that the fish neither rises nor sinks. It can also serve as a noise-producing organ and acts as a resonator in hearing. Species that do not possess or have only a rudimentary gas bladder, such as the darters or Atlantic mackerel, sink to the bottom if they stop swimming.

GONADS   The reproductive organs of either sex.

HETEROCERCAL   A tail having a long upper lobe and a shorter lower lobe, with the vertebral column extending into the upper lobe. It is typical of sharks.

HOMOCERCAL   A symmetrical tail with lobes of equal length; the vertebral column ends at the base of the tail and does not extend into the upper lobe. It is typical of sunfishes.

INCISIFORM TEETH   Flattened, chisellike teeth.

ISTHMUS   The throat or fleshy area that separates the gill chambers.

KEEL   Scales or tissue which form a sharp ridge.

LATERAL LINE   Pored scales extending from the head along the side of the body usually to the base of the caudal fin. Some species do not have a lateral line, while in others it may be incomplete or branched or may extend into the caudal fin.

LINE   A very narrow marking on a fish's body; it may be oriented in any direction.

LUNATE   A tail that is sickle-shaped but not as deeply concave as falcate. It is typical of the tunas.

MANDIBLE   The lower jaw.

MAXILLARY   Pertaining to or denoting the upper jaw.

MOLARIFORM TEETH   Broad, low, flattened teeth used for grinding and crushing.

NAPE   The back of the "neck" from the occiput to the first ray of the dorsal fin.

NARES   The nostrils.

NUCHAL   Pertaining to the nape.

NUCHAL BAND   A band of color transversing the nape.

OCCIPUT   The back of the head.

OCELLUS   A usually round marking on a fish's body surrounded by a halo of a lighter color.

OMNIVOROUS   Eating both plant and animal foods.

OPERCLE   The large posterior bone of the head covering the gills; also called the gill cover or operculum.

ORBIT   The bony eye socket.

PALATINES   Paired bones on each side of the roof of the mouth.

PALATINE TEETH   Teeth occurring on the palatine bones.

PARR   A young trout or salmon, distinguished by dark vertical blotches, called parr marks, on its sides.

PECTORAL FINS   The anterior paired fins behind the gill openings.

PELAGIC   A fish that spends most of its life close to the surface of the sea, such as the tunas. Fish of pelagic habits are opposed to demersal species, which live close to the bottom, such as the cods.

PELVIC FINS   The posterior paired fins on the ventral surface of the body.

pH   A measure of acidity and alkalinity based on a 0–14 scale. Neutral water has a pH of 7; below 7 acidity increases and above 7 alkalinity increases.

PHARYNX   The alimentary canal between the mouth and the esophagus.

PLACOID SCALES   Dermal denticles, resembling a tooth in structure, that form the rough skin covering of most sharks, skates, and rays.

PLANKTON   Animals that float and drift passively in the water of seas, lakes, and rivers as distinct from animals that are attached to or crawl on the bottom. Plankton are mostly of microscopic size and have a large surface area in relation to their weight. Many crustaceans, some mollusks, a few worms, a variety of small larvae, and minute plants (phytoplankton) compose a plankton population.

PREOPERCLE   The anterior bone of the gill cover; it is found in front of the opercle and behind and below the eye.

PYLORIC CAECA   Dead-end fingerlike projections attached to the intestinal tract just ahead of the stomach.

SPINE   The stiff but sometimes flexible rod that acts as a supporting structure in the fins; it is without cross striations and is unbranched.

SPIRACLE   An opening on the posterior portion of the head, above and behind the eye.

SPOT   A round or nearly round marking on a fish's body.

STRIATED   Marked with narrow lines or grooves that are usually parallel.

STRIPE   A horizontal marking on a fish's body.

SUBTERMINAL MOUTH   A mouth that opens ventrally with the lower jaw closing within the upper jaw.

TERETE   A cylindrical and tapering body with a circular cross section.

THORACIC   Pertaining to the chest or thorax.

TRUNCATE   A tail having a vertical and straight posterior margin, such as the tails of groupers.

TUBERCLES   Hornlike projections on the skin that develop on some species during the breeding season, notably many minnows; sometimes called pearl organs.

VERMICULATIONS   Wormlike color patterns on the skin that occur on species such as the brook trout and Spanish mackerel.

VENTRAL   Relating to the abdomen or underside of the fish; opposed to dorsal.

VILLIFORM TEETH   Small, conical teeth in several rows.

VOMER   A median bone at the front of the roof of the mouth.

YEAR CLASS   The fish spawned in any one calendar year.

ZOOPLANKTON   Protozoa and other animal microorganisms living unattached in water. These include small crustacea such as daphnia and cyclops.

MEASUREMENTS AND IDENTIFICATION OF FISHES

Measurements of a Fish

For various purposes a fish may be measured in different ways. Of primary importance to the angler is the total length because this determines the legality of his catch. However, the fishery biologist may use the fork length, while the ichthyologist may use the standard length in his research operations. In the *Field & Stream* Fishing Contest only the fork length is valid. For identification purposes the angler may also want to measure the depth of body, depth of head, and length of body.

Standard length: Length of the body of a fish from the tip of the snout with the mouth closed to the end of the vertebral column (base of caudal fin).

Fork length: Length of the fish from tip of snout with the mouth closed to tip of the shortest ray of the caudal fin (or to the center of the fin if the tail is not forked).

Total length: The overall length of a fish, measured from the tip of the jaw with the mouth closed and extending to the tip of caudal fin. The caudal rays are sometimes squeezed together to give the greatest overall measurement, but this is of no scientific value.

Depth of body: The greatest body depth measured at right angles to the long axis of the body; the number of times the greatest depth is contained in the standard length.

Depth of head: The depth of the head measured vertically from the occiput ("neck"); the number of times the depth of the head is contained in the length of the head.

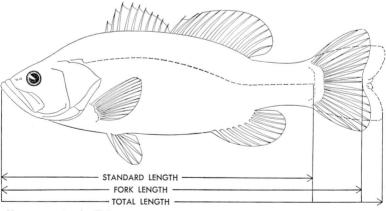

Measurements of a Fish

Scale Counts in Identification

The number of scales on certain parts of a fish's body is a useful aid in identification. The lateral line count is the most important measurement; although it is seldom constant, it will fluctuate within certain limits. In species where the lateral line is incomplete, the number of scale rows above or below the lateral line can be used (see morphology diagram). While it is not practical for the angler in the field to determine counts on finely scaled species of very small fish, particularly without magnification, the method is applicable to species with large scales, such as the sunfishes, herrings, snappers and many of the larger cyprinids (minnows and carps).

In any population of northern spotted bass, for example, the lateral line count varies from 60 to 68 scales. A small percentage will have 59 or 69 lateral line scales and the rare individual will have less or more, but the great majority of northern spotted bass fall within the 60–68 range. This would separate the species from the more finely scaled smallmouth with 69–77. One bass whose scale counts overlap the northern spotted is the northern largemouth, but these are readily separated by the fin ray counts as well as the absence of scales on the interradial membrane at the base of the tail, second dorsal, and anal fins on the largemouth.

Scale counts should be made on a dry specimen. If the bass is large, it's fairly easy to count the pored scales in the lateral line while it's still fresh. The above and below lateral line scale counts run on an angle with the first dorsal and first anal spines as reference points. To make certain that you follow the body contours, use the edge of a sheet of paper as a guide in paralleling the correct sequence from the spines to the lateral line. It helps to raise or move each scale as you count and this can be done with a thin-bladed penknife; however, don't "pick" at the scales too much or they will pop out and confuse any recounting. The scales on the interradial membranes of the fins are often very hard to see, as these are frequently imbedded and it may require considerable picking under a magnifying glass to establish their presence.

Fin Ray Formula in Identification

A fin ray is a bony rod, usually connected to other rays by a membrane (interradial membrane) to form one of the fins of a fish. Rays are generally of two kinds, spines and softrays. Softrayed fishes are exemplified by the trouts, minnows, and suckers, which have only softrays in their fins. Spinyrayed fishes such as the snappers, sunfishes, and perches have one or more spines in their dorsal, anal, and pelvic fins, with the remainder of these fins usually made up of softrays (some fish have one spine in each pectoral fin; spines do not occur in the caudal fin).

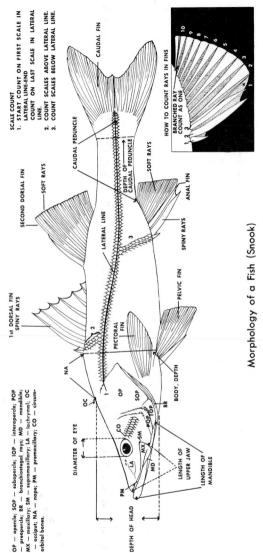

SCALE COUNT
1. START COUNT ON FIRST SCALE IN LATERAL LINE–END COUNT ON LAST SCALE IN LATERAL LINE.
2. COUNT SCALES ABOVE LATERAL LINE.
3. COUNT SCALES BELOW LATERAL LINE.

CAUDAL FIN

SECOND DORSAL FIN

SOFT RAYS

CAUDAL PEDUNCLE

DEPTH OF CAUDAL PEDUNCLE

SOFT RAYS

ANAL FIN

LATERAL LINE

SPINY RAYS

PELVIC FIN

1st DORSAL FIN SPINY RAYS

BODY, DEPTH

PECTORAL FIN

NA

OC

OP

SOP

Bk

DIAMETER OF EYE

CO

MX SM

PM

LA

MD

LENGTH OF UPPER JAW

LENGTH OF MANDIBLE

DEPTH OF HEAD

OP — opercle; SOP — subopercle; IOP — interopercle; POP — preopercle; BR — branchiostegal rays; MD — mandible; MX — maxillary; SM — supramaxillary; LA — lachrymal; OC — occiput; NA — nape; PM — premaxillary; CO — circumorbital bones.

HOW TO COUNT RAYS IN FINS

BRANCHED RAY COUNT AS ONE

Morphology of a Fish (Snook)

Showing Some Features Used in Identification

Spines and softrays take different forms in various kinds of fishes, and a strict definition of either kind of ray is not possible. In some species, such as the mullets, one of the softrays in young juveniles regularly transforms into a spine. In the usual case a spine is rigid, pointed at the tip, and nonsegmented and nonbranched. Softrays are usually flexible, not pointed at the tip (fimbriated), and segmented, and often they are branched.

The kind and number of rays are characteristic of a species and may be described in scientific text by a fin formula with the following abbreviations:

D   Dorsal fin (D_1 and D_2, the first and second dorsal fins when the fin is divided into two units)

A   Anal fin

P_1 Pectoral fin

P_2 Pelvic fin (sometimes given as V when the fin is called a ventral fin, in which case the pectoral fin is designated only as P)

C   Caudal fin

When the fin formula is given, upper case Roman numerals are used to designate spines and Arabic numerals for softrays (at times lower case Roman numerals are used to designate unbranched or unsegmented softrays). The fin formula is not universally standardized, but the following conventions are commonly used: In a single fin containing both spines and softrays, the two kinds of rays are separated by a comma if all the rays are connected by a membrane (D VI, 12 represents a dorsal fin with 6 anterior spines connected to 12 softrays), and by a hyphen if the membrane is discontinuous somewhere in the fin (A II-I, 16 represents an anal fin with two anterior spines separated from the remainder of the fin, which consists of one spine and 16 softrays). When finlets occur in the posterior portion of the dorsal or anal fins, they are separated from the remainder of the fin by a plus sign (for the bluefin tuna: D_1XIII; D_2 I, 14 + 8 represents a first dorsal fin with 13 spines and a second dorsal fin with 1 spine connected to 14 softrays and followed by 8 finlets).

The softrays of the caudal fin are usually given as the unbranched rays in the dorsal part of the fin plus the branched rays plus the unbranched rays in the ventral part of the fin (as C 8 + 15 + 7).

The numbers of rays in some fins may be constant in a species; in others they may vary (D_1 XII to XIII; D_2 I, 14 + 8 or 9 indicates that in the first dorsal fin the spines vary from 12 to 13 and in the second dorsal fin there are constantly 1 spine and 14 softrays and the finlets vary from 8 to 9).

The fin formula is rarely used in this volume, which is designed primarily for the angler.

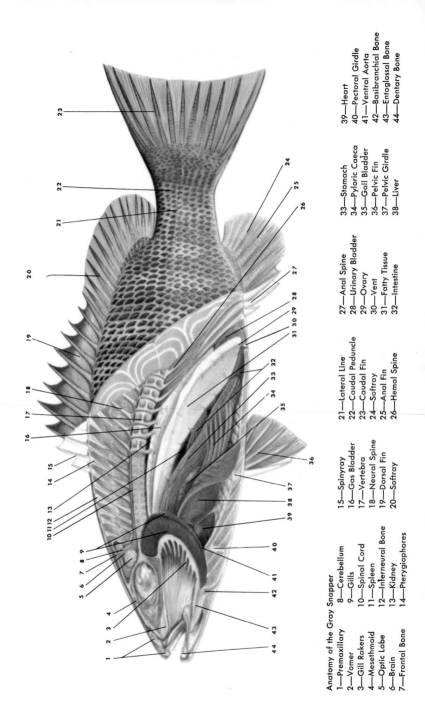

Anatomy of the Gray Snapper

1—Premaxillary
2—Vomer
3—Gill Rakers
4—Mesethmoid
5—Optic Lobe
6—Brain
7—Frontal Bone
8—Cerebellum
9—Gills
10—Spinal Cord
11—Spleen
12—Interneural Bone
13—Kidney
14—Pterygiophores

15—Spinyray
16—Gas Bladder
17—Vertebra
18—Neural Spine
19—Dorsal Fin
20—Softray

21—Lateral Line
22—Caudal Peduncle
23—Caudal Fin
24—Softray
25—Anal Fin
26—Hemal Spine

27—Anal Spine
28—Urinary Bladder
29—Ovary
30—Vent
31—Fatty Tissue
32—Intestine

33—Stomach
34—Pyloric Caeca
35—Gall Bladder
36—Pelvic Fin
37—Pelvic Girdle
38—Liver

39—Heart
40—Pectoral Girdle
41—Ventral Aorta
42—Basibranchial Bone
43—Entoglossal Bone
44—Dentary Bone

Cartilaginous Fishes
Class Chondrichthyes

Sharks

The sharks, which represent a very old group of fishes, lack true bone cells; the skeleton support is received from cartilage. The skin is generally rough and is composed of tiny specialized scales (placoid scales), which are similar in origin to the teeth. The teeth are variable in shape and number, depending on the species and its feeding habits. Fertilization occurs internally and is accomplished through claspers, which introduce the sperm into the female. Some sharks lay eggs (oviparity), the egg case usually bearing filamentous tendrils that attach to grass, algae, or debris. Most sharks produce eggs that hatch within the mother, and the young are subsequently born alive (ovoviviparity); in other species, the young are born alive following contact with the yolk sac placenta (viviparity).

COW SHARK FAMILY Hexanchidae

SEVENGILL SHARK *Heptranchias perlo* Somewhat resembling the sixgill shark, this species has 7 pairs of long gill openings. The body is thin and elongated, the head narrow, and the snout pointed. The large, oval eyes are similar to those of the sixgill shark. The teeth are very similar to those of the sixgill in that the upper and lower ones are unlike, the upper ones being relatively simple, while the lower ones are flattened and have 6–10 cusps. The single dorsal fin is placed relatively far back and is slightly larger than the anal fin. The pelvic fins are large, with their bases well in advance of the dorsal fin. The color is gray with brownish shades, becoming paler below. The caudal and pectoral fins have white edges, and the pelvic and anal fins are pale. There are 2 white spots on the dorsal fin, and both dorsal and caudal fins have black tips. It is a rather small shark, growing only to about 7 feet.

The sevengill occurs on both sides of the Atlantic and in the Mediterranean, being most common in the latter area, and is known from South Africa, Japan, and the North Pacific. A related, if not identical, species occurs in Australia. It resembles the sixgill shark in habits, generally being found in deepwater, but it may enter shallow lagoons in West Africa. Although nowhere numerous, it occasionally becomes abundant in Spanish waters, where it is a predator on commercially important hake.

The breeding habits of this shark are unknown, except that the young are hatched in the mother, where development is completed. The embryos resemble the adult and are about 10 inches at birth. Males mature at $2-2^1/_2$ feet; females mature at about 3 feet or less.

1

SIXGILL SHARK *Hexanchus griseus* This species is recognized by the 6 pairs of gill openings, rather than the usual 5 of most sharks. The single dorsal fin is set far back on the body, almost directly above the anal fin, which is about the same size. The caudal fin is long and about half the length of the body without the tail. The gill openings are rather long, reaching from the ventral midline well up on the sides. The eyes are elliptical, long, and relatively large, particularly in young specimens. The teeth are unusual in that the upper ones are relatively simple. The middle upper teeth have single cusps, and the outer ones 2 cusps; the number of cusps increases to 3 auxiliary smaller cusps at the corners of the mouth. The lower teeth, however, are multicuspate, and all are approximately the same shape, save for the 10 very small unicuspate teeth at the angles of the mouth and the single median tooth on the lower jaw, which is symmetrical. The large teeth are trapezoid in form, with 7–8 pointed cusps regularly decreasing in height. The color is gray-brown to dark gray above, becoming paler below. The eyes are bright emerald-green. Some specimens have a pale area along the well-marked lateral line. Young specimens are slate-gray. The sixgill shark grows to over 26 feet, and individuals of 15 feet are not rare.

This deepwater species occurs on both sides of the Atlantic and in the Mediterranean. In the Pacific it is found from British Columbia to southern California and Chile, and off Japan and Australia. It is found also in the southern parts of the Indian Ocean and off South Africa.

A sluggish species, it is caught in deeper water toward tropical latitudes and shoaler water toward colder latitudes. Specimens have been taken off Portugal at depths of over a mile, while specimens in the North Sea are taken in water as shoal as 90 feet. In the Caribbean, most specimens are taken at depths in excess of 600 feet. The spawning season is not known definitely, but it is reported to be in spring and autumn. Eggs are hatched within the mother, where the young complete their development.

Adults eat fishes (including hakes, dolphins, small marlins, and swordfish), crabs, and shrimps. They evidently feed more actively at night, when they reportedly come to the surface. In Cuba they are caught by the deep-line fishing method, and their flesh is used for oil; in Germany the flesh is reportedly marketed for its purgative action. Specimens are occasionally taken off southern Florida and in the Bahamas in deepwater, and it has been theorized by some anglers that "sea monsters" that take deep-drifted bait, only to snap wire cables, are perhaps giant sixgill sharks.

CARPET SHARK FAMILY Orectolobidae

NURSE SHARK *Ginglymostoma cirratum* This distinctive species is readily recognized by the combination of the 2 dorsal fins, which are about equal in size (*see also* lemon shark), the long barbel at the front of each nostril, and the brown to yellow coloration with (in

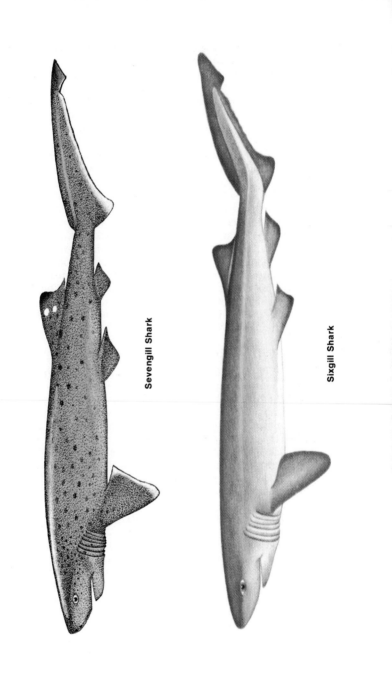

Sevengill Shark

Sixgill Shark

young fish) dark, evenly spaced spots. The caudal fin is relatively long, and the fins generally are large and rounded in comparison with those of other Atlantic sharks. The eyes are very small, and the snout is somewhat blunt and rounded. The fish reaches a length of 14 feet. An 8¹/₂-foot fish weighs about 330–370 pounds.

This widespread species occurs in tropical and subtropical waters of the Atlantic. In the eastern Atlantic it is found off Africa, and in the western Atlantic it is known from Brazil to Rhode Island and throughout the Gulf of Mexico and the Caribbean Sea. In the eastern Pacific, it is known from the Gulf of California to Ecuador.

A shallow-water species, the nurse shark is a reef inhabitant often found resting in caves or under shallow ledges. It may enter mangrove channels as well, occurring either solitarily or in groups. A sluggish species, it is often the target of divers, who attempt to ride it or to grasp its tail; yet it can be extremely voracious, and despite its relatively feeble teeth, it has inflicted painful bites on persons molesting it.

It feeds predominantly on squids, shrimps, crabs, lobsters, and sea urchins. Breeding occurs in shallow water, but almost nothing is known about the details of the period of gestation or the time of birth.

The nurse shark is often caught by anglers, but its comparatively sluggish habits make it not much sought for even by shark fishermen. Its flesh, particularly the fins, is reported to be excellent.

SAND TIGER FAMILY   Odontaspididae

SAND TIGER *Odontaspis taurus* Formerly known as sand shark, this common species is identified by its 2 large dorsal fins of equal size; the large anal fin, which is about the size of the pelvics; and the slender, pointed teeth, which overhang noticeably. The gill openings are all placed in front of the pectoral fins, and the first dorsal is well behind the pectoral fin tips. Its distinctive teeth have a small cusp on either side of the main ones. The fish is pale gray-brown on its upper parts, becoming grayish-white below. Numerous small yellowish spots cover the midparts and posterior parts of the body and fins, giving it a mottled coloration. In some specimens the rear of the fins has black edges.

The sand tiger grows to slightly over 10 feet, and a specimen nearly 9 feet long weighed 250 pounds. Most taken are less than 6 feet long. It occurs in the western Atlantic from Maine to Brazil, in the Mediterranean, and off the Canary Islands and the Cape Verde Islands. Relatively common in the Middle Atlantic and New England area, it is a rather sluggish species that is essentially a bottom dweller in shallow waters. Sand tigers occasionally enter estuaries and penetrate upstream to where the water is quite fresh. They are taken inshore during the warmer months, and it is thought that during the winter they move into deeper water. Spawning habits are not known, but the fish is believed to reproduce in southerly waters. The eggs are hatched

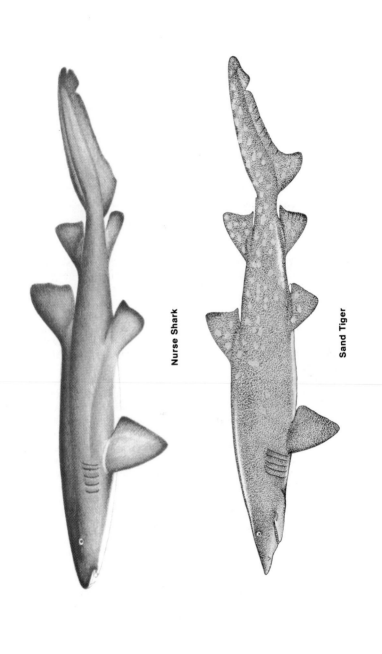

Nurse Shark

Sand Tiger

within the mother, the young eating unfertilized eggs until the time they leave the oviduct.

The adult's chief diet is small fishes, including mackerels, menhaden, flounders, skates, sea trouts, and porgies; crabs and squids are eaten as well.

Although sluggish in its habits, the sand tiger is well equipped with a formidable set of teeth. It has been only recently implicated in an attack on man, but an African relative has been suspected of several fatal attacks. The size of the shark and the muddy coastal waters of the subtropical and temperate zone it inhabits make this species a potential danger.

THRESHER SHARK FAMILY Alopiidae

BIGEYE THRESHER *Alopias superciliosus* This distinctly shaped shark is closely related to the thresher shark, from which it differs in the much larger eyes and longer snout. The tip of the first dorsal fin reaches past the base of the pelvic fins of the bigeye, but falls far short of the base in the thresher. The bigeye's second dorsal fin is well in advance of the anal, while in the thresher the second dorsal tip reaches the anal fin base. The bigeye thresher has far fewer teeth (10–11) than the thresher (about 20) on each side of the jaw.

Its caudal fin, as in the thresher, is enormously long, about half the total length. The pectoral fins are long and are less curved than those of the thresher. Its color is nearly uniformly slate-gray, with dusky edgings to the first dorsal, pectoral, and pelvic fins. It reaches a length of 18 feet.

The bigeye thresher is known from Florida, Cuba, Madeira, and California. Its habits are unknown, although it is believed to occupy deeper waters than its relative, the thresher shark. Hakes, squids, and lancetfish have been found in stomachs of bigeye threshers.

THRESHER SHARK *Alopias vulpinus* Easily recognized by its very long tail, this species can be confused with no other Atlantic sharks except the bigeye thresher, from which it differs essentially in having smaller eyes. The tail is about as long as the body, and the pectoral fins are long and sickle-shaped, although they are relatively shorter than those of the bigeye thresher. The snout is blunt but pointed, and the smooth teeth lack cusps.

The coloration is nearly uniform on the sides and back, ranging from brown to blue-gray or black with metallic hues. The lower parts are white, occasionally with gray mottlings.

The thresher shark grows to 20 feet and a weight of perhaps 1,000 pounds. A 14$\frac{1}{2}$-foot fish weighs about 500 pounds. This shark is predominantly a dweller of the subtropics and warm temperate zone and occurs from Nova Scotia to Argentina, from Ireland to the Cape of Good Hope, and throughout the Mediterranean. In the Pacific it is known from Oregon to Chile and off Hawaii, Japan, China, and

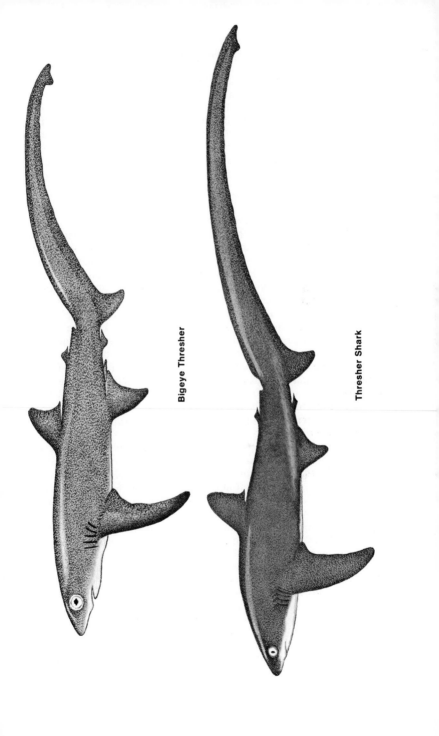

Bigeye Thresher

Thresher Shark

Australia. It is not certain if these forms from the various areas are identical.

Found largely at or near the surface, it occurs predominantly in the open sea and is found offshore during the cold months. It is seldom taken in the tropics, being a fish of cooler waters. It feeds on schooling fishes, such as bluefishes, mackerels, and menhaden, using its long tail to herd and stun its prey. When its prey is extremely common, threshers occasionally congregate to the extent that they become a nuisance to commercial fishermen by tearing their nets. There is no indication that threshers are ever dangerous to man.

MACKEREL SHARK FAMILY Laminidae

BASKING SHARK *Cetorhinus maximus* A giant shark exceeded in size only by the whale shark, it has a streamlined shape similar to that of the white shark and the mako shark. With these sharks it shares the pointed snout, small second dorsal fin, and nearly symmetrical caudal fin. But the huge gill openings, which extend completely around the neck, nearly meeting at the middorsal surface, distinguish the basking from all other sharks. Further, the unique, peculiar teeth are reduced to conical protuberances, their length being only $\frac{1}{8}$ inch in a 12-foot specimen. Long, comblike filaments, like gillrakers of bony fishes, are present on the first gill arch. The mouth is huge, and in the young the snout is particularly long and rather bizarre in shape compared with that of other sharks. The body varies from gray-brown to nearly black, sometimes grading to lighter shadings or even white beneath. This large shark grows to 40–50 feet, and a small free-swimming specimen of about $5\frac{1}{2}$ feet has been taken. California specimens of 28 feet and 30 feet weighed 6,580 pounds and 8,600 pounds, respectively.

Although predominantly an Arctic species, the basking shark regularly occurs as far south as Newfoundland and Norway, straying farther south to Morocco and North Carolina. Closely related, or possibly identical, species occur in the cooler waters of the South Atlantic and off Peru and Ecuador, California to British Columbia, Australia, New Zealand, China, and Japan. The basking shark is sluggish in habits and, as the name implies, is often seen floating at the surface, occasionally on its back, or lazily swimming open-mouthed, ingesting quantities of plankton. The comblike gillrakers sieve out the tiny organisms, which are converted into several tons of shark. Occasionally small crustaceans are eaten.

This species is seen during the warmer months. Usually a solitary species, schools of 60–100 have been seen floating at the surface. It is not easily frightened by man and can be easily approached by boats. The sharks apparently move northward during the summer, possibly retreating southward into deeper water with the onset of cool weather. The breeding season is unknown, but the young are 5–6 feet long at birth, and sexual maturity may occur at 15–20 feet.

A number of sea-serpent stories can be traced to the skeletons of basking sharks, for, in various stages of decomposition, the carcass affords a peculiar sight with its jaws and gill arches, the long vertebral column, and the fin supports. Such a sight on a beach has been sufficient to provoke the imaginations of many people, thus giving rise to innumerable reports of sea serpents.

MAKO *Isurus oxyrhinchus*   Closely related to the white shark, this open-ocean shark resembles it in the nearly symmetrical tail, streamlined shape, and pointed snout. The mako's teeth are long and slender and protrude from the mouth. The second dorsal fin is only slightly ahead of the anal fin in the mako, but it is directly above the anal in the porbeagle. The mako's dorsal and pectoral fins have somewhat rounded tips, while those of the white shark are more pointed. The mako's color is a striking cobalt to bluish-gray in fresh specimens, becoming grayish-brown in dead specimens. Fresh specimens also show a sharp line of demarcation between the colored upper parts and the dead white below.

Makos of 12 feet have been measured, and a $10^{1}/_{2}$-foot specimen weighed just over 1,000 pounds. The Atlantic hook-and-line record is 1,250 pounds, taken off Long Island, New York.

The mako occurs in the tropical and warmer parts of the temperate Atlantic Ocean, being replaced in the Pacific by the closely related shortfin mako. Apparently it is entirely an oceanic species of the blue waters, although a mako has been reported from water about 30 feet deep off Cat Cay, Bahamas. Undoubtedly, most reports of "makos" in shallow water are based on the sand tiger, which has similar teeth and is found inshore. A fast-swimming species, the mako is well known to anglers for its gameness and leaping characteristics. It is apparently a surface- or near-surface-dwelling fish. Tunas, mackerels, and herringlike fishes are staple foods. It is known as an enemy of the swordfish, which it attacks frequently.

The flesh of the mako and the swordfish are very similar in taste, possibly attesting to the importance of swordfish in the mako's diet. The flesh of the mako is indeed a delicacy, but the fish's importance lies chiefly in its attraction for the angler.

PORBEAGLE *Lamna nasus*   The swift-swimming porbeagle, sometimes called mackerel shark, is a heavy-bodied, open-ocean fish closely resembling the mako, shortfin mako, white shark, and salmon shark, being most closely related to the last. It can be distinguished from the white shark by its pointed, slender teeth, each of which has a sharp cusp at the base. The base of the porbeagle's caudal peduncle has a secondary, smaller keel, which is lacking in its Atlantic relatives. The dorsal fin is directly over the pectoral fin in the porbeagle, whereas it is behind the pectoral in the mako; it is only somewhat behind in the white shark. But the second dorsal is located directly

9

above the anal fin in the porbeagle, a feature that separates it from both the mako and the white shark. The porbeagle's caudal fin is less symmetrical as well, the upper lobe being decidedly longer, yet not as long as in the sand tiger. The porbeagle is blue-gray to blackish above to white on the belly, with a white or dusky anal fin. It is not a large shark for this family, the largest recorded being 10 feet, although fish of 12 feet have been reported. A 400-pound specimen was 9 feet long.

Found in the nearshore waters of the Atlantic Ocean, it has been reported from both sides of the Atlantic from the Murman coast south to Africa and the Mediterranean. In the western Atlantic, it has been taken from the Gulf of St. Lawrence to South Carolina. It is a shark of the temperate zone that occasionally enters water that is rather cool. But it apparently moves into deeper strata during the winter to avoid water temperatures that are very low. It is less vigorous a swimmer than its Atlantic relatives and is also found in deeper strata, being reported from depths of 80 fathoms.

Porbeagles feed on schooling fishes, such as mackerels, pilchards, and herrings, and on bottom-dwelling species such as cod, hakes, and flounders. The eggs are hatched within the female, and the young then remain inside for some time afterward. Although embryos have been found in the mother during the winter, evidence suggests that birth occurs during the summer.

SALMON SHARK *Lamna ditropis* This Pacific member of the mackerel shark family is similar in most respects to the porbeagle, but differs in having (in the adult) black blotches on a white background on the lower parts of the body. The color is bluish-black above. The snout is broader and shorter than that of the porbeagle. The salmon shark is reported to reach 12 feet, although $8^1/_2$ feet is the record measurement.

It is found from San Diego to Alaska and Japan, essentially in deeper waters to the south and shallower depths to the north. Warmwaters are avoided, and its distribution, like that of the porbeagle, parallels cooler temperatures. It bears living young, and a $6^1/_2$-foot female from southern California had 4 young, each of which was $2^1/_2$ feet long and weighed 18 pounds. Adults are fast swimmers of the open sea and coastal waters, and they are reported to feed voraciously on salmon and to damage fishermen's nets. This shark is caught by anglers using salmon for bait.

SHORTFIN MAKO *Isurus oxyrinchus* Formerly known as the bonito shark, it differs from the mako only in its lower dorsal fin and shorter head. The streamlined shape of the mako is also characteristic of the shortfin, as are its slender, recurved teeth, pointed snout, and nearly symmetrical tail. The shortfin differs from the salmon shark in having a shallower body depth, the first dorsal fin set entirely behind the pectoral fins and the second dorsal fin somewhat in advance of the

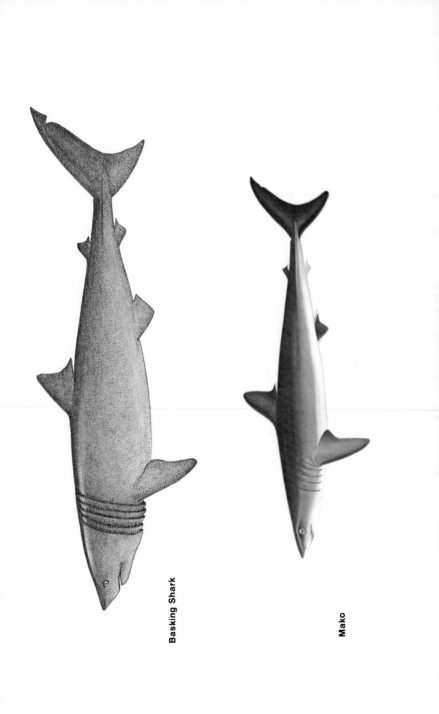

Basking Shark

Mako

anal fin. The shortfin is dark blue above, with an abrupt change to white on the sides and on the lower parts. It reaches a weight of 1,000 pounds and a length of at least 12 feet.

It is found from southern California to Chile, Hawaii, Japan, and the Indo-Pacific. A closely related species is reported from India. Like the mako, it is a swift-swimming species of the open sea and feeds actively on schools of tunas, bonitos, mackerels, and sardines.

Highly prized for its sporting qualities, it is a recognized gamefish in Australia and New Zealand. But its sportiness also makes it a potential danger to man, and it has attacked boats. Its flesh is valued, being similar in flavor to that of the mako.

WHITE SHARK *Carcharodon carcharias*   This is also known as the maneater or great white shark and is recognized by its streamlined shape, pointed snout, triangular, serrated teeth, and crescent-shaped caudal fin, with the dorsal lobe only slightly longer than the lower. It resembles the mako, but can be distinguished by the anal fin, which is nearly completely behind the second dorsal in the white shark. The tips of the dorsal and pectoral fins are more rounded in the mako, and the mako's snout is more pointed. The body of the white shark is much deeper and less elongate than the mako's. The smooth teeth of the mako are more slender, curved inward, and protrude from the mouth. The white shark is grayish-brown, grading to slate-blue or gray, with dirty-white below. In the young, there is a black spot above the pectoral fin that is lacking in large specimens. Large white sharks are leaden-white.

This is a robust shark. A specimen measuring about 8 feet long weighed 600 pounds, while one about 13 feet weighed over 2,100 pounds. It grows to 25 feet. There is great variation in the weight at a given length, depending on the condition of breeding and food intake. The rod-and-reel record from Australia is 2,664 pounds.

The white shark is an oceanic species that roams the tropical and temperate waters of the world. It is nowhere common, but apparently is less common in the tropics than in warm temperate regions.

Fortunately for bathers, this active swimmer usually stays well offshore and also appears to prefer somewhat cooler waters, so that it is not as abundant in the summer months, at least on the Atlantic coast. However, it may enter very shallow water in populated areas, and it has been definitely implicated in several attacks on humans. Its teeth have more than once been removed from boats it has attacked. Its large size makes it a very real potential danger.

It eats a variety of large animals, and other sharks 4–7 feet long have been taken from stomachs. Sea lions, seals, sturgeons, tunas, sea turtles, chimaeras, and squids are also regularly taken. It is also a scavenger on dead flesh and refuse.

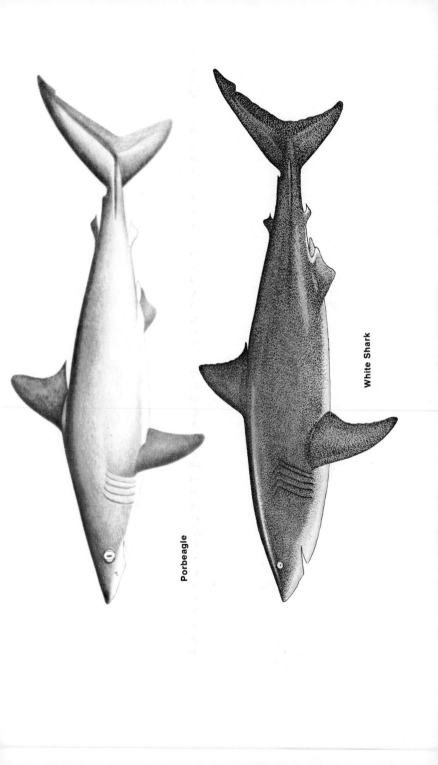

Porbeagle

White Shark

HAMMERHEAD SHARK FAMILY   Sphyrnidae

BONNETHEAD *Sphyrna tiburo*   This shark has a broadly widened head shaped in the form of a shovel, with the eyes at the end of the expanded head. The distinctive head is more broadly rounded in front than in the great hammerhead and its relatives, and there is no deep indentation in its margin opposite each nostril. The pectoral fins are large and broad, and the high dorsal fin, characteristic of this family, is equal to the depth of the body. A slightly indented anal fin also separates this species from the other hammerhead types, which have the anal fin deeply indented. The bonnethead is grayish-brown or gray above on the body and fins, grading to light gray beneath. Occasionally individuals have round dark spots along the sides. Adults are about $3^1/_2$ feet long when sexual maturity occurs. The fish is reported to grow to 6 feet.

In the western Atlantic it strays as far north as southern New England, but it occurs most commonly between southern North Carolina and Brazil and throughout the Caribbean Sea and the Gulf of Mexico. It probably also occurs in the warmer parts of the eastern Atlantic and eastern Pacific oceans. In the warmer parts of its range, it is a year-round resident, but to the north it occurs only during the warm summer months as far as Cape Hatteras. It is one of the commonest shore-dwelling sharks, occurring in less than a foot of water out to at least several fathoms.

GREAT HAMMERHEAD *Sphyrna mokarran*   This species is readily recognized by the hammer-shaped head and the nearly straight profile of the anterior margin with a definite indentation at the center. Its nearly straight anterior margin and the regularly serrated teeth distinguish this fish from the scalloped hammerhead and smooth hammerhead. The pelvic fins are anteriorly convex, and the dorsal fin is less erect than in other Atlantic relatives. Young specimens are brownish-gray to olive above, grading to paler beneath, with dusky shadings on the fin tips. A length of 18 feet is attained, and specimens of 13–14 feet are common.

A warmwater shark, it occurs throughout the tropical and subtropical parts of the Atlantic, the eastern Pacific, and the Indo-Pacific region. It is known in the western Atlantic with certainty from North Carolina to northern Argentina. Apparently it is not as common as some of its relatives, except in southern Florida, where some concentrations have been noted. Sexual maturity occurs at about 10 feet, and the young are born in tropical waters. A large, strong-swimming species, it has been known to attack large tarpons, tunas, and other sharks.

SCALLOPED HAMMERHEAD *Sphyrna lewini*   This shark differs from the bonnethead in having a less rounded anterior margin of the head. The dorsal fin is high, as in all hammerheads, and the head is

Bonnethead

Great Hammerhead

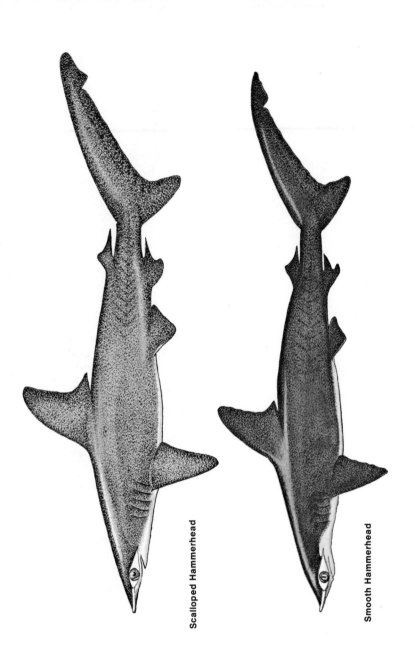

Scalloped Hammerhead

Smooth Hammerhead

tapered in lateral view. The scalloped hammerhead differs from the smooth hammerhead in having a distinct indentation at the midline of the anterior portion of the head, a characteristic it shares with the great hammerhead. It differs from the great hammerhead in having smooth teeth with cusps only on their bases, if at all, and in having the free rear tip of the second dorsal much longer than the anterior margin. A closely related species (*S. tudes*), known from the northern Gulf of Mexico, Brazil, and Uruguay, differs from the scalloped hammerhead in having the posterior margin of the anal fin only slightly concave and the eyes relatively far forward of the front of the mouth. The scalloped hammerhead is light gray above and white below, with black on the ventral surfaces of the pectoral fins.

Specimens of 10 feet are reported, although the maximum size is not known. It occurs in the warmer parts of the Atlantic, as well as the Mediterranean, the eastern and western Pacific, Hawaii, and Australia. It is known with certainty in the western Atlantic from New Jersey to Rio de Janeiro. Males mature at 6 feet, and gravid females occur in south Florida waters, but little else is known about their habits.

SMOOTH HAMMERHEAD *Sphyrna zygaena* This shark is easily distinguished from its relatives by the combination of a slightly convex anterior margin of the head, which is not indented; the high, erect dorsal fin; and the smooth edges to the teeth, which are serrated only weakly and irregularly. The color is dark olive to brownish-gray above and gray-white beneath. The fin tips are dusky, and the pectorals are often black-tipped. The fish grows to 13 feet and a weight of at least 900 pounds.

As is true of other hammerheads, uncertainties of field identification have confused information on the smooth hammerhead with information on related species. The smooth hammerhead has been recorded from the tropical parts of the Atlantic and is believed to occur in the eastern Pacific and throughout the Indo-Pacific. It is widespread in the tropical western Atlantic and has been reported at various localities from Cape Cod to northern Argentina and the northern Gulf of Mexico. A spectacular northward migration is undertaken each summer, and the sharks occur in large numbers at various coastal points during this migration. Most of these migrants are less than 6 feet, but some of 12 feet have been recorded during this coastal movement.

REQUIEM SHARK FAMILY Carcharhinidae

ATLANTIC SHARPNOSE SHARK *Rhizoprionodon terraenovae* This small shark is distinguished by the labial furrows at the corners of its mouth. It is a slender species with a pointed, narrow snout and a high dorsal fin, which is placed relatively far forward. Its slanting teeth are smooth save for a notch on the outer edge. The body is brownish to olive-gray above, with a white belly and white along the rear edge of the pectoral fins; the dorsal and caudal fins are dark-edged.

The sharpnose grows to about 3 feet long. It is known from both sides of the Atlantic Ocean, being found from Uruguay to North Carolina and as an accidental visitor as far north as the Bay of Fundy. In the eastern Atlantic it is known from Morocco to the Cameroons and the Cape Verde Islands. A similar species (*R. longurio*) occurs in the Pacific.

BLACKTIP SHARK *Carcharhinus limbatus*   A widespread tropical shark, the blacktip shares with several other species, including its close relative the spinner shark, the characteristic black tips of the pectoral fins and the lack of a dermal ridge between the dorsal fins. It resembles the spinner shark, but has a shorter, less pointed snout and larger eyes. The eye of the blacktip is about one-fifth the snout distance (compared with about one-ninth in the spinner), and the gill slits of the blacktip are relatively short, the first being about two-thirds of the distance between the nostrils. The teeth are regularly serrated from their bases to their tips. The body is dark gray grading through yellowish to gray-blue above, with white to yellowish-white beneath. A dark band extends along the side up to about the pelvic region. The pectoral fins are black-tipped, as are the dorsal and anal fins and the lower lobe of the caudal fin, especially in young.

This small shark seldom grows to more than about 6 feet. An individual 5^1/$_2$ feet long weighs only about 68 pounds. It occurs through the tropical Atlantic from Madeira to the Cape Verde Islands and from southern Brazil to Cape Cod. The blacktip is also reported from lower California to Peru. Although it is also recorded from the Indian Ocean area, it is not definitely known if this is the same as the Atlantic species. Like the spinner shark, it is an active, strong-swimming shark, frequently seen leaping from the water. It occurs both inshore and off, where it pursues small fishes such as menhaden, sardines, butterfishes, and stingrays.

In the Gulf of Mexico and Caribbean, it is one of the most common sharks and is often caught by sport fishermen. It puts up a determined fight. The blacktip is one of few sharks that will strike artificial lures with any consistency; large bucktail flies, jigs, and plugs are effective. This shark can be stalked on the flats or taken at the edges of channels and banks.

BLUE SHARK *Prionace glauca*   This distinctive, beautifully colored shark is recognized by its very long pectoral fins, the bright cobalt coloration of the back, the snowy-white belly, and the long snout. It is a slender, elongate species, with the first dorsal fin set relatively far back, at about the middle of the body. The teeth are nearly triangular and are serrated along the edges. Although reported to

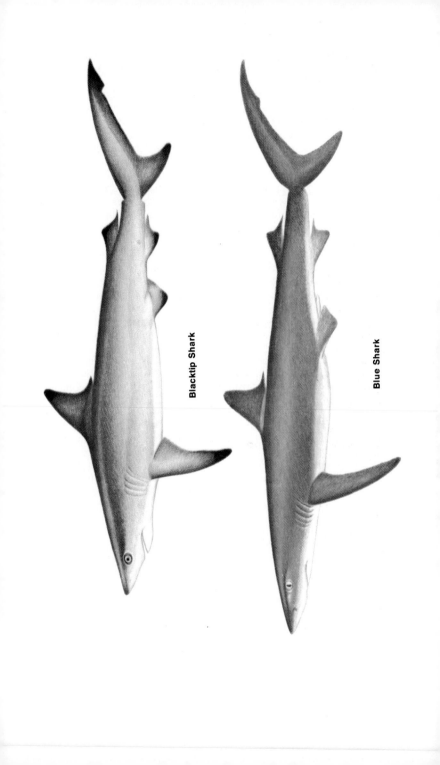

Blacktip Shark

Blue Shark

grow to 20 feet, the blue shark averages less than 10 feet. The rod-and-reel record is an $11^1/_2$-foot shark of 410 pounds taken off Massachusetts.

The blue shark ranges throughout the temperate and tropical waters of the world, being one of the most common of the oceanic sharks. On the Pacific coast, it is frequently seen in shallow waters. In the western Atlantic Ocean, it is more common in northern waters, and although blue sharks are not often caught by anglers fishing on the surface in tropical waters, deep-line or nighttime fishing may produce results. Blue sharks are commonly seen at the surface in northern waters. They rove in packs at times, and at other times are seen singly or in pairs. They also school by sex, with more males being found in some areas (more often the northern and the western parts of the North Atlantic) and more females in others (the more southern and eastern parts of the North Atlantic).

Maturity occurs at 7–8 feet, and as many as 54 young are born at one time, the young being about $1^1/_2$–2 feet long. Food taken includes mackerels, herrings, squids, and other sharks, and in California, flying-fishes and anchovies as well. Sea birds resting at the sea surface are eaten, and blue sharks commonly feed on garbage dumped at sea. These sharks proverbially followed the old whaling ships for long periods, feeding on the carcasses of sperm whales that were thrown overboard.

The blue shark has been implicated in attacks on swimmers and is believed responsible for attacks on military personnel involved in ship accidents or torpedoings during World War II. Although a voracious species, it puts up a poor fight on hook and line.

BULL SHARK *Carcharhinus leucas* The bull shark is easily recognized by its short, broadly rounded snout; large dorsal fin placed well in advance over the pectoral fins; absence of a dermal ridge between the dorsal fins; small eyes; and subtriangular serrated teeth. It is gray to gray-brown above and white below, with dusky markings on the pectoral fins only in the young. A weight of 400 pounds and a length of 10 feet have been reported for this chunky shark, but most seen are less than 8 feet.

It occurs in the western Atlantic from Brazil to North Carolina, straying north to New York. Records of the bull shark are from most of the Caribbean islands, the Gulf of Mexico, and Bermuda. It freely enters freshwaters and occurs in both lakes and rivers in Guatemala and Nicaragua. Throughout its range it is abundant in shallow waters, particularly around harbors, bays, and estuaries. Young are born from May to July in brackish waters, and these same waters are an unusually popular place for the adults to congregate. Feeding is correlated with tidal movements, and this normally sluggish shark becomes a vigorous feeder on other sharks, stingrays, and bony fishes such as mackerels and shad, as well as garbage, which it scavenges actively.

The bull is a vicious shark under some circumstances, and it has attacked bathers and skin divers. The migratory form that enters Lake Nicaragua is responsible for attacks on a number of swimmers.

DUSKY SHARK *Carcharhinus obscurus*   One of the inshore requiem sharks, this fish belongs to the group having a distinct ridge between the dorsal fins. It has a long, pointed snout, somewhat rounded in the dorsal view, and well-developed pectoral fins. The first dorsal fin is high and much larger than the second. The dusky shark closely resembles the sandbar shark, but can be separated from it by the more rearward placement of the first dorsal fin, which originates over or slightly behind the inner corner of the pectoral fin. The dorsal fin is smaller than that of the sandbar, its height being less than the distance from the eye to the first gill opening. The dusky shark resembles the sickle shark, but the free rear corners of its second dorsal and anal fins are much less than twice the height of the fins; in the sickle shark, these rear tips are more than twice as long as the fins are high. The adult is bluish to leaden-gray above and whitish beneath, with a darker coloration of the pectoral fin tips. It grows to nearly 12 feet long, and embryos 3 feet long have been taken.

Dusky sharks apparently occur throughout the tropical and subtropical parts of the Atlantic, although it is not certain if this is the same species on both sides of the Atlantic. A closely related species, *C. galapagensis*, has been identified from the Atlantic and is distinguished by its more erect and more pointed dorsal fin and relatively smaller gill slits. In this area, the dusky shark occurs from Massachusetts to Brazil and throughout the Caribbean. Its center of abundance seems to be around Florida. Although found in shallow water at times, it is largely an offshore coastal species, often taken far from shoalwater. It apparently undertakes spring migrations to the north, and the young are produced over a long season and apparently throughout its range. Fishes are the staple part of its diet.

GRAY SMOOTHHOUND *Mustelus californicus*   Closely related to the leopard shark, this common California shark closely resembles its Atlantic relative, the smooth dogfish. The first and second dorsal fins are about the same size, and the first dorsal is about midway between the pectorals and pelvics. The gray smoothhound can be separated from the similar brown smoothhound (*M. henlei*) by the latter's distinct reddish-brown color and sharp-pointed teeth. The teeth of the gray smoothhound are flat, blunt, and not developed to points, and the fish is dark gray above with a white belly. Maximum length is about 30 inches. It is known only off the coast of California, mostly in shallow waters and most common in southern California.

LEMON SHARK *Negaprion brevirostris*   This common tropical shark is readily recognized by its yellowish-brown color, broadly rounded snout, and 2 dorsal fins of about equal size, both of which

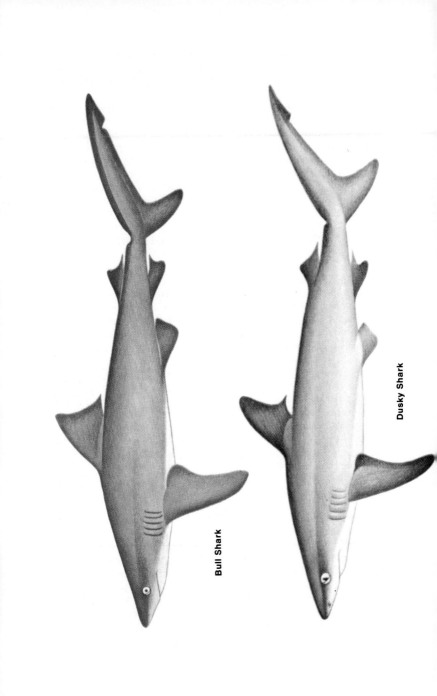

Bull Shark

Dusky Shark

are placed rather far back on the body. The distinctive teeth, which also help separate it from other Atlantic sharks, are symmetrical and erect in the central part of the jaw and lack cusps along their margins. The bases of the teeth of the upper jaw have fine, irregular serrations. The fish reaches a length of about 11 feet, but does not grow as heavy as other species at about the same length.

Lemon sharks are plentiful in the Caribbean and are reported regularly elsewhere from Brazil to North Carolina and the Gulf of Mexico, straying north to New Jersey, as well as off the coasts of tropical West Africa and Ecuador.

Although it is predominantly a shallow-water shark, a few have been taken from 50 fathoms. Young lemon sharks are common in very shallow waters, and adults occur singly or in loose aggregations, usually in schools predominantly of one sex. Young are produced in late spring and early summer, at which times they are abundant in shallow water. They feed on fishes, such as mullets, and crustaceans, apparently feeding more at night than during the day.

This species has been implicated in attacks on humans, and its vicious habits in captivity and its common occurrence in shallow water make it a potential danger to bathers. The lemon is a very common shark on bonefish flats and can provide excellent sport, as it often takes artificial lures such as plugs and flies.

LEOPARD SHARK *Triakis semifasciata* The distinctive color pattern readily identifies this Pacific coast species. It has a general resemblance to the brown smoothhound. It is only somewhat stout anteriorly, tapering rapidly to a narrow caudal peduncle. The first and second dorsal fins are about the same size. The body is gray with about 12–13 dark crossbands on the back and dark spots on the sides. Males grow to 3 feet long, females to 5, and maturity in about half the females occurs at approximately $3\frac{1}{2}$ feet long. Found from Oregon to Baja California, it is fairly common in shallow bays of southern California.

The flesh of the leopard shark is good, and the fish is commonly taken by sport fishermen.

REEF SHARK *Carcharhinus springeri* Although not common in the United States, this is apparently one of the most widespread sharks in the Caribbean and occurs in Florida waters. It closely resembles the dusky shark, but has larger eyes, lobed nostrils, and a larger first dorsal fin with a shorter rear free tip. The distance from the pelvic tips to the anal base is short (about seven-tenths of the anal base in the reef shark and about $1\frac{1}{3}$ times the anal base in the dusky), and the second dorsal is inserted slightly more in front of the anal fin. The reef shark is grayish-olive to olive-brown above and yellowish-white to white below. Specimens up to 9 feet have been caught. In the Caribbean it occurs around deep reefs, occasionally in some numbers. It apparently replaces the dusky shark in these areas.

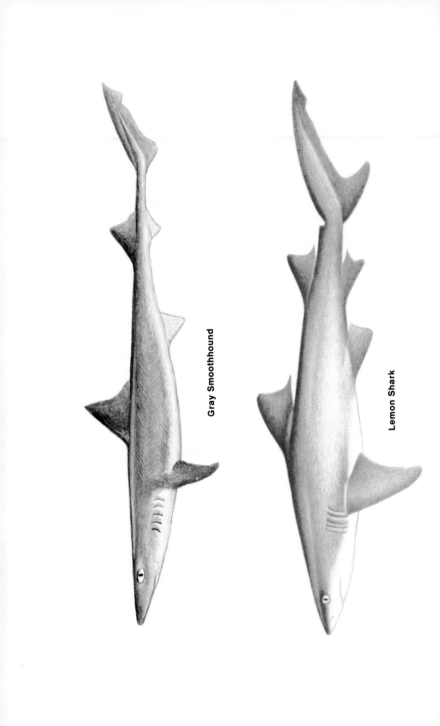

Gray Smoothhound

Lemon Shark

Leopard Shark

Sandbar Shark

SANDBAR SHARK *Carcharhinus milberti* Also known as the brown shark, this very common shark can be identified by the high dorsal fin, which is placed far forward, originating over the inner corner of the pectoral fin; the pointed snout, which is not broadly rounded in dorsal outline; and the short second dorsal fin, whose free rear corner is only about the length of the base. The sandbar resembles the bull shark in general appearance, but the bull shark lacks a dorsal ridge between the dorsal fins. The sandbar's color varies from gray to brown above to white below, and the fins lack markings. It grows to nearly 8 feet and about 200 pounds.

This abundant shark is divided into several populations throughout the warmer parts of the Atlantic Ocean. In the eastern Atlantic, it occurs off Spain and off West Africa, and it is known in the western Atlantic with certainty from New England to southern Brazil. It occurs also in the Mediterranean and the Gulf of Mexico. A shallow-water species, it is found on or near the bottom of depths of 100 fathoms, occasionally moving out in midwater to oceanic habitats. But its commonest haunts lie in 10–30 fathoms.

SILKY SHARK *Carcharhinus falciformis* One of the most common of the offshore sharks, the silky is so called because of its very smooth skin. It superficially resembles the dusky and sandbar sharks, but differs from them in having slender second dorsal and anal fins, which are more than twice as long as they are high. From the bull shark, blacktip shark, and spinner shark, it differs in having a dermal ridge between the dorsal fins. Its body is elongate and the snout long, with the first dorsal set back about midway between the pectoral and pelvic fins. Adults have pectoral fins that are relatively longer than those of other species of *Carcharhinus* and are almost as long as the pectoral fins of the blue shark. But pectoral fins of small specimens are relatively much shorter. The inner and outer edges of the pectoral fins are broadly curved, particularly in small specimens. The silky shark is dark gray to gray-brown, grading to lighter below. The pectoral fin tips are dusky to black, especially in small individuals, but this coloration disappears with age. The fish reaches a length of 10 feet.

The silky shark is known from the warmer parts of the Atlantic, including West Africa, and the Caribbean, from Trinidad to Florida, with a few being reported from North Carolina and off Delaware Bay in late summer and autumn. It also occurs in the tropical eastern Pacific Ocean. Although it is occasionally taken in water as shallow as 60 feet, it is essentially an offshore species of the outer reefs and bluewaters. In the Pacific, squids, crabs, and puffers have been found in the stomachs of silky sharks. Silky sharks from the Pacific have been found carrying an average of 6 young throughout the year, which probably are upward of 2 feet long at birth. Like some other pelagic sharks, this species tends to run in schools of one sex only at certain times of the year.

SMOOTH DOGFISH *Mustelus canis* One of the most common sharks in the United States, this small species is well known to anglers, who catch large numbers during the summer months. It has a slender body. The pectoral fins are long, and the first and second dorsal fins are large and are about equal in size. The teeth are flat and low, without sharp points. The fish is gray or brown above, depending on the type of bottom, with pale coloration beneath. This widespread species is taken from Cape Cod, Massachusetts, to Texas, Bermuda, the Caribbean, and Uruguay. Several closely related species occur in the Caribbean and the western South Atlantic. The maximum size is 5 feet, but most taken by anglers are about 2 feet long.

The smooth dogfish is a bottom dweller, commonly found in depths less than 60 feet, but taken at times as deep as 80–90 fathoms. It enters mouths of bays and estuaries, occasionally entering freshwater. There seem to be several relatively isolated populations of dogfish along the Atlantic coast. A northerly migration occurs in the spring, a southerly drift in the fall, and the winter is spent in deepwater off the Carolinas.

The reproductive period is in early July, and gestation takes about 10 months. The young are about 1 foot long at birth. Sexual maturity occurs at about 3 feet. Crabs and lobsters are eaten, as are squids and fishes, predominantly menhaden and tautogs. Collectively, the large schools of dogfish account for vast amounts of the valuable food supply of the sea.

Despite its common name, the smooth dogfish is one of the requiem sharks and not a member of the dogfish shark family.

SOUPFIN SHARK *Galeorhinus zyopterus* This famous commercial shark is characterized by a pointed snout, a slightly concave head, a large first dorsal fin, and teeth that are notched on the outer edge below the point. The body is deepest at about the middle, tapering sharply to the snout and tail. The second dorsal fin is directly above the anal fin and about the same size, in contrast to the small anal fin of the brown smoothhound. The soupfin is dark or dusky-gray to blue above, shading to pale on the lower parts, with black edges on the anterior parts of the dorsal, pectoral, and caudal fins. It grows to about $6^1/_2$ feet and 100 pounds, the females growing slightly larger than the males.

Found from British Columbia to southern California, it is thought to be identical with a species taken in the eastern Atlantic and Mediterranean, both coasts of South America, and the central, western, and south Pacific. It is taken down to depths of 225 fathoms. Males are more common in northern California and females more common, in shallow water, in the southern part of the state. Males mature at about 5 feet and females at a somewhat larger size. The eggs are hatched within the female, the total gestation period being about a year, and an average of about 35 young is produced in each litter. The soupfin eats predominantly fishes (including flounders, salmon, rock-fishes, sardines, mackerels, barracudas) and squids. In California, an extensive commercial fishery was formerly conducted for the liver of this species, but is not as intensive as it was before the synthesis of vitamin A.

SPINNER SHARK *Carcharhinus maculipinnis* Also known as the large blacktip shark, this long-snouted shark is recognized by its long gill slits, well-marked black tips to the fins, lack of a dorsal ridge, small eyes, and smooth edges of the lower teeth (*see* the blacktip shark for comparison). The spinner is gray above and white below, with a faint dark band on the sides up to the pelvic fins. Individuals of 8 feet are recorded. Known from southern Florida, Cuba, and Puerto Rico, it occurs in schools, and, like the blacktip, is commonly observed leaping from the water and twisting.

The spinner shark, like several other species that seasonally and geographically occur in shallow water (notably the blacktip, hammerhead, and lemon sharks), provides excellent light-tackle angling with artificial lures. Spinning or bait-casting equipment with suitable topwater plugs and the fly rod using large streamer flies will take sharks. There are large concentrations of both spinners and blacktips on the flats around Flamingo, Florida, and as far north as Marco, where conditions for this type of fishing are ideal.

TIGER SHARK *Galeocerdo cuvieri* This is a large, distinctively marked requiem shark of the tropics, characterized by a short, sharp-pointed snout, which is squarish when viewed from above. The first dorsal fin is relatively far forward, and the second dorsal fin is long and low. The caudal fin is long and slender, and the lower lobe is large. A median keel is prominent along the caudal peduncle. The distinctive teeth are recurved and notched at their inner margins, with the tooth margins serrate. A young tiger shark has characteristic bars and spots on the back and upper sides, but a large adult is usually nearly plain-colored brownish-gray.

Maximum size of the tiger is 18 feet, but reports of 30-foot specimens persist. Weight ranges in tiger sharks of 13–14 feet are about 1,000–1,400 pounds, the weight depending largely on the fatness, sex, and reproductive state of the female. The rod-and-reel record is 1,780 pounds. This species occurs throughout the tropical and subtropical regions of the world, and although it is taken offshore, it seems to be more nearly a coastal species, occasionally entering very shallow waters. It is omnivorous on live and dead matter, eating fishes of all kinds, as well as crabs, whelks, lobsters, squids, turtles, and sea lions. Tigers are cannibalistic and eat other species of sharks as well. Their apparently impervious stomachs have yielded cans, bottles, sacks of coal, clothes and shoes, various bits of bird remains, dogs, and even parts of a crocodile.

Spawning apparently occurs throughout the year, and the young are born in shallow waters. Eggs are hatched within the mother, and the young are born ready to swim. From 10 to 82 young have been taken from females, and the young are about 18-19 inches long at birth. A sluggish species under normal conditions, the tiger becomes voracious and strong-swimming in the presence of food.

Because of its size, efficient teeth, and proneness to enter shallow water, it is a potential danger to swimmers, and it has been responsible for a number of attacks on skin divers and bathers.

WHITETIP SHARK *Carcharhinus longimanus* This distinctively marked tropical shark can be recognized by its short, broadly rounded snout and rounded first dorsal and pectoral fins. Further, it has a large, high dorsal fin, and the lower lobe of the caudal fin is convex at its posterior margin. The body is short and relatively chunky, and the free rear tip of the second dorsal fin nearly reaches the caudal pit. The upper teeth are triangular and serrated, while the lower ones are erect and broad-based, and only the tips of the teeth possess fine cusps. The whitetip varies from light gray or pale brown to slaty-blue above and from yellowish-brown to dirty-white beneath. Usually the pectoral, pelvic, and first dorsal fins and the lobes of the caudal fin are light or white-tipped in the adult; in the newborn they may have black tips, which in medium-sized specimens may show as irregular black spots. A few whitetips reach 13 feet, but most are 7-10 feet long.

The whitetip is entirely a pelagic species, occurring far out at sea in the tropical and subtropical parts of the western Atlantic and the eastern Pacific. It is also reported from Madeira. In the western Atlantic it is known from off Long Island to Barbados and throughout the Gulf of Mexico. Almost without exception, it is restricted to waters deeper than 100 fathoms. It travels singly or in packs, being the commonest of the pelagic sharks of the tropical parts of the North Atlantic. Although it is ordinarily a sluggish species in its search for food, it can capture squids and tunalike fishes. The sexes segregate during part of the year, as do many other pelagic sharks. Mating occurs in late spring or early summer, and the young are born after a gestation period of about a year.

Other North American requiem sharks that are not described here include:

Finetooth shark *Aprionodon isodon*
Blacknose shark *Carcharhinus acronotus*
Bignose shark *Carcharhinus altimus*
Smalltail shark *Carcharhinus porosus*
Narrowtooth shark *Carcharhinus remotus*
Night shark *Hypoprion signatus*
Sicklefin smoothhound *Mustelus lunulatus*
Florida smoothhound *Mustelus norrisi*

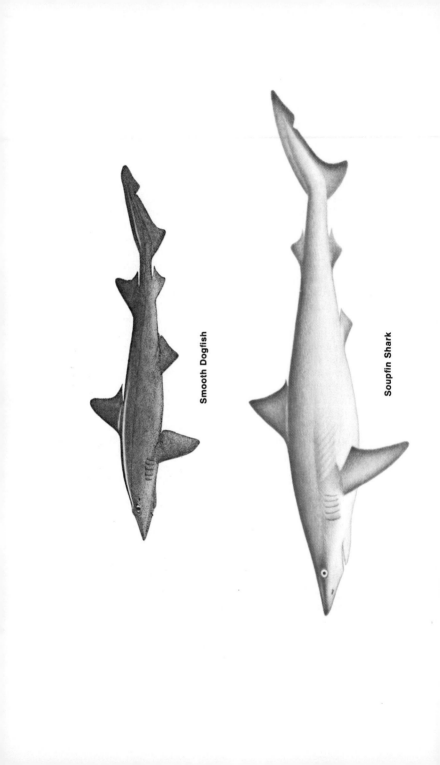

Smooth Dogfish

Soupfin Shark

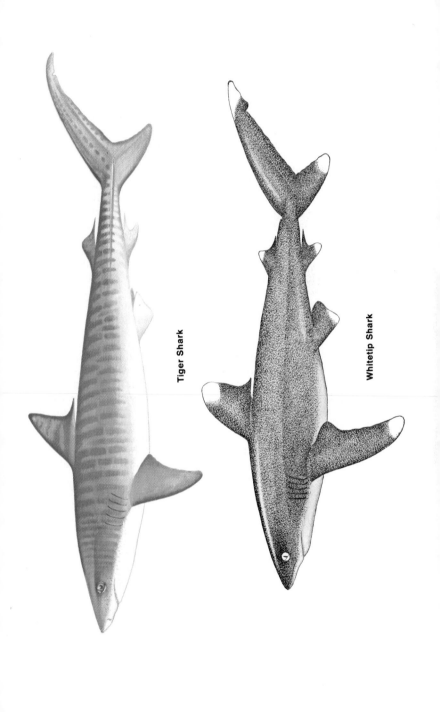

Tiger Shark

Whitetip Shark

DOGFISH SHARK FAMILY Squalidae

GREENLAND SHARK *Somniosus microcephalus* This is one of the larger sharks found on both sides of the Atlantic in Arctic and sub-Arctic waters and southward as far as the Gulf of Maine. It is plentiful around Greenland; hence its name. It is normally found near the surface in winter, but in summer it is usually in deeper water and has been recorded at great depths.

The Greenland shark is easily separated from other Atlantic squalid sharks by the lack of spines in the dorsal fin. It is colored brown or black above as well as below, although the color is variable, and some individuals are slaty-gray all over. The sides and back are crossed by indistinct dark bands, often with whitish spots. It is reported to reach a length of 24 feet and 1 ton in weight, but the largest specimens found in the Gulf of Maine seldom exceed 17 feet. A specimen 11 feet long weighs about 650 pounds.

This shark feeds on fishes, seals, sea birds, and invertebrates; it regularly gathers around whaling stations to devour the offal.

A very sluggish shark, it offers no resistance when hooked or harpooned and may be drawn out of the water very easily. It is sought by commercial fishermen off Greenland, Iceland, and northern Norway, where it is usually caught on hand lines.

SPINY DOGFISH *Squalus acanthias* This very common shark is characterized by the sharp spine in front of each dorsal fin. The head is flat, and the tapering snout ends in a blunt tip. Both dorsal fins are nearly identical, the second being about two-thirds the size of the first. The lack of an anal fin also helps to distinguish this species. The small, reduced teeth are directed toward the corners of the mouth. The fish is usually slate or brown above, grading to pale gray or white beneath. A row of small white spots along the sides occurs in smaller specimens, but those disappear in large adults. Most dogfish are 2–3 feet long, and maximum size is about 4 feet. Weights of 20 pounds have been reported.

It occurs in the northern parts of the North Atlantic and North Pacific. On the United States Atlantic coast it occurs from Nova Scotia to North Carolina, and is replaced in Caribbean waters, apparently, by a closely related species (S. *cubensis*). Essentially a coolwater shark, it migrates inshore with the advent of colder temperatures, moving offshore or northward as temperatures increase inshore. Dogfish swim in swarms of many thousands, roaming over depths from the surf zone to as deep as 100 fathoms.

ANGEL SHARK FAMILY Squatinidae

ATLANTIC ANGEL SHARK *Squatina dumerili* This distinctively flattened shark has pectoral fins that are expanded into winglike structures similar to those of skates. The gill openings are mostly

Greenland Shark

Spiny Dogfish

ventrally placed, rather than on the sides, as in other sharks. The head is broad and blunt, the dorsal and caudal fins are small, and the caudal peduncle is flattened and expanded. The teeth in both jaws are the same and are thin and pointed, with the conelike cusp on a rounded base. Fresh specimens are bluish-gray or ashy-gray to brown above, with hues of red or purple on the head and fins. The lower parts are white, with reddish spots on the throat, the belly, and just behind the anal opening. The pelvics are irregularly banded with red. Specimens of 5 feet are reported, and a 4-foot fish weighed about 60 pounds. Its European relative grows to 8 feet and a weight of 170 pounds.

It is a western Atlantic species, known only from southern New England to southern Florida, the northern Gulf of Mexico, and Jamaica, being most abundant between Virginia and Delaware. Specimens have been taken mostly from shallow water, but several have been captured in depths of about 100 and 700 fathoms. It enters brackish water at times, and is commonly found in the lower reaches of estuaries.

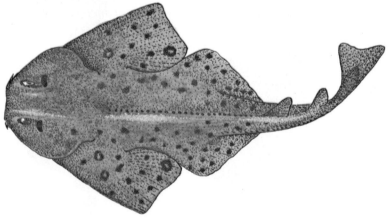

Pacific Angel Shark

PACIFIC ANGEL SHARK *Squatina californica* Closely related to the Atlantic angel shark, the Pacific angel differs primarily in the shape of the inner barbel of the nostril, that of the California species being expanded into a spoonlike structure, while that of the Atlantic species is narrow and tapering. The Pacific angel is reddish-brown, grading through brown to black above, spotted with dark or olive markings. The underparts are white, and the fins are gray on their posterior edges. It usually grows to about 3 feet, although 5-foot, 60-pound specimens have been reported. It is found only along the

Pacific coast of North America, from lower California to southern Alaska. More common along the southern California coast, it occurs on the bottom in shallow, inshore areas.

Skates

Skates are fishlike vertebrates possessing 5 pairs of gill clefts, a cartilaginous skeleton, and generally a flattened body. They differ from sharks in that the gill openings are located on the ventral surface, rather than on the sides. The anterior edges of the pectoral fins are joined to the sides of the head, past the gill openings, producing a flattened appearance; and the upper edges of the eye orbits are not free from the eyeballs. Further, skates lack anal fins, as do rays. Their bodies are strongly compressed, the tail is well marked off from the body, and there are usually 2 dorsal fins and a small but distinctive caudal fin. The skin of most skates has numerous thorns, whereas the skin of rays is generally smooth. Skates do not have a poisonous barb at or near the base of the tail, as is typical of most rays. All skates lay eggs, the young subsequently being hatched from a horny capsule.

SKATE FAMILY   Rajidae

BARNDOOR SKATE *Raja laevis*   One of the largest of the skates, the barndoor reaches a length of 5–6 feet. Its size, together with its pointed snout, smooth skin, pigmented mucous pores on the lower parts, and spines on the tail only, distinguish it from its relatives. The

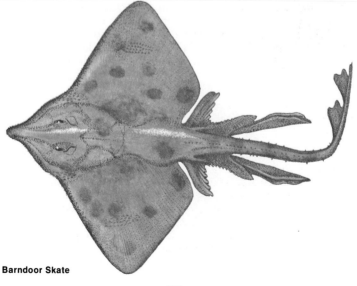

Barndoor Skate

teeth are large (32–36 in each jaw). Round, dark spots or blotches cover the dorsal surface, which is reddish-brown to brown. Each pectoral fin generally has an oval blotch at its base. These skates grow to nearly 40 pounds, and most taken are over 2 feet long; the very small ones are rarely seen.

Known only from the western North Atlantic Ocean, it is recorded from the Newfoundland Banks to South Carolina, but is most common in the New England–Middle Atlantic region. To the north it is taken the year round generally over sand or gravel bottom. It has been taken from the surf zone down to 235 fathoms.

BIG SKATE *Raja binoculata*   This is the Pacific relative of the barndoor skate of the Atlantic. The upper surface of the skin is prickly, and the outer margins of the pelvic fins are slightly concave (in the California skate these margins are slightly convex). The big skate is brown above, covered with numerous light spots scattered about the body. Each wing is characterized by an ocellus or eyespot, which is dark with a white rim. The underparts are pure white with black spots on the mucous pores. The skate grows to 8 feet in length.

Found from northwestern Alaska to southern California, it is most common south of central California, where it is one of the most abundant of the California skates. Eggs are laid, and the egg cases are large for skates, being about 1 foot long and lacking the filaments characteristic of the little skate and its relatives. Each case has 2–7 eggs, and hatching is believed to occur the year round. Adults eat crustaceans and fishes. The big skate's wings are valued as food.

CALIFORNIA SKATE *Raja inornata*   The relatively long snout is extended into a tip, but not so much as in the longnose skate. The front margin of the disk is convex, and there is no eyespot on either side of the disk as in the big skate. The California skate is dark olive-brown above with a dark ring at the base of each pectoral fin; its belly

California Skate

is pale to dusky with irregular mottlings. It grows to $2^{1}/_{2}$ feet and occurs from Washington to southern California in deepwater. Taken by trawlers, it is common enough to enter the commercial catch, and its wings are valued as food.

CLEARNOSE SKATE *Raja eglanteria* The combination of the distinctive subquadrate disk with its markings of bars and dots, the translucent snout on either side of the midline, and the single row of thorns along the midline identifies this species. It resembles the barndoor skate in many respects, but the barndoor has the midrow of thorns only on the tail. The clearnose's dorsal fins are separate, and there are no large circular markings on either wing, as in the roundel skate. The clearnose is reddish-brown to light brown above with numerous dark broken bars interspersed with dark spots. In some specimens darker and lighter spots and bars occur together. The underparts are white. It grows to about 37 inches, but most seen are less than 30 inches, at which size it weighs about 6 pounds.

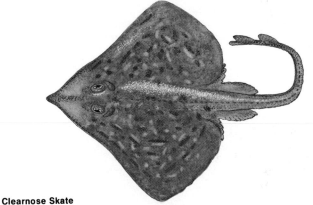

Clearnose Skate

The clearnose ranges from Cape Cod to middle Florida, most commonly between the Carolinas and Long Island. It is a shallow-water species, usually taken in less than 10 fathoms, but it has been taken from depths of 65 fathoms. It breeds inshore during the spring, and the young are hatched from the horny egg cases after 3 months or more. A springtime inshore migration occurs and a converse offshore movement in the fall, the time of movement depending on temperature and latitude.

Although a few are used as food, there is no commercial market for clearnose skates, but they are taken during the summer, sometimes in large numbers, by anglers fishing in inshore waters.

LITTLE SKATE *Raja erinacea* The little skate has a distinctively blunt snout and 3 rows of spines along the midline of the back, most pronounced in the young. The tail is long and covered with spines, and the dorsal fins are touching one another, with no spines between them. The little skate closely resembles the winter skate, but has fewer than 66 teeth, usually fewer than 54, in the upper jaw, while the winter skate has at least 72 and usually more than 80. The females are spinier than the males. The color is grayish to dark brown with dark mottlings or spots above, and white below with the tail dusky. Little skates grow to nearly 2 feet long, and a specimen $1\frac{1}{2}$ feet long weighs slightly over $1\frac{1}{4}$ pounds.

The little skate is a coolwater animal, occurring from Nova Scotia to North Carolina in the shallow surf zones to as deep as 80 fathoms. In New England, it is the commonest of all skates in that region. Taken predominantly close to shore in the winter, it moves offshore during April and May, reappearing in the shallows in October and November. Mating occurs throughout the year in less than 15 fathoms, with a peak from October to January and another peak in June and July. Tough-shelled eggs are laid that contain miniature skates. These egg cases, about 2 by $2\frac{1}{2}$ inches, have filamentlike extensions at each corner and are often seen on beaches.

Little Skate

LONGNOSE SKATE *Raja rhina* Characterized by a distinctively long snout that tapers forward rather gradually, this skate's disk has an irregular shape. The anterior margins of the pectoral fins are decidedly concave. The longnose is dark brown above with irregular spots, often with a distinct large spot, which lacks a white rim, on either wing. The ventral surface is a muddy blue. In size and general characteristics it is somewhat similar to the barndoor skate, growing to a length of $4\frac{1}{2}$ feet. It is recorded from southeastern Alaska to

38

southern California. It lays eggs, each measuring 3–5 inches long and containing a single individual.

ROUNDEL SKATE *Raja texana*   The body of this skate is diamond-shaped, with the corners meeting nearly at right angles. The skin is fairly smooth except for a row of thorns along the tail. On each pectoral fin is a distinct ocellus (a dark spot surrounded by a light area). These ocelli distinguish the roundel from other common skates, except the closely related *R. ackleyi*, which has elliptical ocelli and broadly rounded corners on the disk. The roundel skate is chocolate- to coffee-colored with a translucent area on the snout, as in the clearnose skate. Small specimens are sprinkled with pale spots and blotches. The roundel grows to about 21 inches long. Compared with other skates, this is an uncommon species. It is known only from central Florida to Aransas Pass, Texas.

WINTER SKATE *Raja ocellata*   This species closely resembles the little skate, from which it differs essentially in having 2 large whitish spots near the rear angles of the upper part of the disk. But these spots are sometimes absent, and the large number of teeth in the upper jaw of the winter skate (at least 80 and usually 90–100) separates it from the little skate, which has less than 66, and usually less than 54. The

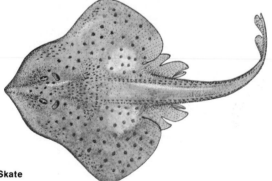

Winter Skate

upper parts are light brown, with numerous black dots that vary in size and number. It grows to about 3¹/₂ feet along and about 10–12 pounds. Specimens have been reported from Nova Scotia to North Carolina, but its center of abundance is between southern New England and New Jersey.

Seldom common anywhere, the winter skate occurs over hard bottoms of sand or gravel from shallow water to 50–60 fathoms. It prefers waters slightly less saline than oceanwater. In addition, it exhibits a tendency to undertake extensive migrations.

Rays

Rays are also closely related to sharks in that they have 5 pairs of gill clefts and a cartilaginous skeleton. But the teeth of skates and rays are pavementlike in contrast to the well-developed, pointed teeth characteristic of most sharks. They resemble skates in having gill openings, which open to the ventral surface, and pectoral fins joined to the head. Their skin is generally smooth; they have a slender tail which lacks a caudal and anal fin; and they usually have one or more well-developed serrated barbs, or spines, at or near the tail base. Rays typically have the embryos developing within the oviduct up to the time of hatching, and thus differ further from the egg-laying skates.

Largely a tropical species, the Atlantic stingray occurs predominantly about Florida and the Gulf of Mexico. It is known from Chesapeake Bay and is questionably reported from Surinam and Brazil. Most records are from shallow coastal waters, from only a few inches to 7–8 feet deep. It tolerates warmwaters and penetrates estuaries, being taken in water that is completely fresh as well as in full-strength oceanwater. In the Gulf of Mexico this stingray occurs in the shallows during spring and summer.

STINGRAY FAMILY Dasyatidae

ATLANTIC STINGRAY *Dasyatis sabina* A prominent, triangularly pointed snout sets this stingray off from its relatives. The disk is rhomboid, and the outer corners are broadly rounded, a characteristic it shares with the bluntnose stingray. But the distance from the snout to the eyes is much greater than the distance between the spiracles, or dorsal gill openings, in the Atlantic stingray. Further, the anterior margin of the disk is slightly indented along either side of the snout. There is a well-developed skin fold along the dorsal and ventral tail surfaces, and a row of thorny tubercles along the dorsal midline extends about one-quarter of the way onto the tail. Otherwise, the skin is smooth. The upper parts are brown to yellowish-brown, with light edgings along the margin, and the ventral surface is whitish. It is a small species, growing only to a length of about 2 feet.

BLUNTNOSE STINGRAY *Dasyatis sayi* This small stingray is characterized by the subcircular shape of the disk and the broadly rounded outer corners of the pectoral fins. Both the anterior and posterior margins of the disk are slightly convex. The tail is long, with a sharp spine about one-quarter of the distance from the base of the tail to the tip. Conspicuous folds are present along the upper and lower surfaces of the tail, and there are no rough thorns along the tail. Except for a row of small thorns along the midline just behind the head and supplementary thorns on either side of the midline, the skin is smooth. Small specimens are yellowish to light brown above; adults are gray to brown or red-brown to greenish. The tip of the tail is black, and the lower surface of the disk is white. Although the average size of a bluntnose off the United States mainland is probably about 1 foot wide, individuals from French Guiana are reported to average about 3 feet, which is about the maximum size reported for North America.

The bluntnose is known from Brazil to Massachusetts and throughout the Caribbean area. In certain places, notably North Carolina, Florida, and French Guiana, it is extremely common in shallow water.

DIAMOND STINGRAY *Dasyatis dipterura* This Pacific stingray closely resembles the southern stingray in that the corners of the disk are rather sharply rounded and the anterior margins of the wings are slightly convex. But the bony tubercles scattered about the disk of the southern stingray are present in the diamond only on the midline in a short row. The tail is quite long, about half again as long as the disk, and there are 1 or more long spines near the tail base. The upper parts are bluish-brown, and the ventral surface is dirty-white. A length of 6 feet is attained.

The diamond stingray occurs from southern California to British Columbia; a closely related, if not identical, form occurs southward to Peru. Common in protected bays and off beaches, it eats crabs and mollusks.

ROUGHTAIL STINGRAY *Dasyatis centroura* The roughtail resembles the southern stingray in general body shape and in having the outer corners of the disk only narrowly rounded. Its long tail is quite thorny, and there are 1 or more long barbed spines near the tail base. The body is rhomboid, with the anterior edges of the wings approximately straight-edged and the posterior margins slightly convex. Along the midline of the back is a series of irregularly spaced low thorns, bordered on either wing by additional, widely scattered thorns of a slightly larger size. There is no fold along the dorsal midline of the tail, but there is a skin fold along the lower surface of the tail. This ray is dark brown to black above with a black tail, and the lower parts are whitish or gray-white, occasionally with dusky to black blotches. It is one of the largest of the stingrays, growing to a recorded length of 10 feet and an estimated length of 13–14 feet and weight of several hundred pounds.

This species occurs in cooler waters than the closely related southern stingray. It is known with certainty from Georges Bank, off New England, to North Carolina, and is believed to occur in Florida. Closely related species occur in the eastern Atlantic and off Uruguay. Its center of abundance is from Delaware Bay to southern New England.

ROUND STINGRAY *Urolophus halleri* The nearly circular shape of the disk distinguishes this stingray from others along the western coast of North America. The skin is smooth, and the tail is short and

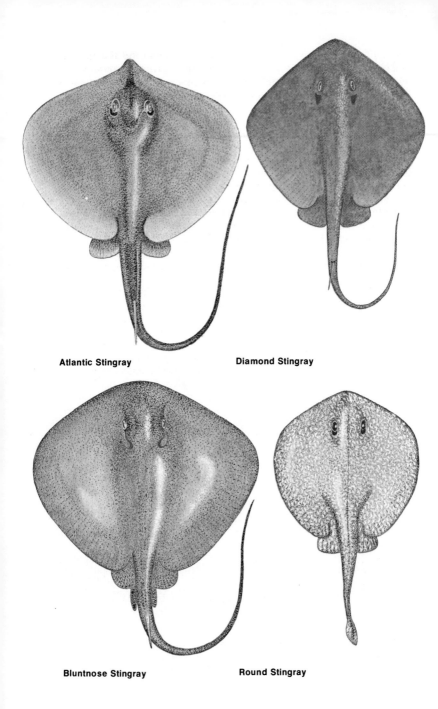

Atlantic Stingray

Diamond Stingray

Bluntnose Stingray

Round Stingray

lacks a dorsal fin. A well-developed spine is located near the tip of the tail. The round stingray is light brown above, with wavy wormlike markings covering the entire surface (occasionally showing up as round spots). It is yellow or yellowish below. The largest recorded specimen is a 22-inch female.

It occurs from Monterey Bay in central California to Panama Bay, where it is common in quiet waters and along sandy or muddy beaches. Most common in 2–3 fathoms, specimens have been taken from a few inches of water down to about 100 feet.

SMOOTH BUTTERFLY RAY *Gymnura micrura* This distinctive ray is recognized by its very broad disk, which is much wider than long, forming a diamond shape. At all stages the tail is very short, and this species has a keel on the upper surface and no tail spine, the latter characteristic distinguishing it from the spiny butterfly ray. It is usually classified with the stingray family, although some ichthyologists prefer to retain it in a separate family. Color varies from gray,

Smooth Butterfly Ray

brown, or light green above with small spots and wormlike markings of lighter or darker color than the background. The tail is pale with 3–4 dark crossbars, and the ventral color of the disk is white with grayish, yellowish, or rosy hues. Characteristic of this species is its ability to vary its color depending on its background. About 4 feet is the maximum width.

The smooth butterfly ranges regularly from Brazil to Chesapeake Bay, drifting northward as far as southern New England. Sand bottoms of shallow coastal waters are its favorite haunt, from a few feet to as deep as about 150 feet. It occurs in warm, shallow waters during the late spring and summer.

SOUTHERN STINGRAY *Dasyatis americana* Its disk is roughly rhomboid in shape, with the anterior edges shorter than the posterior. The tail is long and whiplike, with a barbed spine near the tail base.

43

The southern resembles the roughtail stingray in having the outer corners of the disk narrowly rounded, and both differ in this respect from the Atlantic stingray and the bluntnose stingray, whose disks have broadly and evenly rounded outer corners. The southern differs from the roughtail stingray in having a long, wide skin fold along the

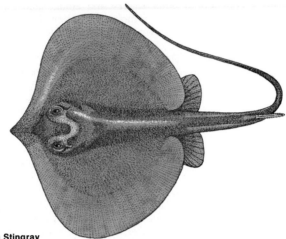

Southern Stingray

lower part of the tail and in lacking well-developed stubby thorns on either side of the tail. The skin is smooth save for a single row of spines along the midline and a small row of secondary, small thorns on either side of the midline. This ray is gray to dark brown to green above and has a light blotch in the middle of its forehead. The ventral surface is gray-white with dark edgings. This species reaches a width of 5 feet and a length of 7 feet.

Its range is in the western Atlantic, from New Jersey to Rio de Janeiro, and throughout the Gulf and Caribbean areas, its center of abundance being from the southern Caribbean to North Carolina. An inshore species, it frequents shallow, open areas of sand and mud bottoms in search of clams, crabs, shrimps, worms, and small fishes.

SPINY BUTTERFLY RAY *Gymnura altavela* The presence of a well-developed tail spine separates this butterfly ray from the smooth butterfly ray. Its disk, like that of its relative, is diamond-shaped and very much wider than long, but the leading edge of the disk is slightly convex instead of concave. Small tentacles behind the spiracles separate it from the smooth butterfly ray. The skin is smooth except in large adults. The disk is dark brown with a red to gray cast, with small spots or blotches. The tail is the same color as the disk in adults, but in small specimens has light and dark bands. The lower parts are whitish, grading to pale brown or rosy, with the disk edged in dusky markings. A western Atlantic specimen nearly 7 feet wide has been reported, but the species has reached 13 feet in the waters off Africa.

YELLOW STINGRAY *Urolophus jamaicensis* This species has a nearly circular disk and a thick tail about as long as the disk length; near the tip of the tail is a well-developed, serrated spine. The distinctive rounded caudal fin curves around the tip of the tail and is longer on the lower surface. Except for a well-developed patch of thorns along the midsection of the back, the skin is smooth. A distinctively beautiful color pattern characterizes this little stingray. The upper surfaces are often covered with wormlike markings of greenish-pinkish or brown on a lighter background.

The yellow stingray is recorded from Trinidad to Florida, with strays occurring to North Carolina, but it is essentially a tropical species limited to the Caribbean. This species seldom grows to more than 1 foot across the disk.

ELECTRIC RAYS   Torpedinidae

ATLANTIC TORPEDO *Torpedo nobiliana* This comparatively large ray differs from its relative, the lesser electric ray, in its size, the straight anterior margin of the disk, and the dark chocolate color that is either uniform or with a few vague, darker spots. The disk is not quite as circular as that of the lesser electric ray. The skin is smooth, and 2 well-developed dorsal fins and a large caudal fin are set on a muscular tail. A maximum weight of 200 pounds has been reported, but any torpedo of over 100 pounds is rare, and most are about 30 pounds. It grows to 5–6 feet long.

This is strictly an Atlantic species, occurring from Nova Scotia to Cuba and from Scotland to West Africa and the Azores. It appears to

Atlantic Torpedo

45

be more common in the cooler parts of its range. Most records have been from shallow water, but torpedoes are believed to be most common in waters 10–40 fathoms deep. Some specimens have been taken off New York in depths of 50–60 fathoms. The torpedo lives on the bottom, capturing fishes such as flounders and eels, but it is apparently able to obtain fast-swimming prey, for specimens taken in England have contained sharks and salmon. This species, like others of the family, can give a considerable electric shock, the power for which is generated through specialized cells in the disk. This shock is used in stunning its prey, and voltages of 170–220 have been recorded for the species.

LESSER ELECTRIC RAY *Narcine brasiliensis* This well-marked species is distinguished from the Atlantic torpedo by its size, its more convex head, the close placement of the spiracles to the eyes, its more rigid snout, and the color pattern. The disk is nearly circular, but the broad pelvic fins appear so nearly confluent with the disk that the disk takes on a triangular appearance. It is dark brown, grading through gray-brown to reddish. The color pattern is highly variable and ranges

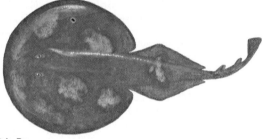

Lesser Electric Ray

from a uniform color to a more common pattern of irregular dark blotches, each of which usually has a light center. Occasionally a band crosses the disk in front of the eyes. The ray grows to a length of about 15 inches.

Found in tropical waters, it is commonest from Brazil to Florida and throughout the Caribbean. A few range into the waters of North Carolina and Argentina. This same species also occurs from the Gulf of California to Panama.

PACIFIC ELECTRIC RAY *Torpedo californica* This species is similar to the Atlantic torpedo in the shape of the subcircular disk, the short tail, and the smooth skin. It is blue-black to lead-gray, with small spots on the dark background of the upper sides of the disk. It grows to at least 50 pounds and 3 feet. Known from British Columbia to southern California in waters that are moderately deep, this ray pos-

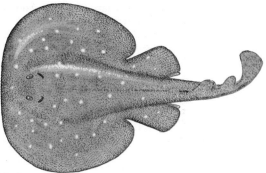

Pacific Electric Ray

sesses the ability of other members of the family to generate a powerful electric shock.

EAGLE RAY FAMILY Myliobatidae

BAT RAY *Myliobatis californica*   Like other members of the family, the bat ray has a conspicuous head set off from the pectoral fins. The disk is much wider than long, and its tapering tips have rounded outer corners. The tail is much longer than the body, and 1 or more sharp spines are near the tail base. A small dorsal fin is located on the tail base next to the pelvic fins. The large eyes protrude on either side of the head, and the teeth are arranged in a flat series. The skin is smooth, and the ray is dark brown to olive or even black above, and white below. Maximum size is just over 200 pounds and about 5 feet wide.

Bat rays range from Oregon to the Gulf of California along sandy bottoms of bays and quiet lagoons, although they are taken on occasion in rocky areas where sand patches are interspersed. They occur singly or in schools, where they are sometimes seen jumping about the surface. They may be seen along the bottom cruising in search of clams, oysters, and shrimps, which they dig by flapping their wings to create turbulence. In more open areas they eat snails and abalones, which they easily crush with their flat, pavementlike teeth.

BULLNOSE RAY *Myliobatis freminvillei*   The broad disk, slender tail, and peculiarly shaped head readily identify this relative of the stingrays. The teeth are in 7 series in each jaw and are platelike in structure. The snout projects noticeably from the disk, unlike the stingrays, and the sides of the snout are partially attached to the pectoral fins. One or two spines are located near the base of the tail. The bullnose resembles the spotted eagle ray, but lacks the spots, the upper surface of the disk being plain reddish-brown to gray-brown, with the margin of the disk pale and the tail dusky to black. The ventral surface is white or whitish with dark hues. The bullnose is a small ray, growing only to about 3 feet wide.

A western Atlantic species, it is known from Brazil and from North Carolina to Cape Cod, being most abundant from Virginia to New Jersey. It should be expected to occur in the Gulf of Mexico and Caribbean, from where it has not yet been recorded. A closely related species, *M. goodei*, separable from the bullnose ray in several proportional characters, is more common in western South Atlantic waters.

The bullnose is found in quiet bays and sloughs, where it searches the sandy and muddy flats for crabs, clams, snails, and lobsters. It visits the north from June to October, disappearing in the cooler months.

COWNOSE RAY *Rhinoptera bonasus* The cownose superficially resembles the spotted eagle ray and bullnose ray. It has a broad disk, pointed pectoral fin tips, and a long slender tail, and is usually included in the same family. But the snout of the cownose ray is deeply indented to form 2 lobes. In side view, the head is deeply indented along its anterior profile. The eyes are located ahead of the pectoral fin margin, slightly protruding from the disk on the peculiarly shaped head. The skin, which is smooth, is brownish above, occasionally with yellow hues, and white or yellow-white beneath. The cownose reaches a width of 7 feet and a weight of perhaps 100 pounds.

Specimens are known from Brazil to southern New England, with records in the Caribbean only from British Guiana, Venezuela, and northern Cuba, although it should be expected anywhere in the Gulf and Caribbean. It browses across mudflats and sandflats in search of food, stirring up food from the bottom with its pectoral fins.

SPOTTED EAGLE RAY *Aetobatus narinari* This beautifully marked ray has regularly arranged spots that vary from white to greenish to yellow on the upper part of the disk. The lower parts are white, and the tail is black. One or more sharp barbs are placed at the base of the long tail, which may be twice as long as the disk. The body is roughly diamond-shaped, with the anterior edges of the disk convex and the posterior edges concave. A shovel-shaped snout with a peculiar duck-billed mouth further characterizes this species. It has only a single series of broad, flat teeth in each jaw, a characteristic that readily separates it from the closely related cownose ray and bullnose ray. Individuals $7^1/_2$ feet wide and up to 500 pounds are known; the body is relatively thicker at the same size than is true of other rays.

The eagle ray occurs from Angola to Cape Verde in the eastern Atlantic, and in the western Atlantic from Brazil to Chesapeake Bay and throughout the Caribbean Sea. It is also known from the Red Sea and the tropical parts of the Pacific.

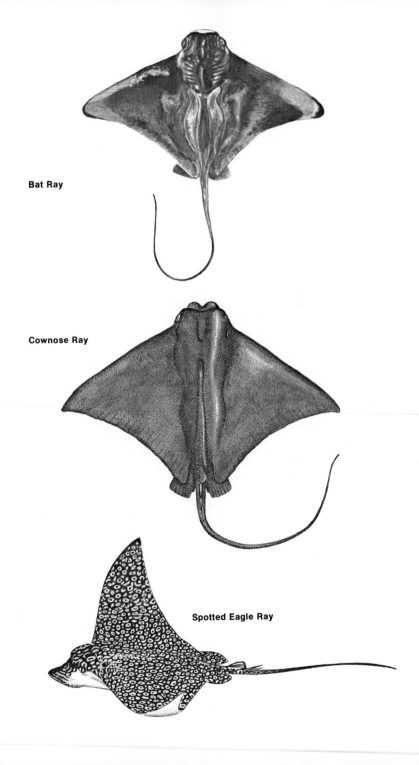

Bat Ray

Cownose Ray

Spotted Eagle Ray

Like other large rays, eagle rays are seen swimming singly or in pairs or in large schools, depending on the time of year. They also share with the other large rays the habit of leaping from the water, during which time they may emit loud croaking sounds. Their duck-billed mouths are used as plows to dig up clams, oysters, and other hard-bodied burrowing organisms, which they crush with their pavementlike teeth. Worms, shrimps, and fishes are also eaten.

MANTA FAMILY   Mobulidae

ATLANTIC MANTA *Manta birostris* This ray is easily distinguished by the 2 hornlike projecting appendages on the front of the head; the large disk, which is about twice as wide as long; and the very long tail. The large eyes are placed on the sides of the distinct head. Its closest Atlantic relative, the devil ray, has its mouth beneath the head; the mouth of the manta is at the tip of the head. Usually a serrated spine is present just behind the dorsal fin. The skin, which is roughened with numerous small tubercles, grades from reddish to olive-brown to black in older specimens. The lower parts are white or white with gray or black blotches. White markings are sometimes present in various patterns on the shoulder, on the posterior part of the disk, behind the eyes, or on the outer surface of the hornlike fins. This manta grows to a known width of 22 feet and a length of 17 feet, at which size it approaches 2 tons.

The manta is known from Brazil to the Carolinas, drifting northward to New England and Georges Bank and Bermuda. In the eastern Atlantic it is known from Madeira and the tropical waters of West Africa. Closely related, if not identical, species occur in the western Pacific and Indo-Pacific regions and in the tropical waters of the eastern Pacific Ocean. These huge batlike rays are encountered at the surface as they swim or bask there, but they probably rest on the bottom as well. They are seen in pairs or in groups of as many as 30, splashing and somersaulting about the surface, with a resounding splash that can be heard at quite a distance.

The head fins are used to channel food into the large mouth, and in this respect the food and feeding habits of the manta differ from those of other rays. Adults eat small shrimps, mullets, and plankton; juveniles eat anchovies, shrimps, and copepods.

Sexual maturity evidently does not occur before a width of 14–15 feet; the young are hatched from eggs and subsequently develop within the mother's body.

DEVIL RAY *Mobula hypostoma* The devil ray resembles the Atlantic manta and Pacific manta in that it has a broad, diamond-shaped disk and 2 well-developed fleshy horns on the head. But the mouth of the devil ray is on the underside of the disk, not at the tip of the head. It is much smaller than the other mantas and grows only to about 4 feet wide. The skin of small specimens is smooth; that of

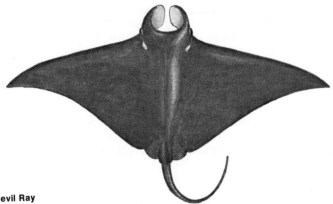

Devil Ray

larger individuals has fine prickles. The tail base lacks a spine, and the tail is long and whiplike, about as long as the body. The disk is blackish-brown above and yellowish to gray-white beneath, with a dark blotch on the lower parts just behind each eye.

The devil ray occurs off Senegal in the eastern Atlantic and is known in the western Atlantic at various places between Brazil and North Carolina and western Florida. A few are seen occasionally, but it is never as common as the Atlantic manta. Like other mantas, it leaps from the water.

PACIFIC MANTA *Manta hamiltoni* Its disk somewhat resembles that of another Pacific ray, the bat stingray, but the hornlike projections on the head readily separate the Pacific manta from the bat ray. The tips of the pectoral fins are pointed, the pelvic fins are short and confluent with the posterior margin of the disk, and there is a short

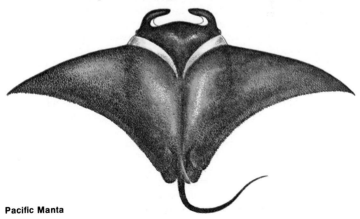

Pacific Manta

dorsal fin. The manta's short tail and the terminal position of its mouth separate it from a southern, closely related species, *Mobula lucasana*, whose tail is nearly as long as the disk and whose mouth is located beneath the tip of the snout. The Pacific manta is black above and white to bluish beneath. All mantas reach a large size, this species growing to 18 feet and over 2,300 pounds.

SAWFISH FAMILY   Pristidae

SMALLTOOTH SAWFISH *Pristis pectinata*   Also called the common sawfish, this ray is found on both sides of the Atlantic. In the western Atlantic, it ranges from New York and Bermuda to middle

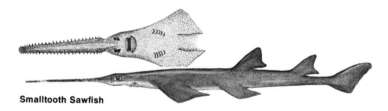

Smalltooth Sawfish

Brazil and the northern part of the Gulf of Mexico. It is a year-round resident in Florida, but northward it is known only as a summer visitor. There are 9 recognized species in the genus *Pristis*. They are found along tropical and warm temperate coastlines in all parts of the world.

The smalltooth sawfish may be separated from the only other sawfish (the largetooth sawfish, *P. perotteti*) known from the western Atlantic as follows: Its first dorsal fin originates about over the origin of its pelvics (rather than considerably in front, as in *P. perotteti*); its caudal fin is much shorter, with lower lobe only faintly indicated; its rostral teeth are more numerous (24 or more on each side); its saw is relatively shorter; its second dorsal has a posterior margin much less deeply concave; and its pectorals are much smaller. *P. pectinata* resembles *P. pristis* of the eastern Atlantic in the shape of its caudal fin and in the position of the first dorsal fin relative to the pelvics, but it differs from *P. pristis* in having numerous rostral teeth.

The smalltooth is nearly uniform dark gray to blackish-brown above, paler along margins of fins, and white to grayish-white or pale yellow below.

This species, like other sawfishes, is almost exclusively restricted to the immediate vicinity of land in water only a few feet deep. It is most often encountered in partially enclosed waters, lying in the deeper holes on bottoms of mud or muddy sand. It regularly runs up large freshwater rivers and perhaps may live permanently in such places. It has been taken from the lower reaches of the Amazon, the

Essequibo, the Atrato and San Juan rivers of Colombia, the lower Mississippi, and in the St. Johns River, Florida.

The smalltooth sawfish preys on various kinds of small animals chiefly by stirring the mud with its saw. This activity has often been seen, and the motion of the saw has been described as principally backward and forward. It has also been seen attacking schools of small fishes by slashing sideways with the saw, then eating the individuals that are wounded. It will readily take a hook baited with freshly cut fish.

This species of sawfish is about 2 feet long at birth and grows to a length of 18 feet or perhaps more. Most of the individuals that wander northward along the Atlantic coast to North Carolina and beyond are large. Specimens 16 feet long have been taken from both North Carolina and New Jersey. An individual of this length weighs about 700 pounds.

Sawfish can utilize their saws by striking sideways with great power. Consequently, even small ones should be handled or approached with caution. Although people have suffered severe injury through handling or disturbing sawfish, there is no evidence of unprovoked attacks.

GUITARFISH FAMILY   Rhinobatidae

ATLANTIC GUITARFISH *Rhinobatos lentiginosus*   This saltwater ray is characterized by its long, flattened body and its lance-shaped snout, which is shaped like an elongated triangle. The dorsal fins are well developed, and the pectoral fins are rounded at their posterior edges. The fish is brown or olivaceous above with numerous light dots; the lower parts are pale. The area on either side of the midline of the snout is translucent. Maximum size is about $2^1/_2$ feet long.

This guitarfish is found along the Atlantic coast from North Carolina to Yucatán, being relatively common about Florida. A limited northward migration of at least a few individuals occurs in the spring and early summer. Inshore habitats are preferred whenever shallow waters are found, but specimens have been found as deep as 60 feet. They are taken in quiet waters or in regions of moderate surf, where they prod for food, predominantly amphipods and mole crabs.

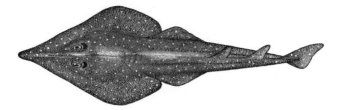

Atlantic Guitarfish

53

SHOVELNOSE GUITARFISH *Rhinobatos productus*   This Pacific ray is very similar in shape to the Atlantic guitarfish and is limited to the area between central California and the Gulf of California. Like that of its Atlantic relative, the snout is sharply pointed and wedge-

Shovelnose Guitarfish

shaped, tapering to a thick tail bearing 2 dorsal fins. The area in the front of the snout is translucent. The back is brownish-gray and the lower parts white, with a black blotch beneath the snout. The young are born alive after being kept, following hatching from the eggs in the mother, for a period of time within the mother. The shovelnose grows to about 4 feet, feeding on worms, crabs, and clams. It has no commercial value and is a nuisance to gillnet fishermen and anglers.

CHIMAERA FAMILY   Chimaeridae

RATFISH *Hydrolagus colliei*   This relative of the sharks has only a single gill opening on either side, rather than the 5–7 that occur in sharks. A fleshy gill cover superficially resembles that of bony fishes. The body is stout anteriorly, tapering to a slim tail. The head is relatively large, with a pointed snout; a clublike projection is located between the eyes of the male. Each of the 2 dorsal fins is preceded by a heavy spine. The body is silvery, with hues of green, golden, blue, or pale metallic-brown; many white spots cover the body in some specimens. The skin is smooth, and the teeth are fused into bony plates that are incisorlike on the upper jaw.

The ratfish belongs to a group that contains about 28 species found all over the world, usually in moderately deep coldwater. The ratfish occurs from northwestern Alaska to Ensenada, Baja Califor-

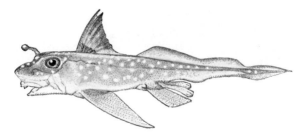

Ratfish

nia. In the southern part of its range it is found in water that is relatively deep, but is taken in relatively shallower water in its northern habitat, usually at depths greater than 40 fathoms. Ratfish occur in large numbers during the fall. They are sluggish swimmers, moving by feeble undulations of the tail and second dorsal fin.

Fertilization is internal, the male introducing sperm via the sharklike claspers. The eggs are tough-skinned capsules deposited vertically in the mud. The young, which resemble the adults upon hatching, have been taken in British Columbia during October.

The ratfish eats mostly fishes, but mussels and other invertebrates are also taken. There is no commercial value to this species, but its liver produces a fine cleaning oil and gun lubricant.

Bony Fishes
Class Osteichthyes

STURGEON FAMILY Acipenseridae

Seven species of sturgeons occur in North American waters, and these are either anadromous or wholly freshwater forms. For descriptions see *McClane's Field Guide to Freshwater Fishes of North America.*

BONEFISH FAMILY Albulidae

BONEFISH *Albula vulpes* This distinctive species, the only living member of its genus, belongs to a family of very primitive bony fishes that dates back to the Cretaceous period (125 million years ago). Like the tarpon and the ladyfish, it possesses an eellike, leptocephalous larval stage. It has a worldwide distribution in tropical and warm waters; on the Atlantic coast of the New World it has been taken as far north as Woods Hole, Massachusetts, but generally does not extend north of Cape Hatteras, and occurs as far south as Rio de Janeiro; on the Pacific coast it has been taken from San Francisco Bay, California, south to Talara, Peru. Two other species of bonefish are presently recognized, *Dixonina nemoptera,* or longfin bonefish, occurring spottily from the Florida Keys to Central America, and the deepwater bonefish *Pterothrissus belloci.* The color of a large bonefish is bluish above and bright silvery on both sides and below. There are dark streaks between rows of scales, at least on the dorsal half of each side, and the dorsal and caudal fins have dusky margins. Very young adults have a double series of dark spots on the back, each just off the median line; these spots soon unite to form about 9 dark crossbands on the back, extending down nearly or quite to the lateral line. The third band crosses the back at the origin of the dorsal fin; the next 2 bands are situated posteriorly under the base of the dorsal fin. The bands persist until the fish reaches a length of about 3 inches. The dark longitudinal streaks of the adult appear shortly before the crossbands become obscure.

Other distinguishing characteristics are a slender body, rounder and less compressed in large specimens than in young adults; firm scales with crenulate membranous edges; 65–71 in lateral series; low head, flat above, its depth exceeding its width at middle of eye by about the diameter of the pupil. The snout is rather long and conical, projecting about a third of its length beyond the mandible. The maxillary does not quite reach to the eye in large specimens.

Dorsal fin somewhat elevated anteriorly, its origin a little nearer to tip of snout than to base of caudal; 17–18, rarely 19, softrays. Caudal

Bonefish

Longfin Bonefish

fin deeply forked, the upper lobe somewhat longer than the lower. Anal fin very small, its origin nearer to base of caudal than to base of pelvic; 8–9 softrays. Pelvic fin somewhat smaller than pectoral, inserted under or slightly behind middle of dorsal base. Pectoral fin with rounded margin reaching less than halfway to pelvic; 16–17, rarely 15, softrays; axillary scale about half as long as fin, adherent to body.

Bonefish attain weights of over 20 pounds. The average fish taken by angling in popular Florida and Bahamian locations is 4–6 pounds and somewhat smaller in Central American and Mexican waters. Fish of 8 pounds or more are considered large, and the rod-and-reel record of 19 pounds was caught off Zululand, South Africa. Bonefish in excess of 20 pounds occasionally enter the commercial markets in Mozambique, Africa, where large individuals are caught by hand line in deepwater.

Although the eellike, leptocephalous larval stage is well known, the spawning season and spawning grounds remain undescribed. Ripe fish and larvae are taken at various times of the year, which indicates a prolonged breeding period. Exceptionally large schools (densely formed and covering an acre or more) are sometimes seen milling in protected shallow bays behind reefs. Both small and very large adults occur together, and these concentrations may be prespawning or spawning bonefish. Evidently, the larvae are dispersed by oceanic currents, as recently metamorphosed juveniles have been collected as far north as Great South Bay, New York. Metamorphosis to the fry stage involves a profound alteration in body form. The eellike leptocephalous grows to a length of about $2^{1}/_{2}$ inches before it starts to develop fins; then it commences shrinking. It continues to shrink for 10–12 days until it is about half its original length. It next metamorphoses into a bonefish form before starting to grow again.

LONGFIN BONEFISH *Dixonina nemoptera* This species resembles the bonefish in having an elongate, torpedo-shaped body, with a slender head and a mouth placed beneath the tip of the pointed snout and extending back to the middle of the eye. The single dorsal fin is placed about in the middle of the body.

The longfin differs from the bonefish in having a more slender body, a longer maxillary bone, a greater number of lateral line scales (76–84 versus about 70), a longer and more conical snout, a larger mouth, and an elongate last ray in the dorsal and anal fins, the length of the fin being less pronounced in the young. The body is bright silvery with dark scale lines along the upper half of the body and dark green about the head. Maximum recorded size is about 16 inches.

The longfin is known in the Atlantic from northern Brazil, Venezuela, Santo Domingo, Jamaica, and, rarely, from the Florida Keys. In the Pacific it ranges from the Gulf of California to Costa Rica.

TARPON FAMILY   Elopidae

LADYFISH *Elops saurus*   This is a fairly common fish, occurring in the Atlantic, Indian, and western Pacific oceans. It is most abundant in the warmer parts of its range and very common around southern Florida and in the Caribbean. Despite the various names applied to this species (such as chiro and 10-pounder), ladyfish seems to be the most acceptable; the name 10-pounder is misleading, as this fish seldom reaches a weight of much over 5–6 pounds. Large ladyfish of 8–9 pounds are reported.

The ladyfish is slender, finely scaled, and generally silver in color with a blue-green back. It has 20 dorsal rays, 13 anal rays, 16–19 pectoral rays, and 13–15 pelvic rays. The scales are very small, about 100–120 along lateral line. Its body is quite elongate. Pectoral fins are inserted low on body. Its dorsal fin is single, on middle of back, the last ray not produced into a whiplike filament as in the tarpon. Pelvic fins are slightly in advance of dorsal fin, about midway between pectoral and caudal fins. Caudal fin is deeply forked. Upper jaw reaches well beyond vertical from the posterior margin of orbit.

The ladyfish occurs in shallow water close to shore over sandy and muddy bottom. It is usually taken in bays, estuaries, and passes. Accessible from shore, piers, and bridges. It also enters freshwater rivers in Florida.

The ladyfish is an excellent light-tackle quarry. It readily strikes artificial lures and leaps frequently when hooked. Its attack is so swift that a great many fish are missed, although ladyfish generally occur in large schools, and obtaining two or more strikes on the same retrieve is common.

A similar species, the machete (*E. affinis*), occurs in the Pacific and has been recorded in southern California.

TARPON *Megalops atlantica*   The tarpon occurs on both sides of the Atlantic; on the western side it has been taken as far north as Nova Scotia, although it does not regularly occur north of Cape Hatteras; it extends southward to at least Natal, Brazil. In the eastern Atlantic it ranges from Senegal to the Congo.

The color is usually dark blue to greenish-black dorsally, shading to bright silver on the sides and belly. Specimens from inland waters sometimes display brownish or brassy colors.

Other distinguishing characters of the tarpon are body with almost vertical sides; dorsal outline of head nearly straight and horizontal, the back somewhat elevated; scales large, firm with crenulate membranous border; 41–48 in lateral series. Lateral line complete, decurved anteriorly, the pores branched. Head moderately short and deep, its depth at middle of eye not quite twice its width at the same place. Mouth superior, mandible projecting far beyond the gape, entering dorsal profile in advance of mouth.

Ladyfish

Tarpon

Dorsal fin high anteriorly with 13–15 softrays, the last ray greatly elongated; origin of fin about equidistant between base of caudal and anterior margin of eye. Caudal fin deeply forked, the lobes about equal in length, generally somewhat longer than head. Anal fin somewhat elevated anteriorly with 22–25 softrays, the last ray elongated in adults. Pectoral fin rather long with 13–14 softrays.

The tarpon is one of the most prolific of all fishes; a single large female may contain more than 12 million eggs. Like the ladyfish and the bonefish, it possesses an eellike, leptocephalous larval stage. Spawning probably takes place in shallow estuarine waters any time from May to September, at least in Florida. The tarpon tolerates a wide range of salinities, often being found in purely freshwater. It seems to prefer the lower salinities of estuaries and the mouths of large rivers. It reaches a very large size; an individual over 8 feet long with an estimated weight of 350 pounds was taken from the Hillsborough River Inlet, Florida.

The tarpon's rate of growth is relatively slow. It probably does not attain sexual maturity until it is about 6–7 years old and attains a length of about 4 feet. Individuals weighing 100 pounds are probably 13–16 years of age. The young fish are common in small brackish or freshwater streams. As they grow larger they move into the larger streams and estuaries. They are carnivorous and are known to feed on mullets, silversides, marine catfishes, and blue crabs.

An often spectacular gamefish, the tarpon is caught on all types of tackle with both live baits and artificial lures.

FRESHWATER EEL FAMILY   Anguillidae

A single catadromous species *Anguilla rostrata,* or American eel, is caught by sport fishermen in salt- and brackish water. For a detailed description see *McClane's Guide to Freshwater Fishes of North America.*

LAMPREY FAMILY   Petromyzontidae

Lampreys occur as anadromous and strictly freshwater populations. For a detailed description see *McClane's Guide to Freshwater Fishes of North America.*

MORAY FAMILY   Muraenidae

Morays are reef fishes found in tropical seas and commonly reaching a length of 6 feet; some may grow to 10 feet. Sometimes, and incorrectly, called moray eels, morays are pugnacious and can be harmful to man if provoked. There are about 12 species common in North American waters, and all have thick, scaleless skins and large mouths with strong teeth (usually pointed and needle-sharp, but blunt in some species). Morays have small, rounded gill openings and are without pectoral or pelvic fins. In some species the dorsal, anal, and

Morays

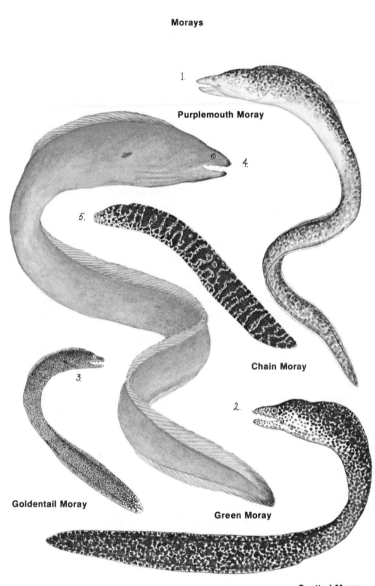

1.

Purplemouth Moray

4.

5.

Chain Moray

3.

2.

Goldentail Moray

Green Moray

Spotted Moray

caudal fins are so small and indistinct (or even hidden under the skin) that the morays appear to be as finless as snakes. Many display lavish colors and patterns.

The color of some morays is affected by a skin coating of algae. The common green moray of Atlantic waters is actually blue-gray in color, but its normal covering of yellow algae gives it a chartreuse hue. Sometimes this species is brown instead of green, and this is probably caused by some different kind of algae.

As a rule, morays are rather poor swimmers. Generally they remain on the bottom—in caves, crevices, or tunnels—and only rarely venture into openwater. When well anchored in rocks or coral, a moray can move the forward part of its body with terrifying swiftness, the movement being much like the strike of a snake.

Of all the fishes commonly associated with coral reefs, none commands more respect from swimmers and divers than the moray. The sight of a huge head, protruding from a hole in a reef, tremendous tooth-studded jaws continually opening and closing and the head swelling at every respiration, is awe-inspiring. And when the moray extends 3–4 feet of its length out of its hole and arches its body, it looks as fearsome as a great cobra about to strike. However, it is normally a docile creature if left undisturbed.

Morays inhabit reefs and rocky areas throughout tropical and subtropical seas. They are found from the shore to a maximum depth of about 150 feet and are rarely, if ever, found in the open sea. They are common in both Florida and California and in these areas reach a maximum length of about 6 feet. Some of the Indo-Pacific species are much larger, possibly exceeding 10 feet.

SNAKE EEL FAMILY Ophichthidae

Snake eels are related to morays, but differ from them in lacking rays at the tip of the tail, which ends in a horny point. The tail projects beyond the dorsal and anal fins. The posterior nostril is placed on the edge of the upper lip, while the anterior nostril is usually a small tube placed near the snout tip. The tongue is attached to the floor of the mouth. The body is elongate and sinuous, and the skin lacks scales.

There are about 40 species in the family in the Western Hemisphere. One of the common species, the sharptail eel, *Myrichthys acuminatus,* has a pointed tail, blunt teeth, and a series of round, yellowish-orange blotches covering the olive to greenish body. The sharptail is commonly seen about coral reefs or, in particular, over grass beds or detritus where a suitable burrow can be made. Secretive in habits, it is commonly mistaken for a sea snake, from which it can be distinguished at a glance by its pointed tail. A sea snake has a flattened tail and is generally banded, besides differing in many anatomical details. The sharptail eel is found from southern Florida to the Lesser Antilles, along shallow reefs, turtlegrass beds, and occasionally in deeper water. It grows to about $2^1/_2$ feet.

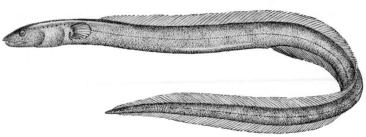

Snake Eel

Snake eels have been found in stomachs of tunas, barracudas, and groupers. Those eaten by groupers often bore through the stomach into the body cavity, where they become mummified.

CONGER EEL FAMILY   Congridae

The congers are true eels, with moderately elongate, scaleless bodies. They have strong jaws, well-developed pectoral fins, and a nearly horizontal mouth. The lateral line is present. The closely related garden eels, subfamily Heterocongtinae, are more elongate, with pectoral fins reduced or absent; the mouth is oblique, and the lower jaw projects. Garden eels are a burrowing form.

There are 8 species of conger eels found in the western Atlantic and 1 Pacific representative, the Catalina conger, *Gnathophis catalinensis*. The most common species is the conger eel, *Conger oceanicus,* which occurs on the continental shelf from Cape Cod south to North Carolina. The American conger reaches 4–6 feet in length, but never attains the size of the European species (*Conger conger*), which has been recorded to 9 feet and a weight of 160 pounds.

CUSK-EEL FAMILY   Ophidiidae

Cusk-eels resemble true eels in appearance, but they differ in having ventral fins in the form of forked, threadlike throat filaments, which probably have some function in finding food. There are 40 known species of cusk-eels, which range from less than 1 foot long when full grown to over 5 feet in length. Most species are small, however, and as they are burrowing creatures, are seldom seen by anglers. Cusk-eels occur in the western Atlantic and Cape Cod south to Florida and in the Bahamas. They are most abundant in southern waters from the shallows out to the edge of the continental shelf. There are 4 species along our Pacific coast. In captivity the cusk-eel has been observed to stand on its tail when at rest; it backs into crevices or holes in the bottom tail-first, leaving only a portion of its head visible.

SAND LANCE FAMILY   Ammodytidae

AMERICAN SAND LANCE *Ammodytes americanus*   Commonly called the sand launce, sand eel, and launce-fish, this small, slender, round-bodied marine species superficially resembles an eel. The family includes 2 other North American species, the northern sand lance (*A. dubius*) and the Pacific sand lance (*A. hexapterus*). The sand lance can be distinguished from a young eel by its separate rather than continuous dorsal and anal fins and by its lack of the rounded caudal fin characteristic of the eel. The sand lance grows to a length of about 6 inches and is important as a food for many gamefish, such as the Arctic char, coho salmon, mackerel, and striped bass.

Schools of sand lances are often abundant in shallow water along sandy shores. For protection the fish can quickly burrow into the sand, snout first, to a depth of about 6 inches. Quantities of sand lances are often dug up in the intertidal zone by people seeking clams. The sand lance makes an excellent bait for many marine gamefishes. It is also a quality food known as whitebait.

American Sand Lance

CUTLASSFISH FAMILY   Trichiuridae

ATLANTIC CUTLASSFISH *Trichiurus lepturus*   Also called the ribbonfish, it is found in the Atlantic, Indian, and western Pacific oceans. In the western Atlantic, it ranges from Massachusetts to Argentina and throughout the Gulf of Mexico. Its only close relative in the Western Hemisphere is the Pacific cutlassfish found on the coast from southern California to northern Peru.

The general appearance is striking, especially the long, silvery body; the tapering, filamentous tail; and the large mouth with sharp, arrow-shaped teeth.

The cutlassfish is a voracious eater of small fishes and is found in large numbers in bays and the shallow parts of the open ocean. It is particularly numerous along the Texas coast and, there, is extensively utilized as bait for the large species of gamefish.

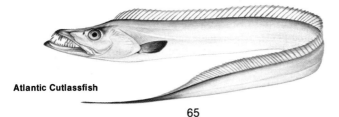

Atlantic Cutlassfish

65

The adults attain a length of about 38 inches and a weight of about 2 pounds. They are readily caught on shrimp or cut bait and will also take small artificial lures.

The cutlassfish is a valued food species in other countries (Japan), but Americans are not accustomed to eating it. Virtually nothing is known about its life history except that sexually mature individuals have been caught in the spring.

WOLFFISH FAMILY Anarhichadidae

ATLANTIC WOLFFISH *Anarhichas lupus* The wolffishes are large blennylike fishes occurring in the cold waters of the North Atlantic and North Pacific. They have well-developed canine teeth and large molars on the vomer and palatine bones. Thus, they are well adapted to feeding on mollusks. The Atlantic wolffish is sometimes called the striped wolffish or loup (France). It is found on both sides of the North Atlantic; in the west it occurs from southern Labrador to Cape Cod and occasionally as far south as New Jersey; in the east it has been taken at western Greenland, Iceland, the Faroes, Spitzbergen, and from the White Sea to the west coast of France.

Its color varies from slaty-blue to dull olive-green to purplish-brown. Usually there are 10 or more dark transverse bars on the anterior two-thirds of the body, some extending onto the dorsal fin. The underside of the head and belly to vent are dirty-white, tinged with the general tint of the upper parts.

Other distinguishing characteristics of the Atlantic wolffish are its compressed and elongated body, which tapers to a small caudal peduncle.

Dorsal fin with 69−77 spines, fin begins over posterior part of head and extends to base of caudal; caudal fin small, very slightly rounded; anal fin with 42−48 softrays, a little more than half length of dorsal and ending under posterior tip of dorsal. Pectorals heavy, rounded, base low in sides, a short distance behind gill openings; pelvics absent. Lateral line absent. Head scaleless, body covered with poorly developed scales.

This species lives in moderately deep water (10−85 fathoms) over hard bottom. Individuals are apparently solitary and are caught in the same areas at all times of the year. Their food consists primarily of whelks, mussels, clams, and other mollusks. Crabs, hermit crabs, sea urchins, and starfish have also been found in their stomachs. The eggs are about $^3/_{16}$ inch in diameter and are attached to the bottom in large, loose clumps.

The Atlantic wolffish is a good foodfish, and catches of about $1^1/_2$ million pounds per year are made in the Gulf of Maine and on the Georges Bank. It is popular table fare in Scandinavia and Spain. It grows to a length of about 5 feet and a weight of about 40 pounds.

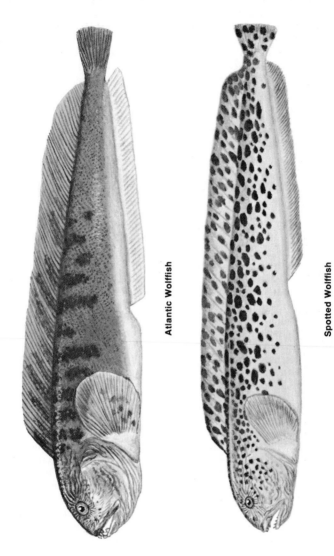

Atlantic Wolffish

Spotted Wolffish

SPOTTED WOLFFISH *Anarhichas minor*   This species is related to the Atlantic wolffish and the northern wolffish as well as the Bering wolffish of the North Pacific. It possesses the same family characteristics as the Atlantic wolffish. The spotted wolffish is also called the leopard fish or spotted catfish. It is found on both sides of the North Atlantic; in the west it occurs from Nova Scotia to Cape Ann, Massachusetts; in the east it has been taken at eastern Greenland, Iceland, the Faroes, Spitzbergen, and from the White Sea to Scotland.

Its color varies from pale olive to chocolate, but the upper parts, including the dorsal and caudal fins, are well marked with blackish-brown spots, irregular in size and shape. Similar spots are on the upper part of head behind the eye.

Other distinguishing characteristics of the spotted wolffish are body stout, elongate, moderately compressed; at about the middle of the pectoral fin, the body tapers to a small caudal peduncle. Head heavy, blunt, profile rounded, mouth terminal, oblique, angle under posterior edge of eye, large canine teeth in front of both jaws; the central patch of vomerine teeth not extending farther back than the flanking rows of palatine teeth on the sides, eyes small.

Dorsal fin with about 78 spines, fairly uniform except the last 3–6 spines are abruptly shorter making an indentation; the fin originates over the posterior part of the head and extends to the base of the caudal; caudal small, slightly rounded; anal fin with about 46 softrays, fin a little more than half the length of the dorsal ending at the caudal base; pectorals longer than broad, rounded, longest rays almost equaling head length, base low on sides of body and a short distance behind gill opening, pelvics absent. Lateral line absent. Head scaleless; body with poorly developed scales.

This species lives in deeper water than the Atlantic wolffish and has been taken as deep as 250 fathoms. Its diet is apparently similar to that of the latter species.

PRICKLEBACK FAMILY   Stichaeidae

These are bottom dwellers inhabiting and feeding on algae in the colder portions of northern oceans, especially the Pacific. They occur from San Diego to the Bering Sea and from Cape Cod to the Arctic. None is of importance in the commercial or sport catch. They are oddities and usually rare, many inhabiting water to a depth of at least 200 fathoms, though a few are taken in the intertidal area.

The membranes of the prickleback's gills are united; the body is long and slender; the dorsal and anal fins are long and usually of nearly uniform height or depth for most of their length; the dorsal fin is supported by spines only; pelvic fins, when present, are thoracic with 1 spine and 3–4 rays. There may be 4 or 1 or no lateral lines.

Many are small, not exceeding 12 inches, but there is a large deepwater species, the giant wrymouth (*Delolepis gigantea*), occurring from northern California to the Bering Sea, which reaches a

Monkeyface Prickleback

length of 46 inches. There is another species whose blood shows through its transparent skin giving it a red color. The largest of the shore species is the rock blenny, reaching a length of 20 inches. In some species the head is decorated with a fleshy crest or plumes or blunt tufts, giving rise to such names as decorated blenny, mosshead prickleback, or cockscomb.

The monkeyface prickleback is the only species that seems to enter the sport catch, and then in only a minor way in central and northern California. It is caught among rocks with a specially made stick with a hook on the end.

WRYMOUTH FAMILY Cryptacanthodidae

WRYMOUTH *Cryptacanthodes maculatus* Also known as the ghostfish or spotted wrymouth, this species is found along the Atlantic coast of North America from southern Labrador and the Grand Bank to New Jersey.

Its background color may be various shades of brown or reddish-brown; the belly is grayish-white; the upper part of the body has 3 irregular rows of small dark brown spots running from the head to the tail; the top of the head is thickly spotted; dorsal and anal fins have smaller brown spots.

Other distinguishing characters of the wrymouth are body very elongate, eellike, greatest depth 14 in total length, much compressed. Head 7 in total length, flat-topped, snout very blunt, mouth terminal, oblique, lower jaw projecting markedly, angle of mouth under posterior edge of eye; stout, conical teeth in jaws and on vomer and palatines; conspicuous mucus-secreting pits on sides of head; eye small.

The first dorsal fin has 73–77 spines, all stout and somewhat hidden by skin; fin begins over middle of pectoral, extends full length of back, and is continuous with caudal; caudal small, oval-shaped, and pointed; anal fin with 47–50 softrays, beginning under twentieth spine

Wrymouth

69

of dorsal, extending to and continuous with caudal; pectorals small, located low on sides behind gill opening; pelvics absent. Lateral line not evident. Body naked. The wrymouth grows to a length of about 3 feet.

The wrymouth lives on soft bottom, where it burrows in mud, sometimes building an extensive branching system of tunnels. It occurs in shallow water and up to 60 fathoms, feeding on amphipods and shrimps.

Two generically different species occur in the Pacific: the giant wrymouth, *Delolepis gigantea*, and the dwarf wrymouth, *Lyconectes aleutensis*.

CORNETFISH FAMILY Fistulariidae

BLUESPOTTED CORNETFISH *Fistularia tabacaria* Also erroneously called the trumpetfish. (*Aulostomus maculatus* is of a different but very similar family to the Fistulariidae.) Related species occur in the eastern Atlantic, Indian, and Pacific oceans. The bluespotted cornetfish ranges to both sides of the Atlantic. In the western Atlantic it is found from the Gulf of Maine and Bermuda to Rio de Janeiro and throughout the Gulf of Mexico.

The body of the cornetfish is very elongate, much depressed, always broader than deep; head very long, the anterior bones much produced, forming a long tube, terminating in a small mouth. Both jaws and usually the vomer and palatines with small teeth; scales absent; bony plates on various parts of the body, mostly covered by skin. A single dorsal fin is placed posteriorly; caudal fin forked, the middle ray produced into a long filament; anal fin similar to the dorsal and opposite it; ventral fins abdominal, far in advance of dorsal with 1 spine, 4 rays; pectoral fins small, preceded by a smooth area.

Color in life greenish-brown above; pale below; sides with a row of blue spots close to the vertebral line on back; sides and back with about 10 dark crossbars, the spots and bars disappearing after capture, leaving the back uniform brown; caudal filament deep blue.

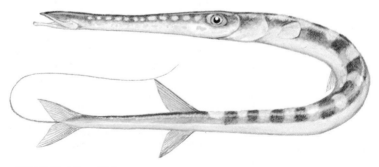

Bluespotted Cornetfish

70

This species is said to reach a length of 6 feet, but most specimens seen are 2–3 feet. It feeds on small fishes and shrimps. Although not a commonly caught fish, it does strike artificial and live baits at times. Another species, the red cornetfish (*F. villosa*), occurs infrequently in south Florida waters.

FLYINGFISH AND HALFBEAK FAMILY Exocoetidae

BALAO Also known as "ballyhoo," a number of similar species are contained in this unique family. One halfbeak, *Hemiramphus balao*, is specifically given the common name of balao, but other halfbeaks are also known under that name. The body is slender and elongate, somewhat flattened from side to side, and the lower jaw projects noticeably, equivalent to the length of the head, the upper jaw being very short. The dorsal and anal fins are set far back on the body, close to

Balao

the caudal fin, the lower lobe of which is the longer. These beautifully hued fish are generally a translucent green on the back, with blue or gold reflections and a silvery band along the sides, becoming pale below. In some species the lower jaw is tipped with red in fresh specimens, and, depending on the species, the lower lobe of the caudal fin may be tipped with yellow or the upper lobe may be tipped with red or orange. Some Pacific species reach 2 feet long, but most species grow to less than 1 foot.

Balaos are found in all tropical seas, some drifting poleward during the warmer months. All are coastal species, generally found over reefs, but some occur over shallow grass flats. They are easily attracted by a light at night and leap from the water when frightened. They travel in vast schools, skimming over the surface and feeding on green algae, bits of turtlegrass, surface detritus, small fishes, and plankton. In turn, they are eaten by barracudas, jacks, groupers, cero mackerel, and other inshore predatory fishes. When sailfish occur over shallow reefs, they feed heavily upon balaos, bunching them into tight schools. Several sailfish will work together concentrating the balaos; then they will slash at the "ball" and feed on the stunned or dead balaos.

Balaos are most important baitfish, and they are primarily trolled for sailfish, marlins, kingfish, wahoo, dolphins, king mackerel, and tunas. They are taken in seines, cast nets, lift nets, hoop nets, and with underwater lights and dipnets.

Although not widely eaten in the United States, they are popular in Caribbean countries, and their flesh is excellent.

FLYINGFISHES   These are swift pelagic fishes, found in all tropical seas, generally far from land.

Structurally, the flyingfishes are of two basic types: those whose enlarged pectoral fins are their only wings and those whose ventral fins are also enlarged and serve as a second set of wings, lower on the body and farther aft.

In both types the pectoral fins constitute the main lifting surfaces. When swimming underwater, the fish keeps these fins folded against

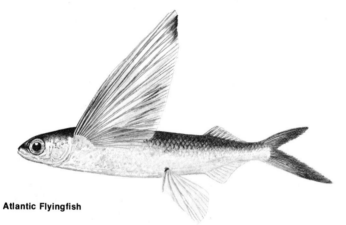

Atlantic Flyingfish

the body and their purpose is obscure. In the 4-winged type the ventral fins give added lift and also act as ailerons (for banking) and as elevators (for climbing and nosing down). In all species the lower lobe of the tail is elongated and serves as a sculling oar for taxiing across the surface before takeoff; the tail also serves as a rudder in flight.

As a rule, the 4-winged fishes make longer flights than the 2-winged fishes and exhibit greater control when aloft. Before taking off the fish swims just below the surface for some distance, its upper tail lobe often breaking the surface; then it turns upward and spreads its pectoral fins, leaving the water except for the lower lobe of its tail. Now vigorously beating its tail back and forth in a sculling motion, it taxis across the surface to gain flying speed. Finally, it extends its ventral fins and rises into the air. Its flight may cover 1,000 feet or more, but the average is much less, perhaps 100–300 feet. Usually it glides no more than 4–5 feet above the water, though it may rise higher in a strong wind, and there are records of flyingfishes achieving heights of 25–36 feet. Most flights last for 10 seconds or less.

Flyingfishes spawn in floating rafts of seaweed or other kinds of surface debris. Some species seem to use sargassum weed almost entirely, building nests by wrapping tightly packed balls of weed with strands of white, elastic material. The eggs are attached to one another and to the nest by thin silken threads. The young, when hatched, strongly resemble the round floats of the sargassum.

At night flyingfishes are definitely attracted by lights. Frequently they fly aboard lighted boats, landing on deck or coming through open portholes. Fishermen in many areas catch them by suspending a lantern over the water and erecting a net or other barrier to arrest their flights.

Flyingfishes are highly valued as food in many parts of the world. Commercial fisheries have operated off California and Barbados.

NEEDLEFISH FAMILY Belonidae

The needlefishes are voracious elongate fishes with a superficial resemblance to the freshwater gars; however, they belong to the order that includes the halfbeaks, sauries, and flyingfishes.

The jaws of needlefishes project into long, thin, and rather fragile beaks, usually with the upper jaw slightly shorter (more so in the young than the adults). A band of long pointed teeth, in addition to a band of shorter ones, arms the jaws.

Seven species of needlefishes are known from the western North Atlantic: the Atlantic needlefish, redfin needlefish, timucu, houndfish,

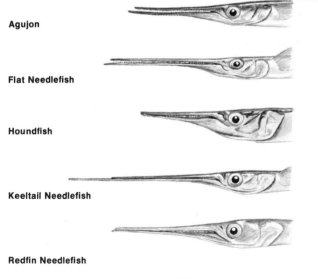

Agujon

Flat Needlefish

Houndfish

Keeltail Needlefish

Redfin Needlefish

agujon, keeltail needlefish, and flat needlefish. Although common in the warm waters of the West Indian region, the Atlantic needlefish is abundant along the eastern seaboard of the United States as far north as Cape Cod. It often penetrates freshwater. The related California needlefish of the cool water of the eastern Pacific ranges as far north as Point Conception, California.

The largest and most heavy-bodied of the needlefishes is the houndfish. It reaches a length of 5 feet. A 52-inch specimen from the Virgin Islands weighed 10 pounds 9 ounces.

Needlefishes live at the surface and are protectively colored for this mode of life. They are blue or green on the back, shading to silvery white on the sides and abdomen. They feed heavily on small fishes. When they, in turn, are threatened by predators, they endeavor to escape by skipping rapidly along the surface, often more out of the sea than in it.

Needlefishes are unique in bearing large eggs. Those of the 10-pound 9-ounce houndfish measured about $1/_6$ inch in diameter. Eggs of most marine fishes tend in general to be less than a quarter of this in size.

Numerous tiny threads can be teased with a dissecting needle from the outer, tough covering of the houndfish eggs. These threads probably serve to attach the eggs to floating objects.

Certain young needlefishes, an inch or so in length, are dark-colored and float motionless and straight at the surface. In this pose they resemble floating twigs. Juveniles about 5 inches long were observed in the Virgin Islands imitating floating pieces of manatee grass (*Cymodocea*). The fish were straw-colored, like many of the grass fragments; they frequently held their bodies in an arc as they floated, seemingly inert, beside curved pieces of the grass.

The larger needlefishes, particularly the houndfish, should be regarded as dangerous to man. At night, when startled by a light, they often execute a series of long leaps from the water. Although apparently not specifically attracted by light, they will at times leap in its direction. Anyone in the path of these living javelins can be impaled on the long, pointed jaws. People have been seriously injured, some fatally, by being struck by these fishes. The needlefish hazard has not received the literary attention it should. By contrast, incidents involving sharks or barracudas are usually widely publicized.

Needlefishes are readily caught on flies, plugs, jigs, and live baits. Their habit of walking on their tails when hooked makes them rather spectacular fighters.

The needlefishes are edible, and their flesh has a very good flavor.

SAURY FAMILY Scomberesocidae

ATLANTIC SAURY *Scomberesox saurus* This small saltwater species found in the North Atlantic somewhat resembles a needlefish. It has no angling value. The saury appears sporadically along eastern shores during the summer months, when it travels in dense schools. Commercial men seldom catch sauries, and there is no market for an otherwise good table fish. There is also a Pacific saury (*Cololabis saira*), which ranges from Japan to California. The Japanese freeze, can, and ship part of their catch to the United Staes during peak periods.

Atlantic Saury

HERRING FAMILY Clupeidae

There are 27 species of herrings found in North American waters, including both anadromous and wholly marine forms. The anadromous species of angling interest are described in *McClane's Field Guide to Freshwater Fishes of North America.*

ATLANTIC HERRING *Clupea harengus harengus* This typical member of the herring family has a compressed body that is more elongate and less compressed than the bodies of most other members of the family. It has a large mouth and a projecting lower jaw that, unlike the shad's jaw, is not notched. Also unlike the shad, this herring has a patch of teeth on the roof of the mouth. Its back is a deep steel-blue to greenish-blue; sides and belly are silver. Fresh specimens are iridescent with shades of blue-green and violet, these colors fading shortly after death. The fish reaches a length of about 18 inches, although the average is less than 12 inches. Maximum weight is about $1^1/_2$ pounds.

The Atlantic herring is found on both sides of the North Atlantic, from Greenland to North Carolina, and from the Strait of Gibraltar to the Bay of Murmansk and Novaya Zemlya, USSR. The species dwells in the surface waters of the open ocean, traveling in huge schools.

Spawning may occur in the spring, summer, or autumn, depending on the locality. Spawning occurs in the open ocean over rocky or

Atlantic Herring

gravel bottoms generally, at between 2 and 30 fathoms, although in the eastern Atlantic, these herrings may spawn as deep as 100 fathoms. The slender, almost transparent larvae grow to about $3^{1}/_{2}$–5 inches during their first year of life. The young feed on copepods, small shrimps, and crustacean larvae. Adults are also plankton feeders, although a few fishes have been found in their stomachs. Herrings are preyed upon by cods, striped bass, mackerels and tunas, salmon, sharks, and squids.

ATLANTIC MENHADEN *Brevoortia tyrannus* Also known as mossbunker, this species is characterized by a large head and comblike edges to the rear portions of the scales, which are straight rather than rounded as in other herrings. The menhaden is dark blue

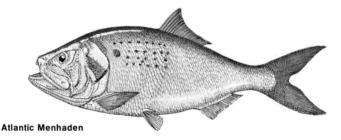

Atlantic Menhaden

to green or dark gray above with shades of brown; the sides, belly, and fins have a brassy sheen. A definite large spot on the shoulder is generally followed by a number of small dark spots on the upper sides. Its numerous long, slender gillrakers differ in structure from those of other members of this family. The menhaden reaches a length of 18 inches and a weight of nearly 4 pounds, although most taken are less than 15 inches long.

This species is restricted to the western Atlantic Ocean, occurring from Nova Scotia to northern Florida and the Gulf of Mexico. The menhaden travels in huge, compact schools and occasionally jumps from the water during its wanderings.

Menhaden are eaten by whales, porpoises, sharks, cods and their relatives, as well as bluefish, swordfish, tunas, and striped bass and other predatory fishes. Small menhaden are excellent bait; the larger ones are cut up for chum.

FALSE PILCHARD *Harengula clupeola* Also called *sardina escamuda*, sprat, and *petit cailleu*, the false pilchard is related to the red-ear sardine and the scaled sardine of the western Atlantic and to two other species in the eastern Pacific. It is a wide-ranging species, found in the Florida Keys, Bahamas, West Indies, and along the mainland coast from Yucatán to Brazil.

Its general coloration is silvery, especially on the lower half of the head and body, with opercular surfaces with iridescent or pearlish reflections; the back is dark brownish or bluish-gray; the body has dark longitudinal streaks more conspicuous on back; the humeral spot is faint; tip of snout and mandible are dusky; upper sector of iris is

False Pilchard

dusky; fins are colorless except caudal, which has some pigment at tips and along inner margin.

This species and its relatives are most abundant in bays and estuaries, where they may be captured with beach seines and cast nets. They are utilized for bait and food throughout the West Indies and Caribbean region.

PACIFIC HERRING *Clupea harengus pallasi* This species is closely related to the Atlantic herring, from which it is separable only on a subspecific level. It is found from northwestern Alaska to San Diego. Its greatest abundance is around Kodiak Island and Sitka, as well as in British Columbia. The Pacific species also ranges from the eastern Soviet Union south to Japan and the Yellow Sea.

Like the Atlantic herring, the Pacific herring reaches a length of about 18 inches. Throughout its range, the Pacific herring seems to be broken up into a number of localized populations that undertake an annual migration between the inshore spawning area and the open ocean feeding ground.

The fishing season is from December into the late summer, when herrings are taken with beach seines, gillnets, and haul nets. Sportsmen in various areas take them with dipnets. During the winter and spring, Pacific herrings enter the bays and shallows to spawn, and the eggs are deposited on weeds and rocks in shallow water. They reach an age of at least 8 years, with occasional individuals living to be 20 years old.

PACIFIC SARDINE *Sardinops sagax* The Pacific sardine is a member of the herring family and is one of the true sardines, being separated from the Pacific herring by the presence of low oblique ridges on the gill cover. The belly does not have a sharp sawtoothed edge, as in the shad, and is less prominent than in the Pacific herring. The body is elongate and round in cross section, with a compressed head and a small mouth, which contains no teeth. The color is dark blue on the back, becoming silvery on the ventral surface, with round black spots forming one or more rows on each side of the body, as well as a row of black dots along the back. The sides are iridescent, reflecting shades of purple and violet.

The range of the species is from southeastern Alaska into the Gulf of California. Close relatives are found in Japan, western South America, Australia, New Zealand, and South Africa.

Spawning occurs in the open sea up to 300 miles offshore, mostly in the southern part of California. The young migrate toward shore at a length of 3−5 inches. When they reach about 7 inches, they move back offshore to resume an open-ocean life, where they become subject to the commerical fishery. An age of at least 13 years is attained, although the average life span is only about 10 years. Regular migrations occur between California and British Columbia, with indications of a northward feeding migration during spring and summer, followed by a southerly movement during the fall and winter.

Pacific Sardine

Owing to fluctuations in the environment, this species has undergone marked changes in abundance during the past years. Water temperature and food supply seem to be responsible for these fluctuations, and on several occasions the commercial fishery has virtually failed. The species is used principally for canning and for production of fishmeal and oil, although a small percentage is used for bait and chum. Young sardines are used as live bait, principally for tunas and mackerels.

ANCHOVY FAMILY Engraulidae

There are 16 species of these small marine fishes common in North American waters. Only 1 species is known to enter freshwater, the bay anchovy (*Anchoa mitchilli*). Five species are found in the Pacific: the deepbody anchovy, slough anchovy, slim anchovy, anchoveta, and northern anchovy. The remainder inhabit the Atlantic.

The striped anchovy is one of the most widely distributed engraulids in Atlantic coastal waters of the United States. It is abundant from Delaware Bay through the West Indies and south to Brazil; it occurs north of Delaware Bay to Maine and the coast of Nova Scotia as a stray. It is a larger (4−5 inches long, rarely to 6 inches) species than the other anchovies identified in the western Atlantic. It has a

Striped Anchovy

very bright silver lateral band and is iridescent pale gray above with faint dusky dots and grayish-white below.

Anchovies are omnivorous feeders, usually on plankton, of both inshore and offshore regions, and are occasionally found in brackish water at the mouths of streams. They travel in densely packed schools, frequently mingling with other baitfish such as the silversides and the so-called green fry of young herring.

Anchovies are of considerable importance as baitfish and foragefish for gamefish such as bluefish, mackerels, striped bass, and tunas.

TROUT FAMILY Salmonidae

The salmonids are strictly freshwater or anadromous fishes. For descriptions see *McClane's Field Guide to Freshwater Fishes of North America.*

SMELT FAMILY Osmeridae

Of the 9 North American smelts only 2 species are wholly marine forms: the night smelt and the whitebait smelt. Of the remainder, 6 are anadromous, and 1 species, the pond smelt, is strictly a freshwater form. For descriptions see *McClane's Field Guide to Freshwater Fishes of North America.*

NIGHT SMELT *Spirinchus starksi* The night smelt, found from southeastern Alaska to Washington, is similar to the whitebait smelt, but it has small teeth, not caninelike, on the vomer. It has short anal fin rays, 62–65 midlateral scales, and 3 rectilinear striae on the gill covers. The night smelt attains a length of about 6 inches.

This species spawns in the surf at night from January through September. Although the sport and commercial catches are minor, the night smelt is an excellent foodfish.

WHITEBAIT SMELT *Allosmerus elongatus* This smelt is almost colorless, with a pale green cast and a silvery, very shiny band on the side. There is a single, large canine tooth on the middle of the vomer. The fish is normally found from the Strait of Juan de Fuca to San Francisco; a single specimen is recorded from southern California. It grows to a length of 9 inches.

Although of minor commercial importance, it forms the major part of the whitebait fishery. Used as bait by commercial and sport fisher-

79

men, it is sometimes taken in the surf by sportsmen with small nets in the spring and summer.

SILVERSIDE FAMILY   Atherinidae

ATLANTIC SILVERSIDE *Menidia menidia*   This species is one of a group of small silvery fishes that inhabits both marine and freshwaters in the eastern United States and Canada. Its closest relatives are the Waccamaw silverside, key silverside, tidewater silverside, Mississippi silverside, and brook silverside. The Atlantic silverside is found along the shore and in estuaries from the southern Gulf of St. Lawrence to Cape May.

The fish is transparent green above with a white belly. A silver band, edged above with a narrow black streak, runs from the upper part of the base of the pectoral fin to the base of the caudal fin. Each scale is outlined with a series of brownish or greenish dots.

Silversides average 3–5 inches in length and are popular as bait for larger gamefish. They also have excellent food value when deep-fried.

Atlantic Silverside

Silversides congregate in sandy shallow water during the summer months, at which time they are easily netted.

CALIFORNIA GRUNION *Leuresthes tenuis*   This small silvery fish, somewhat like a smelt in general appearance, is found chiefly between Point Conception in southern California and Abreojos Point in Baja California. At times they may stray as far north as Monterey Bay. Unlike other fishes, grunions come completely out of the water to spawn in moist beach sand, at which time they are caught by hand. Grunions spawn at night shortly after high tide, but only for 3–4 nights following each full or new moon. The run lasts only a few hours, but thousands of fish may be on the beach at one time. The moon plays a role in their spawning run because the highest tides

California Grunion

80

occur when the moon is full or new. Since wave action erodes sand from the beach as the tide rises and deposits sand as the tide falls, the grunions unerringly time their arrival for the falling tide. The female deposits her eggs about 2 inches below the sand, and they are buried deeper by the outgoing tide. The eggs remain buried for about 10 days, at which time the next series of high tides erodes the beach, and minutes after they are free the baby grunions hatch.

KILLIFISH FAMILY   Cyprinodontidae

Killifishes are small, soft-rayed fishes with cycloid scales on both body and head. The absence of a lateral line and the presence of scales on the head distinguish killifishes from members of the minnow family (Cyprinidae). There are about 50 killifish species in North America, of which only 5 are strictly marine forms: the Gulf, diamond, striped, spotfin, and goldspotted killifishes. For other descriptions see *McClane's Field Guide to Freshwater Fishes of North America.*

CALIFORNIA KILLIFISH *Fundulus parvipinnis*   This is the only killifish species occurring in the Pacific; it inhabits salt- and freshwater as well as brackish water, and is commonly found in estuaries. It also ascends clear sand-bottom streams in the southern part of its range. It is distributed from Morro Bay, California, to northwestern Baja California. It grows to about 3 inches.

California Killifish

SHEEPSHEAD MINNOW *Cyprinodon variegatus*   A small member of the killifish family occurring in both fresh- and saltwater, this common species is characterized by its short, stubby body, with a rather high-arched back and a high, short dorsal fin. The small mouth is studded with a row of well-developed incisor teeth. The tail is broad and square-edged. Unlike other killifishes, its dorsal fin is well forward of the anal fin. The head and body are covered with large scales. The color of the males is particularly captivating during the mating season, being steely-blue with green hues on the upper part and orange-red to salmon on the belly. At other times, both sexes are brassy-olive above, grading to buff or white below. The young and the females have black bands; in adult males the bands become pale.

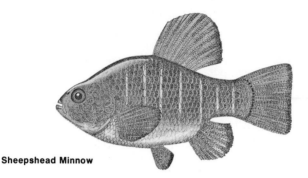

Sheepshead Minnow

The minnow grows to about 3 inches. A coastal, inland form, it is found from Cape Cod to Mexico in shallow brackish and hypersaline bays and marshes. It is extremely abundant in such areas, occurring over a wide range of temperature and salinity.

STRIPED KILLIFISH *Fundulus majalis* This killifish is characterized by the vertical bars of the female and the distinctive stripes of the male. It resembles the mummichog in body shape. The striped killifish has a pointed snout that is much longer than the eye diameter. The body is less stout and the caudal peduncle less deep than in the mummichog, and the pointed shape of the fins is distinctive. The species is olive-drab to brassy olive-green above and has a pale olive belly; the male has black longitudinal stripes. During the breeding season, the colors of the male are intensified. It is one of the largest of the family, reaching a length of 8 inches.

Striped Killifish

It is a shallow-water coastal species occurring all year from Massachusetts to Florida in bays, lagoons, and estuaries. Sand or sandy-mud bottom and salt marshes are favorite haunts, and large, loose schools can be seen in such areas, occasionally in the company of the mummichog.

Spawning occurs from April to September in shallow-water habitats. The eggs are large, and only a relatively small number is produced.

SEA CATFISH FAMILY Ariidae

GAFFTOPSAIL CATFISH *Bagre marinus* The gafftopsail catfish is confined to the western Atlantic and ranges from Cape Cod to Panama and throughout the Gulf of Mexico. Its closest relatives are 2 species that occur along the Pacific coast of Mexico.

The body of the gafftopsail catfish is rather robust, its greatest depth a little greater than the width, tapering posteriorly; the profile from tip of snout to origin of dorsal is straight; the mouth is broad; the cleft reaches or almost reaches anterior margin of eye; teeth are small, in villiform bands on jaws, vomer, and palatines; 2 pairs of barbels are present, the maxillary barbel flattened and ribbon-shaped reaching from base of ventrals to opposite anal base; the mandibular barbels are small, failing to reach opercular margin.

The color is uniform steel-blue above, silvery below, with or without dark spots; dorsal fin is more or less dusky anteriorly, usually yellowish-green; the adipose is dusky; caudal with upper lobe is somewhat dusky, the lower lobe yellowish-green; the other fins are pale with perhaps some dusky markings.

The gafftopsail catfish prefers intermediate salinities, being usually taken where the salt concentration is 5–30 parts per thousand. This

Gafftopsail Catfish

means that it tends to gather in brackish bays and estuaries. However, it is very sensitive to cold and migrates offshore during the worst part of the winter. Usually none is reported by fishermen during November, December, and January.

The maximum length is about 2 feet, and an individual of this size would weigh about 5–6 pounds. Although the gafftopsail catfish is usually caught by bottom-fishing methods with live or cut bait, it will occasionally strike artificial lures such as jigs or plugs. Contrary to popular belief, it is a good foodfish.

SEA CATFISH *Arius felis* Also called the hardhead, this species is confined to the western Atlantic and is mainly found in warm temperate waters. It ranges from Cape Cod to the West Indies and throughout the Gulf of Mexico. It has several relatives that occur along the tropical parts of the Pacific coast.

The body of the sea catfish is rather elongate and rounded, tapering to the slender tail; the profile from tip of snout to origin of dorsal is slightly convex. Teeth occur on the vomer in two small separate groups that may or may not be continuous with the much larger rounded patches of palatine teeth; all teeth are villiform. Maxillary barbels extend to or nearly to the end of the operculum; outer mandibular barbels are about half the length of head.

The color of the back varies from steel-blue to grayish or gray-green. The sides and belly are white to yellowish.

In contrast to the gafftopsail, the sea catfish seems to prefer high salinities, most individuals being caught where the salt content is 30 or more parts per thousand. However, a wide salinity range can be endured, and the very young fish tend to occur in the more brackish waters.

The maximum length is about $1\frac{1}{2}$ feet, and such a fish would weigh about 3 pounds. This species is easily caught with hook and line by bottom fishing with bait. Although not generally regarded as food-fish, the flesh of the sea catfish is edible.

Both the sea catfish and the gafftopsail possess a single sharp spine at the anterior end of the dorsal and pectoral fins. These spines are enveloped by a thin layer of skin called the integumentary sheath.

Sea Catfish

Within the epidermal layer of the sheath is located a series of glandular poison cells. These will rupture and release their contents when the spine penetrates the body of a victim. The result can be a painful wound, although it is usually not severe. If extensive, the wound should be thoroughly washed in seawater and then soaked in hot water. After this, it should be treated with an antiseptic and a sterile dressing.

TOADFISH FAMILY   Batrachoididae

OYSTER TOADFISH *Opsanus tau*   This species is a member of a small family of shallow-water marine fishes with a worldwide distribution in tropical and temperate waters. Two related species belonging to the same genus occur in Florida waters and in the Gulf of Mexico, and a third occurs in the Bahama Islands. The oyster toadfish is found from the Gulf of Maine south to Miami, Florida.

Its color on back, sides, and head is predominantly dull greenish or brownish with dark vermiform markings.

Other distinguishing characteristics of the oyster toadfish are a stout, scaleless body, with loose wrinkled skin and an obscure lateral line; numerous flaps or cirri on the head; a very wide mouth with fleshy lips and a single row of blunt teeth on jaws, vomer, and palatines.

In the northern part of its range the oyster toadfish spawns in June and July. The eggs are deposited in a single layer within a shell or some other nesting cavity. Each egg is attached to the substrate by means of a peculiar adhesive disk. Even after hatching, each larva remains attached to its disk until the egg yolk is well absorbed.

The nest is guarded by the male, who expends considerable energy in keeping the eggs clean. He will remain with the nest even if it becomes exposed at low tide. Incubation takes 2–3 weeks.

Oyster Toadfish

This species attains a maximum length of about 18 inches and a weight of a little over 1 pound. The males become larger and live longer than the females (to 12 years compared with 7 for the females). Food consists mainly of bottom-dwelling crustaceans and mollusks.

The flesh of the oyster toadfish is edible, but individuals need to be handled with care, as both the dorsal and opercular spines are poisonous.

GOOSEFISH FAMILY Lophiidae

GOOSEFISH *Lophius americanus* The goosefish is an inshore relative of a highly specialized group of deepsea anglerfishes. The body is strongly flattened, and the fish appears to be mostly head, with an enormous, tooth-filled mouth. The head is very broad, and the small eyes are partially protected by horny protuberances on the top of the head. Modified dorsal spines form a "fishing lure," which is located just behind the upper lip. On the first spine, a flap of skin is used as an attractant to prey. In this species and its relatives, a rapid movement of the lure can be effected, with the resulting attraction of curious prey. The body tapers sharply to a narrow caudal peduncle. The peculiar pectoral fins, modified into footlike structures, are in front of the gill openings, a characteristic typical of the anglerfishes. The skin lacks scales and is thin, pliable, and slippery to the touch. The lower

85

jaw is fringed with fleshy flaps. Maximum size is 4 feet and 50 pounds. A specimen slightly over 3 feet weighed 32 pounds.

The goosefish occurs in the western Atlantic from the Grand Banks (Newfoundland) southward to North Carolina. It is found at the tideline during cool months, retreating to deeper water in the warmer season. A wide range of temperatures can be tolerated, but apparently, sudden drops in temperature affect the fish, for following cold snaps goosefish are sometimes found dead or moribund in the shore zone.

The appetite of this species is notorious. Sea birds, including cormorants, gulls, and ducks, are part of its regular fare. Lobsters, crabs, squids, and other assorted invertebrates are also taken. It is a good foodfish, and while some are eaten locally, the low market for them in the United States hardly compares with the demand in Europe.

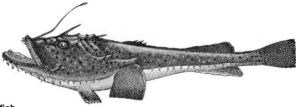

Goosefish

FROGFISH FAMILY Antennariidae

SARGASSUMFISH *Histrio histrio* The frogfishes are characterized by their globular bodies, more or less rough skin, limblike pectoral fins, and gill openings restricted to a pore near or behind the axilla of each pectoral fin. The first dorsal fin spine is free and bears a lure at its terminus. Of the approximately 54 species, 20 are found in American waters.

The sargassumfish is one of nature's best camouflage artists. Its coloring matches that of the weeds in which it lives. It has irregular dark markings like those of the branching fronds and golden rings on its sides exactly resembling the air bladders of the sargassum. White dots even simulate with remarkable fidelity the white encrustations of tiny marine animals living on the sargassum plants. The fish even has the trick of changing its skin coloring to match the background of its changing environment. In the drifting world of weeds, *Histrio* is hidden from view, but when a smaller fish, shrimp, or worm passes by, the sargassumfish approaches each, not in the form of the ferocious predator it is, but in the guise of an innocuous vegetable. Its flexible fins, which can be used much the same as arms, wrists, and fingers, enable the animated weed to clamber about its home. *Histrio* frequently moves by a series of thrusts of jets of water from its small round gill openings, one under each "arm." This allows it in many

Sargassumfish

cases to approach its prey without being detected. It can draw near with closed mouth, and, suddenly opening its mouth, take in the unsuspecting prey in an instantaneous gulp. A *Histrio* gulp is no ordinary gulp, for when this fish opens its mouth to catch a victim, its jaws open so suddenly and widely that a powerful suction is created; the unfortunate prey is sucked down a capacious throat. *Histrio* can also use this technique in self-defense. If attacked, it can throw open its jaws, swallow water, and pump itself up to a size too large for its attacker to swallow.

BATFISH FAMILY   Ogcocephalidae

LONGNOSE BATFISH *Ogcocephalus vespertilio* This batfish species is occasionally caught by angling and is sometimes observed along the bottom in tropical marine habitats. The fish seldom exceeds 1 foot in length and is distinguished by its broad body and flattened

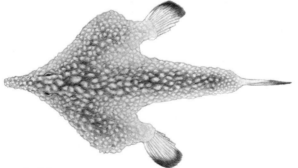

Longnose Batfish

head, the anterior portion of which is elongated into a snout process with an inferior mouth. The large pectoral fins are inserted horizontally, and the skin is covered with bony tubercles. Related species in the Atlantic are pancake batfish (*Halieutichthys aculeatus*), tricorn batfish (*O. mcgintyi*), shortnose batfish (*O. nasutus*), roughback batfish (*O. parvus*), and polka-dot batfish (*O. radiatus*); in the Pacific Ocean, the spotted batfish (*Zalieutes elater*). Batfish vary in color from black to shades of red. They feed on small fishes, crustaceans, and mollusks.

The batfish usually does not swim fishlike, but uses its pelvic and pectoral fins in the manner of limbs by trotting, hopping, or jumping forward along the bottom. Like the anglerfishes, the batfish uses the modified dorsal spine underneath the forehead as a nasal lure to attract its prey.

STARGAZER FAMILY   Uranoscopidae

STARGAZERS *Astroscopus* spp.   This genus is characterized by its robust body and large bony head, with small eyes placed on top of the head directed upward. The mouth is large, obliquely upturned nearly vertically, and fringed with fleshy filaments. The body is relatively small and tapers abruptly backward to a small tail. The pectoral fins are broad and large. The first dorsal is composed of short sharp spines; the second dorsal is long and much higher. The body is dark with numerous small white spots.

Two species, the northern stargazer, *A. guttatus*, found from North Carolina to New York, and the southern stargazer, *A. y-graecum*, found from North Carolina to Brazil, occur on the Atlantic coast.

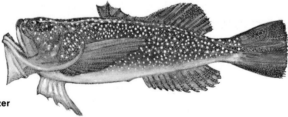

Stargazer

They are separated by the positions of the nostrils relative to the eyes and the shape of the top of the head. The northern species has small, closely spaced white spots on top of the head and body; the southern species has large, widely spaced white spots. Most northern stargazers are less than 1 foot long; the southern species grows to about 15 inches. Both species have a specialized area just behind the eyes that contains modified muscles capable of giving an electric shock. The mechanism is used in capturing food and possibly also for protection against enemies. Small fishes and crustaceans are eaten. The stargazer habitually lies partially buried in the sand, with only the eyes and lips exposed. It is also able to live out of water for many hours. Young stages of the northern stargazer have been found offshore, at a length of about $^1/_2$–$^3/_4$ inch. The young fish, too, has a large head, which is provided with long spines similar to those of the flying gurnard. Spawning possibly occurs in spring and early summer in deepwater, the young subsequently drifting inshore and settling to the bottom.

Stargazers are occasionally caught in nets and traps, and the flesh is edible.

FLYING GURNARD FAMILY   Dactylopteridae

FLYING GURNARD *Dactylopterus volitans*   The flying gurnard resembles the searobins in general appearance. The head is large and bony, and the pectoral fins are long and winglike. However, the first 5–6 pectoral rays are connected to one another, but are separate from the remainder of the pectoral, and the first 2 dorsal spines are free and not connected to the rest of the fin by a membrane. A bony spine projects rearward behind the eye to the middle of the first dorsal fin, and a second, at the lower level of the opercle, reaches just past the dorsal fin origin. The body tapers backward gradually, and the dorsal and anal fins are about equal size. The caudal fin has 3 brownish-red bars. The coloration of this brilliant fish is virtually indescribable, but the predominant colors are brown to greenish-olive and paler below. Pink to orange markings variously mottle the body. Intricate vermiculations cover the winglike pectorals with blue streaks, spots, and bars over a reddish-brown background. The young are silvery with cobalt-blue reflections above, and yellow or pinkish-orange eyes. The fish reaches about 16 inches long.

The flying gurnard is found in the eastern Atlantic and from Brazil to Massachusetts; a stray has been taken in Nova Scotia. But it is largely a warmwater form, where spawning apparently takes place. The silvery young are common at times where bluewater is relatively close to shore. The young can perform repeated short jumps over the surface, but cannot glide as do flyingfishes. Adults lie on the bottom with the pectorals spread and can walk over the bottom using the ventral fins, rather than the pectoral fins as searobins do.

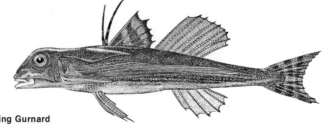

Flying Gurnard

89

SEAROBIN FAMILY Triglidae

SEAROBINS *Prionotus* spp. Several searobins are found along the Atlantic coast and from time to time are common in anglers' catches, depending on season and locality. One of the most common, the northern searobin, *P. carolinus*, occurs from the Bay of Fundy to South Carolina. Like its relatives, its large head is covered with bony plates and spines. The large pectoral fins are fan-shaped, each with 2 dusky blotches. The fish has a spiny and a soft dorsal fin, and the ventral fins are located beneath the pectorals. The first 3 rays of the pectoral fins are free and unconnected to the remaining rays by a membrane. The body is reddish to red-brown or gray, with fine black markings and saddlelike blotches. The fish grows to about 16 inches and $1^3/_4$ pounds. Most specimens are less than 1 foot long. A closely related species, the striped searobin, *P. evolans*, has a distinct stripe on each side of the body, and the pectoral fin has only a single broad blotch. It grows to 18 inches and has about the same distribution as the commom searobin.

Searobins are bottom dwellers, but they can be taken close to the surface, and apparently they can swim rapidly in short bursts. The modified pectoral rays are used in walking along the bottom and in searching for or stirring up food. The fish may be on the bottom with the pectoral fins spread, but if disturbed it burrows into the sand, exposing only the top of the head and the eyes. Northern searobins occur over a depth range from the tidal zone commonly to at least 40 fathoms and to a maximum of 93 fathoms; striped searobins are found in shoaler water. Both species appear in shallower waters during the summer and move offshore during the cold months.

They are omnivorous and voracious and eat fishes, shrimps, crabs, amphipods, squids, clams, and worms. Spawning occurs from at least June to September. The eggs float at the surface, and the young grow rapidly, reaching 7 inches at the end of the first year.

Although the meat is good, few searobins are eaten, even though large numbers are taken and would provide inexpensive and tasty fare.

Striped Searobin

POACHER FAMILY Agonidae

Members of this family, which includes sea poachers and alligator-fishes, have a body covering of bony armor made up of rows of shields that do not overlap and do not have free margins. They are small fishes, found on rocky or muddy bottoms. They are most abundant in the North Pacific into Arctic seas, but are also found in the North Atlantic and the east and west coasts of South America. Rarely are they found deeper than 3,000 feet and can occur in shallow water in tide pools. Though abundant, they are of no commercial value.

Long, slim, and angulated for the most part, the agonids' bony shields give an 8-angled appearance to the body. The pelvic fins are thoracic, each with 1 spine and 2 rays. Poachers are separated from alligatorfishes in having a single dorsal fin compared with the latter's 2 dorsals.

They reach a length of 12 inches, but most specimens are much shorter.

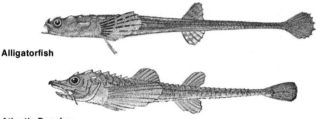

Alligatorfish

Atlantic Poacher

SCULPIN FAMILY Cottidae

This large fresh- and saltwater family is made up for the most part of small fishes. Species vary in length from 2 to 30 inches. A few are large enough to be used as food, and some are taken for use as bait, but only a half dozen or so are of any commercial or sport importance. They are found from very shallow waters to great depths. Some remain onshore between tides.

The family is most numerous in the North Pacific. There are 84 known species in the United States and Canada, exclusive of about 45 that occur only in Alaskan waters.

CABEZON *Scorpaenichthys marmoratus* The species is one of the largest sculpins on the Pacific coast, reaching a length of 30 inches and a weight of 25 pounds. Even though the flesh is of varied colors, it is an excellent foodfish, except for the roe, which is poisonous. It is found from central Baja California to northern British Columbia.

The cabezon has a large head and high, closely set eyes. The skin is smooth and thick; the snout has a prominent flap (cirrus). The spined portion of the dorsal fin is notched; there are large marbled pale areas on the dorsal and caudal fins and body, and a spine and 5 rays in the pelvic fins. Body color may be from green to cherry-red and changes with the environment.

The fish carries as many as 100,000 greenish eggs and spawns from the fall to March, depositing the ova in a mass. Its food consists largely of crabs, but other crustaceans and fishes are taken. It is found on many types of bottom and in kelp beds in shallow inshore waters to depths of about 200 feet. Maturity in the males is at 2–3 years of age, and in the females at 3–5. The cabezon has been known to reach 13 years of age. The young are pelagic, and are blue and silver in color. It does not move rapidly unless in pursuit of food.

GREAT SCULPIN *Myoxocephalus polyacanthocephalus* A large Pacific sculpin reaching a length of 30 inches, it is common and found from Washington to the Bering Sea at moderate depths. The great sculpin has small, fleshy papillae scattered over the body; a large, heavy blunt, short preopercular spine, equal to the eye diameter; a lateral line decurved below the soft dorsal fin. It is dark olive to black dorsally, white to cream ventrally; a pale band crosses the body, and there are black markings on all but the pelvic fins.

NORTHERN SCULPIN *Icelinus borealis* One of the small members of the family, it is dark olive-gray or brown above and white to cream below and has 4 dark saddles across the body. Narrow brown bars are present on the lips, cheeks, and all fins except the pelvic and anal. The male can be distinguished by 2 black spots on the spinous dorsal fin. The spinous dorsal has 9–10 rays and is separate from a soft dorsal fin with 15–17 rays. The anal fin has 12–14 rays.

This sculpin attains a maximum length of 4 inches. It is found at depths of 10–60 fathoms in the ocean from Puget Sound to northwestern Alaska.

PACIFIC STAGHORN SCULPIN *Leptocottus armatus* This abundant Pacific coastal sculpin is important as a baitfish. Some anglers for striped bass use it exclusively. It is often a nuisance, taking bait intended for more desirable fishes. Its sharp preopercular spines are formidable weapons thrust upward as the fish flattens its head when disturbed. It is found in bays and inshore, also in and near freshwater at the mouths of streams, from northern Baja California to northwest Alaska. It grows to 12 inches.

SHORTHORN SCULPIN *Myoxocephalus scorpius* Found on the northern Atlantic coast at least as far south as New England, the shorthorn sculpin reaches a length of 25 inches. It is distinguished by the presence of a small slit or pore behind the last gill arch. The dorsal fin has 9 spines and 15 rays; the anal fin has 14 rays. It lives primarily

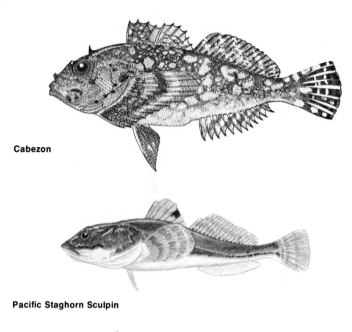

Cabezon

Pacific Staghorn Sculpin

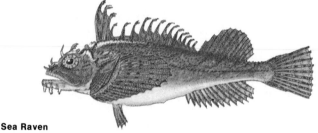

Sea Raven

inshore in the summer, migrating to greater depths in winter. It spawns in the fall and winter. It feeds on crustaceans and small fishes.

SEA RAVEN *Hemitripterus americanus* This sculpin is common north of Cape Cod but occurs to Chesapeake Bay. It has the ability to inflate the belly when disturbed. Its colors vary from purple to reddish-brown or yellow. It grows to a length of 25 inches and a weight of 5 pounds. It is distinguished by the fact that the spinous dorsal is larger than the softrayed portion. There are 4 spines in the first part of the dorsal fin, 12 in the second, and 1 spine and 12 rays in the last.

STICKLEBACK FAMILY   Gasterosteidae

There are 6 species of sticklebacks found in North American waters, of which only 2 are strictly marine forms: the tube-snout (*Aulorhynchus flavidus*) of the Pacific, and the blackspotted stickleback (*Gasterosteus wheatlandi*). For descriptions see *McClane's Field Guide to Freshwater Fishes of North America.*

BOXFISH FAMILY   Ostraciidae

This family includes the trunkfishes and cowfishes. The boxfishes are named because the head and most of the body are enclosed in a hard, boxlike shell composed of polygonal plates. This carapace is so rigid that the fish is able to move only its caudal peduncle, fins, eyes, and mouth.

In the scrawled cowfish, *Acanthostracion,* the carapace is more or less triangular in cross section, the ventral surface being essentially flat. There are 2 preocular spines on the head, which are directed anteriorly, and another pair projecting posteriorly from the lower rear part of the carapace (hence the specific name *quadricornis*). The cowfish is colored with bright blue or blue-green spots or short lines on the cheeks usually arranged to form several horizontal bands. The ground color is usually yellowish or olive.

In the western Atlantic there is a second species, the honeycomb cowfish (*A. polygonius*), which is less common than *A. quadricornis.* It has circular or hexagonal blue markings, one in each of the hexagonal plates except dorsally on the carapace and on the head, where there is a reticulum of blue. It has 12 instead of 11 pectoral rays, as in *A. quadricornis.* There seems to be a distinction in habitat in the West Indies, *A. quadricornis* being found most often on seagrass flats and *A. polygonius* on reefs.

The cowfish reaches a total length of about 18 inches. It is found in the western Atlantic Ocean from Massachusetts southward to Brazil, including Bermuda, the West Indies, and Gulf of Mexico. It is not common north of the Carolinas.

Other western Atlantic trunkfishes include the blackspotted *Rhinesomus bicaudalis*, which has a single pair of spines extending from the ventroposterior part of the carapace; the common smooth trunkfish (*R. triqueter*), which has no spines and is spotted with white; and the large *Lactophrys trigonus*, which has the pair of posterior spines, a highly arched sharp dorsal ridge on the carapace, and an isolated small plate dorsally on the caudal peduncle behind the carapace.

PUFFER FAMILY   Tetraodontidae

NORTHERN PUFFER *Sphoeroides maculatus*   Commonly known as blowfish, swellfish, and globefish, the puffer derives its name from its ability to inflate its body with air or water by means of a sac, which

Honeycomb Cowfish

Scrawled Cowfish

Smooth Trunkfish

Spiny Boxfish

is a ventral extension of the stomach. When alarmed or touched, the puffer quickly expands to a large size until it is almost globular; this protects the puffer from its enemies. When left alone, it soon deflates and assumes its moderately slender proportions. The northern puffer occurs from Cape Cod to Florida, where a similar species, the southern puffer, replaces it.

The northern puffer has a very small mouth, located at the tip of the snout. It does not have true teeth; the bones of the upper and lower jaws form cutting edges, which are divided in the middle giving the ap-

95

Northern Puffer

Northern Puffer (Inflated)

pearance of two large incisors both above and below. The skin is scaleless, but the head and body are covered with small, stiff prickles creating a heavy sandpaper texture. The gill openings in front of the pectorals are small and run obliquely backward and downward. The soft dorsal fin has 8 short rays and is twice as high as it is long. The anal fin has 7 rays and originates just behind the dorsal fin when a vertical line is drawn. There are no ventral fins. The northern puffer may reach 14 inches, but is usually less than 10 inches.

An inshore species, the northern puffer is seldom caught in water more than a few fathoms deep. Puffers are primarily bottom feeders and consume shrimps, crabs, amphipods, isopods, mollusks, worms, sea urchins, and other invertebrates. They spawn from mid-May through June according to the location, the eggs sinking and adhering to any object. The larvae are brilliantly pigmented with orange, red, yellow, and black. Puffers only $^1/_2$ inch long can inflate themselves to a greater extent than the adult, until the expanded skin completely hides the anal and dorsal fins.

Puffers are caught incidental to some other bottom species and are often considered a nuisance because of their ability to strip a bait from the hook. Occasionally, they will also strike artificial lures, such as small jigs. The northern puffer is highly regarded as a table fish and is sold commercially as sea squab, but we do not recommend the use of any puffer as food. The viscera and skin are toxic. The roe should never be eaten.

SMOOTH PUFFER *Lagocephalus laevigatus* Also known as rabbitfish, the smooth puffer is distributed on both sides of the Atlantic. In the western Atlantic it ranges from Massachusetts south to Argentina, including the Gulf of Mexico. This puffer is distinguished from other Tetraodontidae in its geographical range by its smooth skin (only the belly has short prickles), large dorsal and anal fins, and the concave caudal fin. The smooth puffer is not able to expand its body as greatly as the northern or southern puffers, possibly because of its larger size. It may grow to 2 feet and 7 pounds.

SOUTHERN PUFFER *Sphoeroides nephelus* Known from southeastern Florida and throughout the Gulf of Mexico, southern puffers occur in a variety of habitats, including both grassy and smooth, unvegetated bottoms. They often are found near pilings and rocks as well.

In life they are brownish above, with small black and green spots; white below. There are 7–8 irregular black bars on the sides posterior to the pectoral fins and a black spot in front of the pectorals. There is a dark brownish area at the base of the dorsal fin and between that fin and the caudal. The dorsal and anal fins are plain; the pectoral pale brownish-yellow; the caudal yellowish-brown. Said to reach a length of 14 inches, specimens seldom exceed 10 inches.

Of no commercial or sport value in themselves, southern puffers often are considered a nuisance inasmuch as they steal bait by nibbling it with their beaklike dental structures and themselves often are caught instead of desired species. The flesh of the southern puffer is frequently toxic and should not be utilized as food.

SEA BASS FAMILY   Serranidae

In addition to the sea basses, hamlets and groupers are included in this family. The name grouper is usually applied to the large serranid fishes belonging to such genera as *Epinephelus, Mycteroperca, Paranthias,* and *Dermatolepis.*

BLACK GROUPER *Mycteroperca bonaci* A common grouper in southern Florida and throughout the tropical American Atlantic, this fish may reach 50 pounds in weight and a total length of over 3 feet.

The black grouper has 11 dorsal spines; its dorsal rays number 16–18, usually 17; anal rays 11–13, usually 12; and pectoral rays usually 17. Posterior nostril is about as large as the anterior. Insertion of pelvic fin is under or somewhat behind lower end of pectoral base. Posterior margin of caudal fin is straight or somewhat convex. The sides of the body have rows of rectangular dark blotches or irregular pale lines forming a chainlike or reticulate pattern.

This grouper is distinguished from the others by the color pattern. The gag is commonly called black grouper in Florida waters, but can be separated by its plain coloration and lunate caudal fin.

Young individuals may occur close to shore, but the larger adults are found on rocky bottom in deeper water.

The black grouper is a good fighter, especially when taken by trolling with natural bait, or plugs, spinners, or spoons. Very good eating, it is a grouper of some commercial importance.

BLACK SEA BASS *Centropristis striata* One of the most popular bottomfish species of the northeast Atlantic coast, the sea bass ranges from southern Massachusetts to northern Florida, with its chief center of abundance from New York (Long Island) to North Carolina. Sea bass are exclusively marine fish and, in contrast to the related striped bass, never venture into rivers. They are found in bays, sounds, and along the inshore and offshore zones. The sea bass can readily be identified by its moderately stout body, which is 3 times as long (not counting the caudal fin) as it is deep. It has a high back but a flat-topped head, moderately pointed snout, and 1 sharp spine near the apex of each gill cover. The dorsal fin contains 10 spiny rays and 11 softrays; the caudal fin is rounded. Like many fish that inhabit rocky bottoms, the color of the sea bass is variable. It ranges from smoky-gray to dusky-brown to a blue-black or indigo. The color is sometimes mottled or has the appearance of being barred with longitudinal spots of a lighter shade because the bases of the exposed parts of the scales are paler than the margins.

Sea bass are not large fish. The smallest, sometimes called pin bass, range from a few ounces to a pound or so. The average is about $1^1/_2$ pounds, and they are seldom heavier than 5 pounds. A few have been recorded at a weight of 7 pounds. The larger males are nicknamed humpbacks because of a pronounced rise just in back of the head.

Sea bass live offshore in the winter (where they are commercially netted in Virginia and North Carolina waters). In the spring, populations of them move inshore. Some remain in the ocean, while others forage in sounds and bays. This spring sport-fishing run usually begins in May and lasts throughout the summer, reaching its zenith in the warmer months. When autumn chills the water sea bass swim offshore to spend the winter. Depending on water temperatures, the seaward journey can occur as late as October or even early November.

These fish are essentially bottom dwellers, spending most of their time on, or a short distance above, the sea floor. They favor hard bottoms in water that is clear and fairly deep. In the ocean they are caught down to depths of 100 feet. In bays and sounds they often show a preference for water 20–50 feet deep.

The largest specimens are those hooked by deepsea anglers. The usual weight range is $1^1/_2$–3 pounds, but at the height of a run the occasional sea bass will weigh up to 4–5 pounds. In bays and other confined waters the general run of fish is smaller, with sizes up to 2 pounds.

CONEY *Cephalopholis fulva*   This is one of the most common and perhaps the smallest of groupers. It is fairly abundant in southern Florida and much more so in the West Indies. It occurs throughout the tropical American Atlantic. It seldom reaches over 15 inches in total length.

The coney has 9 dorsal spines; dorsal rays 14–15, usually 15; anal rays usually 9; and pectoral rays usually 18. Posterior nostril about as large as the anterior. Insertion of pelvic fin is under or behind lower end of pectoral base. Posterior margin of caudal fin is convex. General coloration is variable: red, brown, or yellow, usually with small, light blue spots; 2 black spots on top of caudal peduncle.

The number of dorsal spines distinguishes this grouper from the others except the graysby. It is distinguished from the latter by the more numerous dorsal, anal, and pectoral rays and by the 2 black caudal spots.

The coney is an excellent eating, pan-sized grouper, highly valued as a foodfish in the West Indies.

GAG *Mycteroperca microlepis*   This species is fairly common along the South Atlantic and Gulf coasts of the United States, from North Carolina to Louisiana. Although reported from as far south as Brazil, it is apparently very rare in the West Indies. This grouper may reach a weight of about 50 pounds and a total length of over 3 feet.

The gag has 11 dorsal spines, 16–19 dorsal rays, and usually 11 anal rays. Posterior nostril is somewhat larger than the anterior. Insertion of pelvic fin is under or somewhat behind lower end of pectoral base. Posterior margin of caudal fin is concave. Color uniform gray without distinctive markings, or with dark vermiculations tending to group in clusters.

The gag is distinguished from the other groupers by the plain coloration and the lunate caudal fin.

GRAYSBY *Petrometopon cruentatum*   This is a small grouper frequently taken in southern Florida, but apparently more abundant in the West Indies. It occurs throughout the tropical American Atlantic and seldom reaches over 15 inches in total length.

The graysby has 9 dorsal spines, usually 14 dorsal rays, usually 8 anal rays, and usually 16 pectoral rays. The posterior nostril is somewhat larger than the anterior nostril. Insertion of the pelvic fin is under or slightly in advance of lower end of pectoral base. Posterior margin of the caudal fin is convex. General coloration is reddish or

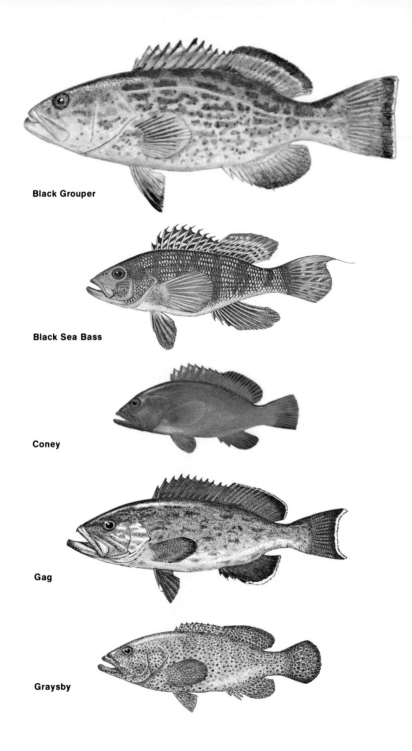

Black Grouper

Black Sea Bass

Coney

Gag

Graysby

brownish, profusely spotted with red. Several black spots are usually present along the dorsal fin base.

The number of dorsal spines distinguishes this grouper from the others except the coney. It is distinguished from the latter by the fewer dorsal, anal, and pectoral rays, and by the black spots along the dorsal fin base.

JEWFISH *Epinephelus itajara*   This is perhaps the largest of the groupers and reaches a weight of 700 pounds. It is fairly common in southern Florida and throughout the tropical American Atlantic. It is also called spotted grouper and in Spanish *guasa*.

The jewfish has 11 dorsal spines; 15–16 dorsal rays, usually 16; 8 anal rays; and usually 19 pectoral rays. The posterior nostril is about equal to, or somewhat larger than, the anterior. Insertion of pelvic fin is under, or somewhat behind, the lower end of pectoral base. Posterior margin of caudal fin is convex. There are irregular dark bars and dark spots on the sides of the body.

In addition to the large size, the color pattern distinguishes this grouper from the others.

This is a shallow-water species usually found under ledges not far from shore. Usually, small individuals and often large ones occur in estuaries and in waterways among keys. The jewfish takes live or dead bait and frequently it will also take artificial lures. The very large size it attains makes this fish a spectacular catch, although it is not a good fighter. Its habit of swimming into a hole as soon as hooked presents quite a challenge to the angler. Small specimens weighing a few pounds can be taken on fly, spinning, or plug tackle. These are much better fighters than the large adults.

The jewfish is excellent eating at any size. In the West Indies, it was salted, dried, and sold as imported salt cod during World War II.

MARBLED GROUPER *Dermatolepis inermis*   This fairly rare grouper is taken occasionally off southern Florida. It occurs throughout the tropical American Atlantic. The few specimens available in museums or studied in the field measure usually less than 20 inches in total length.

The marbled grouper has 11 dorsal spines, usually 19 dorsal rays, and usually 9 anal rays. It has 18–19 pectoral rays, usually 19. The posterior nostril is 2–3 times larger than the anterior. Insertion of pelvic fin is behind the lower end of the pectoral base. Posterior margin of caudal fin is slightly convex, straight, or slightly concave. Head, body, and fins are marbled or mottled with irregular light blotches and spots on a dark background.

MISTY GROUPER *Epinephelus mystacinus*   Also called the mustache grouper, this rather rare deepwater species may reach a weight of 50 pounds. It is found throughout the tropical American Atlantic, including extreme southern Florida. The name mustache grouper refers to the black mustachelike band on either side of the snout parallel to the upper jaw. Called *cherna del alto* in Spanish, it is a commercial fish in some of the Antilles, but is rarely seen in the markets.

It has 11 dorsal spines, usually 15 dorsal rays, 9 anal rays, and 18–19 pectoral rays. The posterior nostril is much larger than the anterior. Insertion of pelvic fin is under, or in advance of, the upper end of the pectoral base. Posterior margin of caudal fin convex. There are dark bars on the sides of the body. A dark bar around the caudal peduncle is much darker on top but does not form a well-defined saddlelike black blotch.

The much enlarged posterior nostril distinguishes this grouper from the others, except the snowy grouper. The latter, however, has an entirely different color pattern.

The misty grouper occurs on rocky bottoms, usually along the edge of the shelf, in depths of 80–120 fathoms.

Because of its occurrence in deepwater, this grouper has little or no angling value in the usual sense. When taken with a wire line, however, it provides the thrill of an unusual catch by an unorthodox method. It is taken on hand lines by West Indian fishermen.

MUTTON HAMLET *Alphestes afer* This is a distinct species but has a close relative in the tropical eastern Pacific. The mutton hamlet is confined to the western Atlantic and extends from Bermuda and southern Florida all the way south to Argentina and the Falkland Islands.

Its color may be described as olive, blotched and mottled with darker olive to brown. There are some dark orange spots on the body. The pectoral fins are dull olive-red with bluish spots, the vertical fins olive with darker markings. Some pale spots are present on the ventrum and the anal fin. The lower part of the head is yellowish. Above the maxillary there is a dark reddish-brown "mustache." At night this pattern is lost and 2 dark bands cross the body.

Other distinguishing characters of the mutton hamlet are 11 dorsal fin spines, 18–19 softrays; 3 anal fin spines, 9 softrays; scales covering head and body, reduced in size at nape and everywhere on head except opercles, where they are larger than on body.

The fish attains a length of about 1 foot. Females with well-developed eggs have been taken as small as 7$\frac{1}{2}$ inches. This is an important foodfish in the West Indies, but its life history is unknown.

NASSAU GROUPER *Epinephelus striatus* Among fishermen, this is one of the best-known groupers in southern Florida and throughout the tropical American Atlantic. It is also one of the most common of the important commercial groupers. Although it may reach over 3 feet in total length, the usual size is less. The common name probably refers to its being more abundant in the Bahamas than in Florida.

The Nassau grouper has 11 dorsal spines; 16–18 dorsal rays, usually 17; 8 anal rays; and 18, rarely 17, pectoral rays. Its posterior nostril is somewhat larger than (up to about twice as large as) the anterior. The insertion of the pelvic fin is behind the lower end of the pectoral base. The posterior margin of the caudal fin is convex. Dark bars occur on the head and body. There is a saddlelike black blotch on top of the caudal peduncle. Scattered black specks are present around the eyes.

This grouper is distinguished from all the others by the color pattern. It somewhat resembles the red grouper, but the latter is much paler and lacks the black blotch on top of the caudal peduncle.

The Nassau grouper prefers rocky bottom in shallow to medium-depth water. Small individuals may occur close to shore; large adults are usually found in somewhat deeper water around coral heads and reefs. It takes live bait as well as artificial lures. One of the best fighting groupers, it is difficult to keep away from holes if hooked on light tackle.

Excellent eating, it is one of the most important commercial fishes in the southern United States and the Caribbean. The skin is tough and strongly flavored. The firm white fillets should be cut in fingers for deep frying or in chunks to make chowders.

ROCKHIND *Epinephelus adscensionis*   Although frequently taken in southern Florida, this species is more abundant in the Bahamas and throughout the Caribbean area. It is a relatively small grouper, reaching a length of usually less than 30 inches.

The rockhind has 11 dorsal spines; 16–17, usually 17, dorsal rays; 8 anal rays; and usually 19 pectoral rays. The posterior nostril is about equal to the anterior. Insertion of pelvic fin is behind the lower end of the pectoral base. Posterior margin of the caudal fin is convex. The head, body, and fins have dark red spots which are larger on the ventral area. There are three dark blotches along base of dorsal fin. There is a saddlelike black blotch on top of caudal peduncle.

This species is found on rocky bottom in relatively shallow water. It is frequently taken around coral heads in water only a few feet deep, although it may occur in much deeper water. The rockhind takes live or dead bait and artificial lures. It is good eating and of commercial importance throughout the tropical American Atlantic.

SAND BASS *Paralabrax nebulifer*   This is a small Pacific marine species of minor angling importance. Anglers take sand bass from boats, piers, and barges usually in the vicinity of kelp beds. The sand bass attains a length of about 18 inches. It is often lumped with a very similar species, the kelp bass, *P. clathratus*, as a rock bass in commercial and sport catches.

SCAMP *Mycteroperca phenax*   This grouper, apparently very rare in the West Indies, is fairly common along the South Atlantic and Gulf coasts of the United States. The usual size is less than 30 inches in total length.

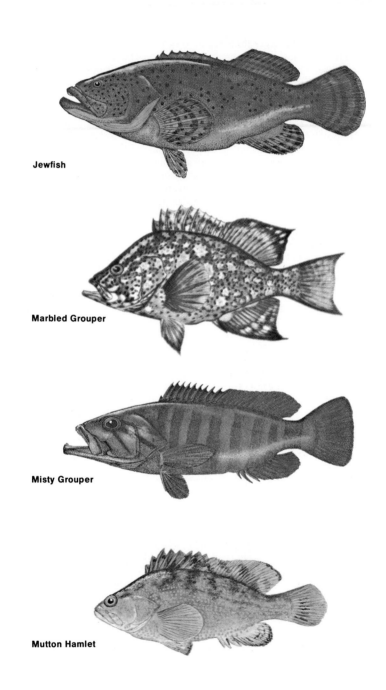

Jewfish

Marbled Grouper

Misty Grouper

Mutton Hamlet

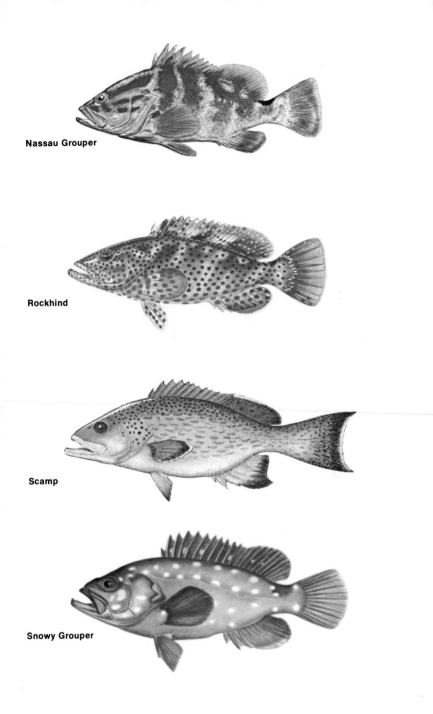

Nassau Grouper

Rockhind

Scamp

Snowy Grouper

The scamp has 11 dorsal spines, usually 18 dorsal rays, and usually 11 anal rays. The posterior nostril is much larger than the anterior. Insertion of pelvic fin is under the lower end of the pectoral base. Posterior margin of the caudal fin is concave. Coloration is light brown with small dark spots arranged in round or elongate clusters.

This grouper is distinguished from the others by its color pattern.

The scamp occurs in shallow water to water that is moderately deep. It is a good fighter, especially when taken by trolling with natural bait, plugs, spinners, or spoons.

It is a foodfish of some importance in the southern United States.

SNOWY GROUPER *Epinephelus niveatus* This is a deepwater grouper occurring in southern Florida and throughout the tropical American Atlantic. The common name refers to the snow-white, round body spots of the young. Large adults are called golden groupers and may reach a total length of 4 feet.

The snowy grouper has 11 dorsal spines; 13–14 dorsal rays, usually 14; 9 anal rays; and 18 pectoral rays, rarely 19. The posterior nostril is much larger than the anterior. Insertion of pelvic fin is under, or in advance of, the upper end of the pectoral base. Posterior margin of the caudal fin is convex (young), straight or slightly concave (adult). The body has white spots in longitudinal and vertical rows. The top of the caudal peduncle has a black saddlelike blotch. These color marks gradually disappear with age and are absent in specimens over 15 inches in total length.

The enlarged posterior nostril distinguishes this grouper from the others, except the misty grouper. The latter, however, has an entirely different color pattern.

Adults are taken on rocky bottom along the edge of the continental shelf, at depths usually around 80–120 fathoms. Large adults have been taken in 250 fathoms, probably a depth record for groupers. Juveniles and young occur in water as shallow as 50 feet.

Since it occurs mostly in water that is very deep, this grouper has little angling value. It provides, however, an unforgettable experience when taken on a wire line. It is taken on hand lines by West Indian fishermen.

SPECKLED HIND *Epinephelus drummondhayi* This rather rare species occurs off southern Florida and throughout the tropical American Atlantic. It is one of the smaller groupers, rarely reaching over 20 inches in total length. It is also called calico grouper in reference to its color pattern.

The speckled hind has 11 dorsal spines; 15–16 dorsal rays, usually 16; 9 anal rays; and usually 18 pectoral rays. The posterior nostril is about equal to, or somewhat larger than, the anterior. Insertion of pelvic fin is under the lower end of the pectoral base. Posterior margin of the caudal fin is straight or slightly concave. The head, body, and fins are profusely speckled with white spots on a dark background.

This species is distinguished from the others by the unique, striking color pattern.

One of the least known of the groupers, the speckled hind occurs in water that is moderately deep. It is a rewarding catch owing to its scarcity and beautiful color pattern.

TIGER GROUPER *Mycteroperca tigris* This is a rather uncommon species occurring throughout the tropical American Atlantic, but rarely taken. It is known to reach a total length of over 20 inches. The common and scientific names refer to the tigerlike crossbanded color pattern.

The tiger grouper has 11 dorsal spines, 16–17 dorsal rays, 10–11 anal rays, and usually 17 pectoral rays. The posterior nostril is much larger than the anterior. Insertion of pelvic fin is under the lower end of the pectoral base. Posterior margin of the caudal fin is straight or somewhat concave. The sides of the body have several oblique, narrow, light bands.

The color pattern distinguishes this grouper from the others.

Not much is known about the habits of this species. It occurs on rocky bottom in waters of medium depth and takes live or dead bait. It is a good fighter, but not known to have been taken on artificial lures.

WARSAW GROUPER *Epinephelus nigritus* This is one of the largest of groupers, reaching a weight of several hundred pounds. It occurs in the tropical American Atlantic including southern Florida. It is also erroneously called black grouper in reference to its color.

The Warsaw grouper has 10 dorsal spines; 13–15 dorsal rays, usually 14; 9 anal rays; and 18–19 pectoral rays, usually 18. Posterior nostril equal to, or somewhat larger than, the anterior. Insertion of pelvic fin in advance of upper end of pectoral base. Posterior margin of caudal fin convex. Coloration nearly uniformly dark, sometimes with a few scattered white spots.

This species is distinguished from the other Atlantic groupers by the number of dorsal spines. The others have 8, 9, or 11.

A bottomfish occurring in offshore waters of moderate depth, it takes live or dead bait and will occasionally strike artificial lures.

The large size attained makes this fish a spectacular catch. It is one of the best fighting groupers. Since it does not occur close to shore, a boat is required. Small individuals can be broiled in chunks or fingers, and the larger fish can be chunked to make an excellent chowder. The flesh must be skinned.

YELLOWEDGE GROUPER *Epinephelus flavolimbatus* This deepwater grouper occurs in the tropical American Atlantic including southern Florida. The common name refers to the yellow margin of the dorsal fin, which is a distinguishing mark for the species.

The yellowedge grouper has 11 dorsal spines; 13–15 dorsal rays, rarely 15; 9 anal rays; and usually 18 pectoral rays. The posterior nos-

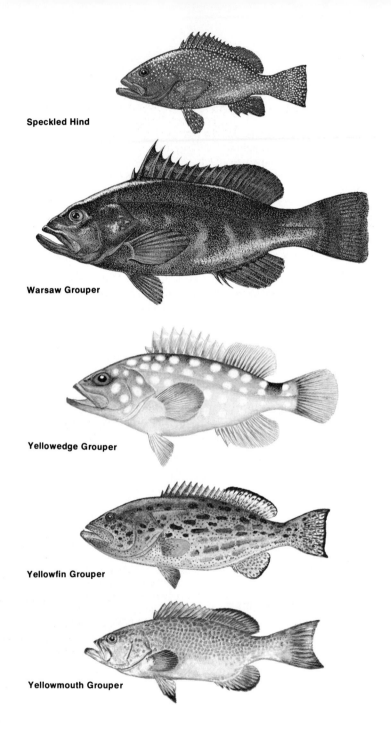

Speckled Hind

Warsaw Grouper

Yellowedge Grouper

Yellowfin Grouper

Yellowmouth Grouper

tril is about as large as the anterior. Insertion of pelvic fin is under, or in advance of, the upper end of the pectoral base. Posterior margin of the caudal fin is convex (young) and straight or slightly concave (adult). The sides of the body have white spots in longitudinal and vertical rows (young). The top of the caudal peduncle has a black saddlelike blotch (young). These color marks gradually disappear with age and are absent in specimens over 15 inches in total length.

The yellow margin of the dorsal fin distinguishes this grouper from the others. The white body spots and the caudal peduncle blotch also occur in the young of the snowy grouper, but in the latter, the posterior nostril is much enlarged.

Juveniles and young occur in shallower water; adults, especially large specimens, are taken on rocky bottom at 80–120 fathoms.

YELLOWFIN GROUPER *Mycteroperca venenosa* This medium-sized grouper is fairly common in southern Florida and throughout the tropical American Atlantic. The usual size is 3 feet or less in total length. The common name refers to the yellow margin of the pectoral fin.

The yellowfin grouper has 11 dorsal spines, usually 16 dorsal rays, usually 11 anal rays, and usually 17 pectoral rays. The posterior nostril is larger than the anterior. Insertion of the pelvic fin is under or somewhat behind the lower end of the pectoral base. Posterior margin of the caudal fin is concave. The head and body have red spots and irregular longitudinal rows of rounded or quadrangular dark blotches. The outer third of the pectoral fin is yellow.

The color pattern, especially the yellow margin of the pectoral fin, distinguishes this grouper from the others.

The yellowfin occurs on rocky bottom in shallow to medium-depth water. It is frequently taken around coral heads with live or dead bait or artificial lures.

YELLOWMOUTH GROUPER *Mycteroperca interstitialis* A fairly common grouper in southern Florida and throughout the tropical American Atlantic, its usual size is less than 20 inches in total length.

The yellowmouth grouper has 11 dorsal spines; 16–17 dorsal rays, usually 17; usually 11 anal rays; and usually 16 pectoral rays. The posterior nostril is much larger than the anterior. Insertion of the pelvic fin is usually somewhat behind lower end of the pectoral base. Posterior margin of the caudal fin is concave. Coloration is uniform dark brown or with light lines forming reticulations enclosing small dark spots.

The color pattern distinguishes this grouper from the others.

The yellowmouth occurs in shallow to moderately deep water and takes live or dead bait and artificial lures.

Good eating, it is a fish of some commercial importance in the West Indies.

TEMPERATE BASS FAMILY Percichthyidae

Of the 6 temperate basses found in North American waters, only the Atlantic wreckfish and the giant sea bass of the Pacific are strictly marine forms. The white perch and striped bass are anadromous; the white bass and yellow bass, strictly freshwater species. The striped bass is partially described here for identification purposes because of its popularity in the saltwater sport fishery. For details on the temperate basses see *McClane's Field Guide to Freshwater Fishes of North America*.

GIANT SEA BASS *Stereolepis gigas*   This large sea bass occurs from central California south to the Gulf of California, Mexico. It has been recorded to 557 pounds. It is known to live from 70 to 75 years. It is usually found close to shore, but only small numbers are caught by anglers, and these seldom exceed 100 pounds.

The giant sea bass has 2 dorsal fins with more spines (11) than soft-rays (9–10). In adults the dorsal spines are shorter than the dorsal rays and the color is dark brown to blackish above, somewhat paler below. The young are very different in both shape and color. In specimens about 1 inch long the spiny part of the dorsal fin is higher than the soft, the body is nearly as deep as it is long, and the pelvic fins are longer than the pectorals. The body is brick-red with distinct brownish or blackish spots. As the fish grows it gradually takes on the typical adult appearance. The dark spots on the sides are often evident in fish up to 30 pounds.

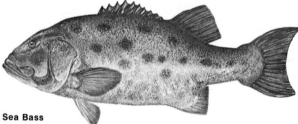

Giant Sea Bass

STRIPED BASS *Morone saxatilis*   An important marine gamefish regionally known as the rockfish (south of New Jersey) and infrequently called squidhound or greenhead, the striper is easily identified.

The trunk of the striped bass is $3^1/_2$–4 times as long (to the base of the caudal fin) as it is deep. The fish has a long head, a moderately pointed snout, and a projecting lower jaw. The 2 dorsal fins are about of equal length, and both are triangular in outline; these fins are separated. Although the color may vary, as a rule the striped bass is dark olive-green (hence the name greenhead) to steel-blue or almost black

110

above, becoming silvery on the sides and white on the belly. The sides have 7–8 longitudinal dark stripes that follow the scale rows; 3–4 stripes are above the lateral line, 1 on it, and 3 below it. The upper stripes are the longest and may reach to the caudal fin. The stripes are often interrupted or broken and are usually absent on young fish of less than 6 inches. There is little chance of confusing striped bass of over 10 inches with any other species of fish along the Atlantic or Pacific coasts. The prominent stripes, separated dorsal fins, and the general outline are unique. In young specimens of less than 7 inches it may be difficult to distinguish the striped bass from the related white perch. However, the dorsal fins of the white perch are connected.

The striped bass has been successfully hybridized with the related white bass and stocked in southern U.S. waters, where it is known as the whiterock or sunshine bass.

Striped Bass

WRECKFISH *Polyprion americanus*   Relatively rare in the western Atlantic, this species is found from Norway to the Canary Islands and in the Mediterranean. The body is flattened and the head rough with bony protuberances over the eye and nape; there are strong spines on each gill cover. Rough scales extend over the base of softrayed fins. The wreckfish attains a size of at least 5 feet and weighs over 100 pounds.

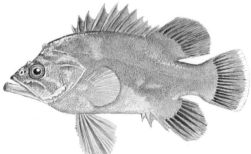

Wreckfish

PORGY FAMILY Sparidae

GRASS PORGY *Calamus arctifons* Known from Florida to the West Indies, the grass porgy is fairly common on the west coast of Florida and in the Gulf of Mexico, especially in shallow water in aquatic vegetation.

Like the sheepshead porgy, it has comparatively large scales, 45–53 in the lateral line. Unlike the latter, the dorsal outline of the body does not form a regular arch. Instead, its greatest depth is before the middle of the body. This porgy is a banded fish, with the fins variously mottled with darker spots. The olive-colored body is speckled with white spots, and there are 6 yellowish spots on the lateral line. The fish rarely exceeds 1 foot in length.

Commercially it is generally taken with a haul seine and is a good foodfish. Anglers use shrimps or cut fish for bait.

JOLTHEAD PORGY *Calamus bajonado* This is one of the larger members of this wide-ranging genus. Although common to the Western Atlantic, porgies of the genus *Calamus* also occur in the eastern Pacific on the mainland shores of southern North America, Central America, and northern South America, and in the Galápagos Islands. The most frequently encountered species along the coast of the southeastern United States is the whitebone porgy. While primarily a West Indian species, the jolthead porgy is distributed along the Atlantic seaboard as far north as Rhode Island, and in the Gulf of Mexico. It also occurs in Bermuda and as far south as Brazil.

Jolthead Porgy

The body color of the jolthead porgy is silvery with violet and blue overtones. Although said to be dull in color, in life it is often beautifully marked with chestnut-brown blotches; these disappear or diminish in intensity when the fish are living on light sand bottoms or when the specimen is dead. The dorsal fin usually contains 12 spines and 12 softrays; there are 3 spines and 10 softrays in the anal fin and 50–57 scales along the lateral line.

The jolthead porgy, as well as other members of this genus, has conical teeth in the front of the mouth, rather than incisors, and molariform teeth behind. The posterior nostril is slitlike, which distinguishes it from the often confused genus *Pagrus*, the red porgy, which possesses an oval posterior nostril.

PINFISH *Lagodon rhomboides*   There is but one species in this genus, ranging with little variation from the south side of Cape Cod south to the Yucatán Peninsula in Mexico. It also is found at Bermuda, but records from other islands, such as Cuba, Jamaica, and the Bahamas, apparently are erroneous. The pinfish probably is one of the most abundant of inshore fishes, especially in the more southern parts of its range.

Pinfish

In life, the ground color of the pinfish is bluish-silver, darker above than below. There are 4–6 dark crossbars (varying in intensity) on the sides and numerous longitudinal golden stripes on the length of the fish. There is a dark shoulder spot. The fins are yellowish, with tinges of blue.

Like many American sparid fishes, the pinfish has a series of humanlike incisor teeth in the front of the jaws. However, it can be distinguished from members of the other genera by the conspicuous notching of these teeth. Using these teeth, the pinfish grazes, and its food is quite varied; the bulk apparently consists of small animals, particularly crustaceans, and perhaps plant material to some degree.

Spawning is believed to take place offshore, for gravid females are found only in a few areas, despite the wide distribution of the species, and postlarvae smaller than about $1/_2$ inch rarely are seen, but are common larger than this after they have migrated or been swept inshore. Spawning usually occurs in the late fall and early winter.

Inshore, pinfish occur most commonly on shallow, fully marine grassy flats, but they also come up rivers into water that is essentially fresh, and the larger adults occur at or near the bottom far beyond the zone of vegetation. Pinfish apparently are quite tolerant of changes in their environment, and this may account in part for their great abundance.

Members of this species form a major portion of the diet of a number of gamefish, and consequently often are used for bait. Larger specimens, sometimes reaching nearly 14 inches, are used to some extent as foodfish.

RED PORGY *Pagrus sedecim*　Although a closely related species occurs in European waters, only this one species is found in the western Atlantic, from New York to Argentina and in the Gulf of Mexico.

P. sedecim has conical teeth and a rounded posterior nostril (instead of slitlike, as in members of the genus *Calamus*). In life, the color basically is reddish-silver, with numerous minute blue spots.

No data are available on food and spawning habits, but the fish likely is carnivorous and an offshore winter spawner.

The red porgy occurs in water that is rather deep, more so on the average than do other American sparids, but it often forms part of the catch in sport bottom fishing. It may reach a length of 3 feet. Good numbers often are taken in bottom trawls fished off the coast of the southeastern United States and in this way enter the commercial fishery. The red porgy is erroneously known and often marketed as silver snapper.

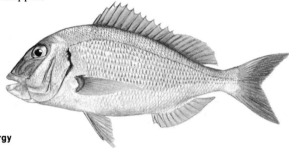

Red Porgy

SCUP *Stenotomus chrysops*　This fish is commonly known as porgy along the northeastern United States coast. Apparently there are only 2 species in this genus, *S. chrysops* and the common species of the Gulf of Mexico, the longspine porgy, *S. caprinus*. *S. chrysops* ranges from Nova Scotia south to the Atlantic coast of Florida, but has not been shown to occur in the Gulf of Mexico as some writers have supposed. *S. caprinus*, on the other hand, does occur off the Carolina and Georgia coasts along with *S. chrysops*. *S. aculeatus*, the so-called southern porgy or scup of the Atlantic coast, apparently is identical with *S. chrysops*.

The scup has lanceolate incisor teeth, which distinguish the members of this genus from other American sparids.

In life, the ground color is silvery to brownish, without distinct markings except sometimes for traces of darkish vertical bars on the

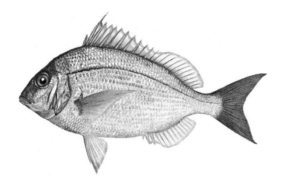

Scup

sides, the bar midway the length of the body being usually more distinct than the several others. The scup sometimes reaches about 18 inches and 3–4 pounds.

The scup often enters importantly both the commercial and sport catches, especially in the more northern parts of its range. Although it readily takes bottom-fished baits, the scup is often regarded as a nuisance by anglers seeking larger species. It is a good table fish.

SEA BREAM *Archosargus rhomboidalis*   The species is primarily tropical and ranges certainly from south Florida to Rio de Janeiro. It questionably has been recorded from as far north as New Jersey. Although common in the proper habitat in the West Indies, it has not been recorded from the Bahamas. This species probably replaces the pinfish *Lagodon* in the tropics, for the two forms have similar ecological and food habits.

In life, the color is much like that of the pinfish: basically bluish-silver with several indistinct dark crossbars, which vary in intensity, on the sides; numerous longitudinal golden stripes on the sides (somewhat wider, more distinct, and less regular than in the pinfish); and a dark shoulder spot. The fins are yellowish, with tinges of blue. In size, the sea bream may reach about 1 foot.

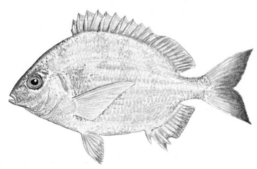

Sea Bream

115

The sea bream lives on grassy flats and feeds on small animals and on plant materials, using its lunately edged incisor teeth in a typical grazing type of feeding behavior. Records of *Lagodon* from the West Indies actually are the sea bream, and where the two occur together, as in the Florida keys, they usually are not distinguished by local fishermen despite the deeper body and different tooth form of the sea bream. Spawning apparently takes place not far offshore in winter.

SHEEPSHEAD *Archosargus probatocephalus* There are 3 named species in the genus *Archosargus* that apparently, at best, are only of subspecific rank within the species *probatocephalus*. One of these subspecies, *probatocephalus*, occurs from Nova Scotia south to the northeastern Gulf of Mexico. The second subspecies, *oviceps,* ranges from the northeastern Gulf of Mexico to the Yucatán Peninsula in Mexico. The third subspecies, *aries,* is known from British Honduras to Brazil. There are no records of *A. probatocephalus* from any of the West Indian islands or from Bermuda, and apparently it is restricted to mainland coasts, where it is often quite common.

In life, the ground color is silvery, darker above than below, and there are usually 5–6 distinct dark vertical bars on each side, which give this species the sometimes used common name of convict fish. There is some variation in this color pattern, and the bars *may* be higher in number, lower, or different on different sides of the fish, or odd in shape so that they cannot really be counted at all.

The sheepshead is a popular game- and foodfish in some areas, particularly in Florida, and some sport fishermen specialize in them because they often are such a challenge to catch. They commonly reach a size of 2 feet, although individuals over 3 feet in length have been reported.

The sheepshead is a very suspicious quarry. When the experienced angler locates sheepshead, he frequently chums the area with crushed fiddler crabs to stir them into feeding. Fiddler crabs, hermit crabs,

Sheepshead

116

shrimps, and sandbugs are popular baits. Sheepshead rarely strike an artificial lure, although they may display interest in small flies and jigs. They are excellent table fish.

SPOTTAIL PINFISH *Diplodus holbrooki*   Four members of the genus *Diplodus* occur in western Atlantic waters, but except for the Atlantic waters of central and southern Florida, the species usually encountered in the continental waters of the United States is *D. holbrooki.* It ranges from about Chesapeake Bay south to about New Smyrna Beach, Florida, and from the Florida Keys to the northwestern Gulf of Mexico. The West Indies islands species, *D. caudimacula,* appears to replace *D. holbrooki* from about New Smyrna Beach to the Florida Keys. The other two American species are confined one to Bermuda and one to the mainland coast of South America.

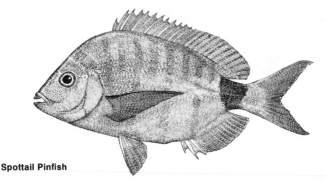

Spottail Pinfish

In life, the body of the spottail pinfish is plain silvery, sometimes with several faint, narrow crossbars on the sides. However, a distinct dark blotch or saddle on the caudal peduncle distinguishes it and other American members of the genus *Diplodus* from the other American sparids.

WHITEBONE PORGY *Calamus leucosteus*   This probably is the most frequently encountered member of this large (some dozen species in all) and wide-ranging genus in the southeastern United States. It is found in the Atlantic waters off the Carolinas, Georgia, and Florida, and also in the eastern Gulf of Mexico. Other members of the genus range from New England to the central Atlantic coast of South America. In the West Indies, in particular, species of the genus *Calamus* are primary foodfish for human consumption, some species reaching nearly 3 feet. *C. leucosteus* may reach about 18 inches.

Members of this genus, including the whitebone porgy, have conical teeth in the front of the mouth, rather than incisors. The posterior nostril is slitlike.

117

The color of the whitebone porgy is silvery, with irregular, dark markings of varying intensity on the sides of the body, more like splotches than spots. There may be a tendency for the sides to bear darkish crossbars. There is no distinct axillary spot.

Most species of the genus *Calamus* occur in the western Atlantic, but the genus also is represented in the eastern Pacific on the mainland shores of southern North America, Central America, and northern South America, and in the Galápagos Islands.

Like other American sparids, *C. leucosteus* apparently spawns offshore in the late fall or winter.

Food habits of this species are poorly known, but inasmuch as whitebones readily take a hook, they are presumed to be primarily carnivorous. They provide considerable sport as bottom dwellers in places where such fishing is pursued.

DRUM FAMILY Sciaenidae

Also known as croakers, drums are characterized by the presence of a lateral line that extends onto the caudal fin. Usually there are 1 or more barbels on the lower jaw.

ATLANTIC CROAKER *Micropogon undulatus* The Atlantic croaker has a temperate distribution ordinarily extending from Rhode Island to Cape Kennedy and, in the Gulf of Mexico, from Tampa Bay across to the southern Gulf of Campeche. There are records from southern Florida, but these are probably the result of occasional southward migrations under the stress of unusually cold winter conditions.

Its color is a very light silvery-gray above with a vertical pattern of interrupted bars giving a faintly spotted effect. The lower one-third of the body is white. During the spawning season, the fish becomes a distinct bronze or yellow color and, for this reason, is occasionally called the golden croaker. The iris becomes golden on the dorsal margin, the pelvic fins yellow, and the pectorals blackish at their bases. The inside of the mouth becomes a pinkish-red, the anal fin a bronze-yellow, the caudal a faint yellow, and the preopercle bronze.

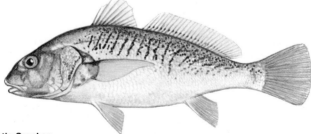

Atlantic Croaker

Other distinguishing characteristics of the Atlantic croaker are 28 dorsal rays (26–30); gillrakers 15 (14–16) on lower limb of first arch; scales above lateral line 8 (7–9); orbit 22 (15–27) percent of head length; without conspicuous black lines along the back.

In the Chesapeake Bay area, the postlarval and juvenile stages migrate into the estuaries and return to the ocean as yearlings. Adults have been observed to move into the bays in the spring and leave in the fall. In the winter, the adults move out to the deeper, warmer waters of the shelf and may also migrate to the south. Along the Texas coast, adults in spawning color appear in the passes and bays from mid-October into November. Apparently, the spawning takes place in the open Gulf near the passes.

Along the Gulf coast, most Atlantic croakers spawn and die at the end of their second year. The adults seldom reach more than 2 pounds, considerably smaller than the 4–5 pounds the fish of the Chesapeake Bay area attain.

BLACK DRUM *Pogonias cromis*   This fish occurs along the Atlantic coast of the Americas from southern New England to Argentina. It is common from New York southward. The species is known to reach a weight of 146 pounds. Most of the specimens caught weigh 20–40 pounds. The rod-and-reel record, a specimen 4 feet 8 inches long, weighed 111 pounds and was caught at Cape Charles, Virginia.

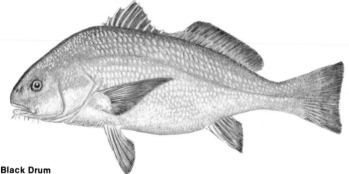

Black Drum

The black drum has a short, deep body (less than 3 times as long as it is deep to the base of the caudal fin). Its back is high-arched, and the ventral surface is somewhat flattened in appearance. The mouth is low and horizontal, the upper jaw projecting beyond the lower. The maxillary does not reach to the posterior margin of the orbit. Chin barbels are present. The throat of the black drum is armed with large pavementlike teeth which the fish uses to crush shellfish. In life the body coloration is silvery with a brassy sheen, which turns to a dark

119

gray after death. The fins are blackish. There is no black spot at the base of the caudal fin, as in the case of the red drum. The black drum has 11 dorsal spines, 20–22 dorsal rays, 2 anal spines, 6–7 anal rays, and 41–45 scales along the lateral line.

A bottomfish that feeds on crustaceans and mollusks, the black drum is usually taken with natural baits such as clams, mussels, crabs, or shrimps. Although its strike is slow, the fish puts up a strong fight. Basically a shoreline fish, the black drum is caught from party boats, piers, skiffs, and in the surf. In the Gulf states it is most commonly caught in bays and lagoons; a spring run along the lower mid-Atlantic coast (from Delaware to the Carolinas) produces large specimens to the surfcaster.

KINGFISH *Menticirrhus* spp.   Four species of kingfishes frequent the Atlantic and Gulf coasts of the United States. The southern kingfish, *M. americanus*, ranges all the way from New York to Argentina and to the northern Gulf of Mexico. The Gulf kingfish, *M. littoralis*, extends from Virginia to Florida and throughout the Gulf of Mexico. The northern kingfish, *M. saxatilia*, is found only on the Atlantic coast from Maine to Florida. The minkfish, *M. focaliger*, is confined to the Gulf of Mexico. There is one Pacific species, the California corbina (*M. undulatus*), which is a small shore fish usually found over a sandy bottom.

The group is characterized by having a small subterminal mouth; teeth in bands in both jaws; a single barbel on the chin; short gillrakers; 10–11 rather high, slender dorsal spines; an anal fin with a single sharp spine; an asymmetrical caudal fin, the upper lobe sharp, the lower rounded; and no air bladder.

Along the Texas coast, the southern kingfish and the Gulf kingfish are the most common species. The former is most common in the bays, although it migrates out to deepwater during the coldest weather, and the latter mainly inhabits the surf. Both species are bottom feeders, existing on crabs, shrimps, and various mollusks. Spawning takes place any time from spring to early fall.

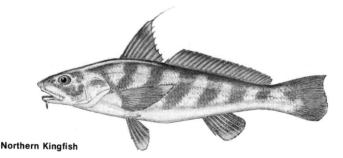

Northern Kingfish

120

The kingfish, regionally known as whiting, are of minor importance to the sport fisherman mainly because the adults are small, seldom reaching over 1 foot in length. However, they are good eating and are fished commercially in the Chesapeake Bay area.

ORANGEMOUTH CORVINA *Cynoscion xanthulus*   The species is much sought after. It is known as the yellow-finned corvina in Mexico. The orangemouth corvina is the chief gamefish in the Salton Sea, where it was introduced beginning in 1950. From a small introduction of about 275 fish, the population in the sea has increased to an estimated millions. Here the orangemouth has reached a maximum recorded weight of 32 pounds. It is a common corvina from the head of the Gulf of California to Mazatlán.

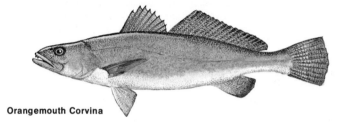

Orangemouth Corvina

The mouth of this species is a bright orange-yellow. The body is long and slim. Its back is tan or blue, and the flanks are silvery. The middle rays of its caudal fin are longer than the top or bottom ones. There are 7–9 anal rays; gill cover lining black; caudal fin yellow.

In the Salton Sea the species reaches $2^1/_4$ pounds by the second winter, $5^1/_4$ pounds in the third, and 11 pounds by the fourth. Plankton is utilized in the sea as food until the fish reaches $1^1/_4$ inches. Large fish are piscivorous. The species spawns in April and May.

The orangmouth corvina is a popular gamefish and will take a variety of lures and live bait. It is readily caught on gold wobbling spoons. The corvina is an excellent foodfish.

RED DRUM *Sciaenops ocellata*   This species is better known along the South Atlantic and Gulf coasts as redfish and as channel bass in some other localities along the Eastern seaboard of the United States. Red drum occur along the Atlantic coast of the United States from Massachusetts to Texas. Specimens weighing more than 50 pounds are rare, but many of the individuals taken weigh up to 40 pounds, usually much less. The largest specimen on record weighed 90 pounds and was caught in North Carolina.

The red drum can be distinguished from the black drum by the absence of chin barbels and the presence of a black spot or "ocellus" on

121

the base of the tail; occasional specimens may have 3 or more ocelli. The body coloration is copper- or bronze-colored rather than silvery or gray. Otherwise the fish are generally similar in appearance. The red drum has 11 dorsal spines; 23–25 dorsal rays; 2 anal spines; 8 anal rays; and 40–45 scales along the lateral line. There are 8–9 gillrakers on the lower limb of the first arch. The upper jaw projects beyond the lower. The maxillary reaches to, or beyond, a vertical from the posterior margin of the orbit.

Red Drum

Comparatively little is known of the life history of this gamefish. Studies have shown that red drum in the Gulf of Mexico do not undertake extensive coastal migrations; in fact there is little movement between bays. Great fluctuations in abundance have been caused in the Gulf area by mass mortalities due to freezing weather, plankton blooms, and excessive salinity. Along the northerly part of its range in the Atlantic, the red drum is apparently migratory and seasonal in abundance.

A bottomfish, it feeds mostly on crustaceans and mollusks, although it consumes other fish (notably mullet) at times. The red drum is a favorite of surfcasters along the Southeast coast of the United States. Popular live baits include crabs, clams, bloodworms, sandbugs, mossbunker, and cut mullet. Red drum also hit spoons, plugs, metal squids, and leadhead bucktails. The larger drum are usually caught in the northern part of their range along the Carolina coast to New Jersey. Young "puppy drum," generally weighing less than 10 pounds, are also taken in southern Florida and along the Gulf coast on fly, plug, and spinning tackle.

SAND SEATROUT *Cynoscion arenarius* Also called the white trout, the sand seatrout occurs from the west coast of Florida to Texas and Mexico as far south as the Gulf of Campeche. Its body coloration is pale, without well-defined spots, yellowish above, silvery below, the center of the scales above the level of the gill opening sometimes forming faint oblique rows of cloudy areas. The back of a young sand seatrout is cloudy, the cloudy areas tending to form indefinite crossbands.

Sand Seatrout

Other distinguishing characteristics of the sand seatrout are the 11 soft anal rays (sometimes 10–11); total number of gillrakers usually 13–14, but frequently 15.

The life history is not well known. The young are found in the shallow bays of the Gulf coast and seem to be particularly abundant where the salinity is reduced. There is a general migratory movement from the bays into the Gulf with the onset of cool weather in the fall. Also, in the spring and summer there is a spawning migration of adults into the Gulf. The young move into the bays from April to September, indicating that this species has a prolonged breeding season.

This is a small species, the adults usually ranging from 12 to 15 inches in length. The food seems to be mainly small fishes and shrimps. The sand seatrout supports a minor commercial and sport fishery.

SILVER SEATROUT *Cynoscion nothus* Also called the silver trout, it is related, but not closely, to the other members of its genus. The fish occurs from Chesapeake Bay to Florida and throughout the Gulf of Mexico. Its color is pale, without conspicuous pigmentation, the upper part usually straw or walnut, the lower part lighter silvery; sometimes there is an indication of irregular rows of faint spots. Small individuals, up to about $3^1/_2$ inches standard length, have the upper part more or less faintly clouded, the cloudy areas tending to form transverse bands.

Other distinguishing characteristics of the silver seatrout are the 9 anal softrays, sometimes 8 and infrequently 10 in specimens from the Atlantic coast. Total number of gillrakers on the first arch in individuals of 1–6 inches is a mode of 13, frequently 12–14, rarely 15. Most common number of gillrakers on the first arch is 3 + 10 (3 on upper, 10 on lower limb).

The snout is rather short, shorter than the least depth of the caudal peduncle. The caudal peduncle is short, the length of the rather short maxillary is greater than the distance from posterior end of insertion of dorsal to base of caudal on midline. The eye is conspicuously larger than in the other species. The dorsal is rather long, the usual number of softrays 28–29, frequently 27, less frequently 30, the number of rays increasing in more northern latitudes, and the mode being 28 in Gulf specimens.

Very little is known about the life history. In contrast to the sand seatrout, this species is more common in the ocean than in the bays. In fact, it seems to enter the bays only during the cooler months of the year. It spawns offshore, probably in deepwater, in the early fall. Young have been reported (Gulf coast) only in October and November. This is the smallest seatrout, the adults seldom growing to more than 10 inches.

SPOT *Leiostomus xanthurus* A small, well-known member of the croaker family, the spot is distributed along the Atlantic coast from Cape Cod into the Gulf of Mexico as far as Campeche, Mexico. Its most common occurrence is south of New Jersey.

The spot can be separated from the Atlantic croaker in that the body is comparatively short and deep and there are no barbels on its lower jaw. The mouth is small and horizontal; teeth are present on the lower jaw of the young but are lacking in adults. The body coloration is usually bluish-gray with gold or bronze reflections above and a silvery cast below. There are 12–15 oblique yellowish bars on the sides, which become indistinct with age. The maximum size is about 14 inches, weighing less than 2 pounds, but the average is generally smaller than 10 inches.

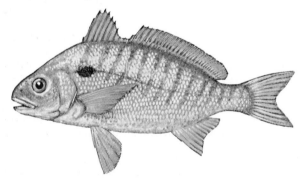

Spot

Spots range from freshwater to salinities nearly twice that of oceanwater. Sometimes they occur in large schools, from the shallows of coastal marshes to at least 112 fathoms, and occasionally they are extremely abundant in deepwater. They appear to be more common in deepwater during fall and winter. Spots occur over mud and sand bottom, as well as oyster and shell reefs.

They eat a variety of animals and plants, principally small planktonic and bottom-dwelling crustaceans, although worms are also of importance. Young spots feed more heavily on plankton; older fish eat worms and small fishes. In turn, spots are fed on by striped bass. Like other croakers, the male spot makes a drumming sound using the swimbladder.

During peak runs, spots are readily caught on hook and line and cut bait, such as clams or worms.

SPOTFIN CROAKER *Roncador stearnsi* This is a distinctive species with no close relatives. Its range is confined to the warm temperate Pacific coast from Point Conception to San Juanico Bay, Baja California. Distinguishing characteristics: lower jaw included; dorsal spines 10 in the first dorsal fin, 1 in second, 21−24 dorsal softrays, anal fin with 2 spines and 8−9 softrays; chin without barbels; a large black spot at base of pectorals.

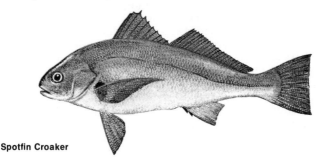

Spotfin Croaker

A shallow-water species that prefers beaches and sloughs, the spotfin often congregates in bottom depressions just outside the breaker zone. Its food is mainly small mollusks and crustaceans. Best fishing in late summer with sand crab, clam, mussel, or pileworm bait. Maximum weight about 9 pounds; greatest length about 26 inches.

SPOTTED SEATROUT *Cynoscion nebulosus* One of the most popular inshore saltwater gamefish in the southern United States, it occurs from New York to Florida and throughout the Gulf of Mexico. The spotted seatrout is not closely related to other members of its genus. Also called speckled trout or simply trout, the fish is widely caught on artificial lures as well as live bait.

The body coloration of the spotted seatrout is dark gray above, with sky-blue reflections, shading to silvery below. The upper parts of its sides are marked with numerous round black spots, the spots extending on dorsal and caudal fins. Very young fish have a broad, dark lateral band, and blotches of the same color on the back; the base of caudal is black. Fins are pale to yellowish-green; the dorsal and caudal fins are spotted with black in the adult.

The spotted seatrout has 10 spines (rarely 11) in the first dorsal fin, 1 spine and 24−26 softrays in the second dorsal fin. The anal fin has

2 spines followed by 10–11 softrays. There are 90–102 scales in the lateral line. The body is elongate and somewhat compressed. The back is a little elevated, while the head is long and low. The snout is pointed, the maxillary reaching nearly or quite opposite the posterior margin of eye. Teeth are similar to those of *C. regalis;* gillrakers are rather short, 8 on lower limb of first arch. The scales are small, thin ctenoid, extending forward on head, cheeks, and opercles, not present on fins, 11–12 between origin of anal and lateral line; the dorsal fins are contiguous or separate, spines of the first weak, flexible, the longest spines scarcely longer than the longest softrays; the caudal fin is pointed in the very young, becoming straight to somewhat emarginate in adults; the anal fin is small, the spines very weak, base of fin ending about an eye's diameter in advance of the end of base of dorsal; the ventral fins are rather small, inserted a little behind the base of the pectorals.

The life history of the spotted seatrout is quite well known. Spawning takes place from March through November, primarily within the coastal bays and lagoons. The larval and juvenile development is in the protected beds of vegetation found in many parts of the inland waters. The egg and larval stages have not been described, but are apparently similar to those of the weakfish (*C. regalis*).

The majority of the young fish are found within 50 yards of a shoreline, usually in the marine vegetation. The vegetation affords the small fish protection and contains many small crustaceans and fishes upon which the juvenile trout feed. The young fish remain in the shallow, grassy areas until winter approaches, when they move into deeper waters.

Although part of the population moves out into the ocean during the winter, becoming distributed up and down the beaches, the majority remains within the bays, where they are killed by the millions during cold weather. Such kills occurred along the Texas coast in 1962 and 1963, and earlier instances have been reported in the literature.

Shrimps are the preferred food, and when shrimps are in abundance the spotted seatrout feed on them almost exclusively. When shrimps are scarce, they turn to fish and seem to prefer mullets or silversides.

As far as the Gulf states are concerned, the spotted seatrout is the most popular of the bay fishes for the sport fisherman. Live shrimps are the most widely used bait, but good catches are often made on small live fishes, cut mullets, or small crabs. Plugs, both topwater and sinking types, as well as jigs, spoons, streamer flies, and popping bugs are all successful lures of regional importance. As a rule, plugs with silver-flash finishes and those that imitate mullets and needlefish are very popular.

WEAKFISH *Cynoscion regalis* This popular marine gamefish generally resembles the spotted seatrout in appearance. The name weakfish refers to the delicate mouth structure from which a hook can easi-

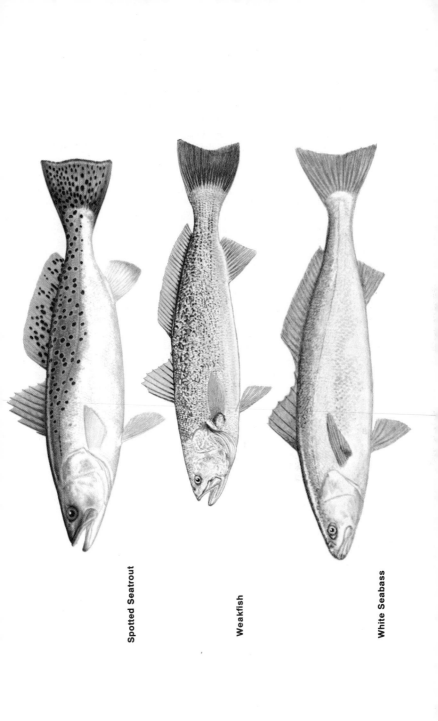

Spotted Seatrout

Weakfish

White Seabass

ly tear free. It is also regionally called gray weakfish, squeteague, and yellowfin.

The weakfish is a slim, well-shaped fish, about 4 times as long as deep (to the base of the caudal fin). Its color along the dorsal surface is a dark olive or greenish or greenish-blue. The sides are burnished in tones of blue, green, purple, and lavender, and have a coppery or golden tinge. The back and upper sides are peppered with small, vaguely defined spots of black, dark green, and sometimes bronze. Some of these spots are confluent to form irregular lines that extend diagonally downward and forward. The spotting is confined mostly to the upper part of the body. The underside is white or silvery. The weakfish has a head (nearly one-third the body length) characterized by a large mouth, a somewhat pointed snout, and a lower jaw that projects beyond the upper. It has a well-developed tail with a slightly concave outer edge. This caudal fin is dusky or olive, sometimes with a yellow tinge on its lower edge. The shorter, higher first dorsal fin has 10 spines. The longer second dorsal is soft and has 26–29 rays. The dorsal fin color is dusky, usually with some yellow tinges. The ventral, pectoral, and anal fins are also tinged with yellow.

The extreme general range of weakfish is on the Atlantic coast of the United States extending from Massachusetts southward to Florida's eastern seaboard. The largest populations are concentrated between the Chesapeake Bay region and New Jersey and New York. Centers of abundance include Chesapeake Bay, Delaware Bay, coastal areas of New Jersey, and the Peconic Bay system of Long Island.

Within their range, weakfish are found in the surf and in sounds, inlets, bays, channels, and saltwater creeks. They also enter estuaries of rivers, but do not venture into freshwater. By nature they are schooling fish, with a marked preference for shallow, sand-bottom areas.

The food of weakfish includes sea worms, shrimps, squids, sand lances, crabs, mollusks, and small fishes such as silversides, killifish, butterfish, and young menhaden. Because of this varied diet, weakfish seek prey at different levels of the water. Frequently they feed right at the surface or close to it. This near-surface feeding can occur in shoal areas, such as over the sandflats of bays and other places where killifish, silversides, and other forage species are available.

An excellent gamefish, the weakfish has been recorded to $17^1/_2$ pounds (Mullica River, New Jersey).

WHITE SEABASS *Cynoscion nobilis* This species is one of the drums and not a true seabass. It is closely related to the totuava and the shortfin seabass of northern Mexican waters. The white seabass is known as white corvina in Mexico. It is found from Alaska to Chile, but is uncommon north of San Francisco. Although the white seabass reaches 80 pounds and 4 feet, weights over 40 pounds are rare.

The dorsal fins of the white seabass are at least in contact; the pectoral fin more than half of head length; caudal fin yellow; second dorsal base longer than base of anal fin; no enlarged canine teeth in upper jaw; lower jaw protrudes slightly; belly with a raised ridge from vent to pelvic fin base.

The body color is gray to blue on back, silvery on sides, white on belly; pectoral with inner basal dusky spot; 3–6 crossbars in young fish.

White seabass are found near kelp beds. They spawn in spring and summer and are most numerous from May to September in California. Males spawn at about 24 inches in length, females at about 27 inches. The species feeds on other fishes, crustaceans, and squids.

Although much live-bait still-fishing is done for white seabass, they are also taken by trolling and surf-casting with feathers, underwater plugs, spoons, and metal squids. Night fishing is often most productive. White seabass are reluctant to strike fast-moving lures; they should be worked slowly and near the bottom.

COD FAMILY Gadidae

ATLANTIC COD *Gadus morhua* This cod is recognized by its 3 dorsal fins and 2 anal fins, in combination with the pale lateral line and a single large barbel at the tip of the chin. As in other members of the cod family, the mouth is large and contains many small teeth in both jaws.

It differs from the haddock in its pale lateral line and can be readily separated from the pollock by the large barbel and the projection of the upper jaw beyond the lower. It resembles the tomcod, which has small, narrow pelvic fins that are prolonged as feelers and in which the outline of the caudal fin is broadly rounded, whereas in the cod it is square to slightly concave.

The color is variable; there are two color phases, the red and the gray. The red phase varies from reddish-brown to orange to brick-red; the gray phase ranges from black to brownish-gray to greenish. The sides are covered with numerous dark spots.

Most fish taken in the New England area range from 6 to 12 pounds, although 50–60 pounders are not at all unusual. The largest cod on record weighed over 210 pounds and was over 6 feet long, although any fish taken now over 100 pounds is unusual. This species is taken in the North Atlantic, from western Greenland and the Hudson Strait, south to Cape Hatteras, North Carolina, where it occurs in deepwater. In the eastern Atlantic, it is found throughout the Baltic Sea and the northern part of Scandinavia, eastward to Novaya Zemlya, USSR, south to the Bay of Biscay.

This common New England species occurs from the surface to a depth of more than 1,500 feet, the young being found in shallow water, and the large cod generally in depths exceeding 60 feet. During the winter, many come into the shallow water, and during the summer they are found in deeper water.

Some cod populations participate in fairly extensive migrations; others are relatively sedentary. Spawning occurs from December to late March in about 20 fathoms of water in the Gulf of Maine area. The cod, in general, lays great quantities of eggs, and a 75-pounder was estimated to contain over 9 million eggs. Its eggs float and are thus at the mercy of winds and currents, as well as numerous predators. The very young cod feed upon copepods and other small crustaceans while they are found in the surface layers; later, they drop to the bottom and feed upon shrimps, barnacles, and small worms. Adults feed upon clams, snails, mussels, crabs, lobsters, worms, squids, and various small fishes.

The cod is a popular sport fish in the New England area, being taken by anglers using clam, herring, and squid. Party boats are the mainstay of the sport fishery, although small boats and jetty-fishing account for large numbers of cod taken.

Cod are cold-weather fish, a detail that imposes limits on the angling season throughout much of their range. In three of their most important sport-fishing regions—southern New England, New York, and New Jersey—the season begins in autumn and continues through the winter on into early spring. Depending to a great extent upon the water temperatures involved, the cod season may begin as early as mid-October and last on into April. In general, the season starts in November and ends sometime in March. Exceptions are certain deepwater areas in the vicinity of Montauk Point, New York, and Block Island, Rhode Island, There, a combination of coldwater and good food supply makes for a cod sport-fishing season that lasts to some degree the year around.

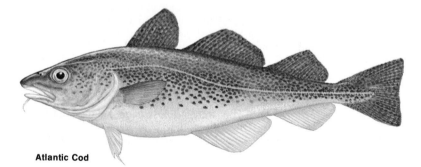

Atlantic Cod

ATLANTIC TOMCOD *Microgadus tomcod* This small member of
the cod family resembles the Atlantic cod in general body shape and
the presence of 3 dorsal fins and 2 anal fins, with a heavy body tipped
with a large, subterminal mouth. It differs from the Atlantic cod in the
long ventral fins that taper into filaments. The posterior margin of the
tail of the tomcod is rounded rather than straight or slightly concave.
In addition, the eyes of the tomcod are quite small in comparison. In
coloration, instead of being spotted as is the Atlantic cod, it is olive- or
muddy-green above with dark spots or blotches forming a mottled
pattern on the sides. Unlike the plain fins of the cod, those of the tom-

Atlantic Tomcod

cod have wavy or mottled markings. This small species grows to 15
inches and a little over 1 pound, but most are 6–12 inches long.

The tomcod is found along the North American coast from
Labrador and the Gulf of St. Lawrence south to Virginia, and is common locally from Long Island northward. This inshore fish seldom is
taken deeper than 2–3 fathoms. It may be commonly taken in
brackish water and occasionally in freshwater during winter. This
hardy species is also resistant to changes in salinity and to sudden
cold spells.

It spawns in either brackish or saltwater from November to February, the eggs sinkng to the bottom and attaching to algae and rocks.

The tomcod lives close to the bottom, utilizing its chin barbel and
ventral fins as sensory organs to detect food. Shrimps, amphipods,
worms, clams, squids, and small fishes are eaten.

This delicious fish is taken by anglers in large quantities during the
colder months in the spawning season. It is also caught commercially
in small numbers.

HADDOCK *Melanogrammus aeglefinus* An important member of
the cod family, the haddock is characterized by 3 dorsal fins and 2
anal fins, and generally resembles the cod. It is easily distinguished
from its close relatives by a black line along each side and the black
patch midway between the first dorsal fin and the pectoral fin. Its 3
dorsal fins distinguish it and its close relatives from the silver hake.

In a freshly caught haddock the top of the head, back, and sides are a dark purplish-gray, becoming silvery-gray with pinkish reflections below the lateral line; the belly and the lower sides of the head are white.

The largest haddock on record weighed 37 pounds and was 44 inches long, but the majority are about 1–2 feet long, and weigh about 1–5 pounds.

Generally, haddock are found in deeper water than cod, most being taken in 25–75 fathoms of water. The haddock is found on both sides of the Atlantic, from the North Sea and Iceland to Newfoundland and Nova Scotia, southward to New Jersey, and occasionally in deepwater to Cape Hatteras, North Carolina. It is common on

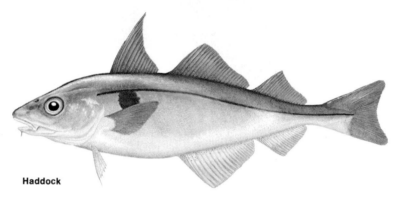

Haddock

smooth, hard bottom composed of broken shells, sand, and pebbles. It prefers slightly warmer waters than cod, although generally it is a coldwater species. Unlike the Atlantic tomcod, it never enters brackish water.

Although there is some seasonal migration to the north in the spring and south in the fall, the haddock is a relatively sluggish species, and, unlike its relatives, it seldom actively feeds upon fishes. Generally, crabs, snails, worms, clams, and sea urchins are eaten by the adults; young haddock eat copepods, as do cod. Fishes and squids are also taken by the adults of the species whenever the opportunity presents itself.

During the spawning season, between January and June, large concentrations are found at 20–100 fathoms of water. The young live on the surface for several months, after which they move on to live a bottom existence. They grow to an age of about 14 years, but those taken in the commercial fishery are less than 8 years old.

PACIFIC COD *Gadus macrocephalus* A close relative of the Atlantic cod, this Pacific species differs from its Atlantic kin only in minor details, mainly in the pointedness of its fins. The heavy body is elongated, bearing 3 dorsal fins and 2 anal fins. A well-developed barbel on the chin and a large mouth help to typify this species. The position of the anal opening, placed below the anterior part of the second dorsal fin, and the large barbel, which is about equal to the eye diameter, distinguish it from the Pacific tomcod. The body is brown to gray on the back, becoming lighter on the belly, with scattered brown spots on the upper parts. The fins are all dusky and are edged with white on their outer margins. Specimens have been taken in excess of 3 feet, but the species does not attain the size of its Atlantic relative.

It generally occurs from Oregon to the Bering Sea; it has been recorded from northern and central California, but is more common to the north. Specimens have been taken from shallow water to nearly 800 feet.

PACIFIC HAKE *Merluccius productus* This cod is distinguished from its other Pacific relatives by the 2 dorsal fins and the single anal fin; the second dorsal and anal fins are deeply notched, so that each fin appears to be divided. As in other cods, the head is large, but this species has a very large mouth, with strong, sharp teeth. The lower jaw projects and lacks a barbel. The body is elongate and tapered, ending in a square caudal fin. The thin scales fall off readily. It is a dull silvery-gray to metallic-black above, grading to silvery-white on the lower parts. The head and body are usually covered with irregular black dots. The lining of the mouth and gill covers is black. It is larger than the Atlantic hakes, reaching about 3 feet.

Found from the Gulf of California to Alaska, it is most common from central California to Washington in moderate depths.

Spawning occurs largely from February through April, and the larvae are extremely abundant from Baja California to San Francisco, up to 300 miles offshore. To the north, the young are taken in shrimp trawls in 300 feet or more of water, but adults have been taken off California, as deep as 3,000 feet. Small fishes and squids are eaten.

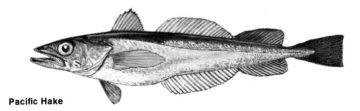

Pacific Hake

133

Because of its abundance, this hake is common in commercial and sport catches, but its flesh is not valued and has poor keeping qualities.

PACIFIC TOMCOD *Microgadus proximus* A small Pacific member of the cod family, it resembles the Atlantic cod and Pacific cod, but it differs from the latter in having the anus positioned beneath the first dorsal fin and by its small barbel, which is equal to about half of the eye diameter. Codlike in appearance, it has a large mouth with fine teeth, a large head, and 3 dorsal and 2 anal fins. The body is covered with small thin scales. It is olive-green to brown on the back and white to silvery on the lower sides and belly, with dusky edges to the light-colored fins. It reaches a length of about 1 foot.

It is known from central California to Alaska, in 60–300 feet, occasionally entering shallower water. It occurs in otter trawls sporadically and is of only minor commercial importance, although the flesh is good. In central California it has some value as a sport fish.

POLLOCK *Pollachius virens* This sportier member of the cod family is popular with anglers. It resembles the Atlantic cod in general body form, but it can be easily distinguished from the cod, haddock, and tomcod by the projection of the lower jaw beyond the upper and the deep, plump body ending in a pointed snout. Its long lower jaw, forked tail, and light lateral line readily separate it from its relatives.

Pollock

The freshly caught pollock is a striking olive-green, varying from rich olive-green or brownish-green above to yellowish or gray on the lower sides, becoming silvery-gray on the belly. This species attains a maximum weight of about 35 pounds corresponding to a length of about $3^1/_2$ feet, but most caught are around 4–15 pounds.

RED HAKE *Urophycis chuss* Formerly called the squirrel hake, the red hake is brownish-gray or reddish on the upper sides of the back, with more or less dark mottlings, and usually yellowish on the underside with some dusky spots. The lateral line is pale. Its maximum size is about 30 inches, and its weight about 8 pounds. Most of the commercial catch runs between 2 and 5 pounds.

It is distributed from the banks of Newfoundland and the Gulf of St. Lawrence as far south as Chesapeake Bay. It is normally found

Red Hake

over soft bottoms; few are taken over rocks. It is found from the tide-mark down to about 1,800 feet.

The red hake spawns in June and July in the Massachusetts Bay region. The eggs float at the surface and young hake 1–4 inches long are often found under floating eel grass or other vegetation. When slightly larger it takes to a bottom existence.

It feeds on shrimps, amphipods, squids, and fishes.

It readily takes a hook baited with herring or clam. It apparently forages mostly at night, as the largest catches are taken at that time. Commercially it is taken with line trawls and is a fine table fish.

SILVER HAKE *Merluccius bilinearis* This member of the cod family is distinguished from the cod, pollock, tomcod, and haddock by the presence of only 2 dorsal fins, the second of which is long and low, somewhat similar in shape to the anal fin. The first is a short and relatively high fin. The body is long and slender, with a large mouth well armed with sharp teeth. The silver hake lacks the chin barbel typical of the cod and haddock and most other relatives of the cod family. The general body shape is slender; the head is flat-topped. The body is dark gray above with brown and purplish reflections; the sides and belly are silvery with gold and purple hues; the belly and lower parts are silvery as well.

Although this hake reaches a maximum length of about 2¹/₂ feet and a weight of about 8 pounds, the average length is less than 14 inches.

This continental shelf species is found from the Newfoundland banks southward to off South Carolina, being taken in large numbers between Cape Sable and New York. Closely related forms are taken in the southern parts of the United States and in the Gulf of Mexico. It occurs in shallow waters to depths of about 1,800 feet, although, generally speaking, many of the adults are found in deeper waters. They are found in comparatively deeper water than their relatives, but they travel in pursuit of prey into very shallow water. These voracious swift swimmers travel in large schools, and thus they occasionally strand themselves while in aggressive pursuit of schools of their prey. The feeding habits of the silver hake make it a ready sport fish, although somewhat sluggish in character.

SOUTHERN HAKE *Urophycis floridanus* Also known as Gulf hake, this fish is characterized by dorsal fin rays that are not elongate and scales that are small, there being about 120 in transverse series. Its color is reddish-brown above and lighter below, with a small dark spot above each eye, a vertical series of 3–4 spots behind each eye, and 2 spots on each opercle. The lateral line is black and is interrupted at intervals by white spots. The fish's maximum length is about 12 inches.

The southern hake is found in the Gulf of Mexico, where it comes inshore during the winter, usually from February to May. In the summer it is found in deep offshore waters. It feeds mostly on invertebrates and fish taken near the bottom.

This hake is caught on hook and line during the winter, when it frequents the shallows. It is occasionally taken on small jigs with light spinning tackle.

WALLEYE POLLOCK *Theragra chalcogrammus* This cod is sometimes known as whiting and is distinguished from its other Pacif-

Walleye Pollock

136

ic relatives by the projecting lower jaw, large eyes, the placement of the anus midway between the first and second dorsal fins, and the reduced or absent barbel on the lower jaw, in contrast to the Pacific cod and Pacific tomcod. The lateral line is arched somewhat higher than in these two species. Like other closely related forms, it is a heavy-bodied, large-mouthed species, with 3 dorsal fins and 2 anal fins. It is greenish to olive on the back, with mottlings similar to those of the Atlantic tomcod, and silver to white on the sides and belly. The fins are dark or dusky. The young are distinguished by 2 yellow lateral stripes. The walleye attains a length of 3 feet.

It occurs from northern California to northwestern Alaska and is abundant in waters of moderate depth, where it feeds on planktonic crustaceans. An excellent foodfish, it is taken commercially by seines and trawls and is of some importance locally as a sport fish.

SCORPIONFISH FAMILY   Scorpaenidae

This large family of marine fishes is widely distributed in tropical, temperate, and boreal waters, and contains about 250 species, many of great sport and food value. They have firm, white, tasty flesh. Most of the North American commercial catch is filleted for the fresh-fish trade. Scorpionfishes are usually abundant where found and are easily taken by means of cut or whole bait or jigs. The Pacific rockfishes are often called rockcod but have no close relationship with the true cod.

BLACK-AND-YELLOW ROCKFISH *Sebastodes chrysomelas* The species is one of the most highly esteemed rockfishes of central California. It is a favorite of the angler as well as the commercial fisherman.

The black-and-yellow rockfish is characterized by strong spines on the top of its head; lower jaw not projecting; interorbital space concave; and a broad pectoral fin with thick rays. The general coloration is olive-brown to black tinged with yellow; there are several large, irregular yellow blotches on the body; indistinct dark stripes radiate from each eye. This rockfish reaches a length of 15 inches. It is found from northern Baja California to northern California.

BLACK ROCKFISH *Sebastodes melanops* This rockfish is common inshore in shallow water from Point Conception, California, to the Gulf of Alaska. It reaches a length of 20 inches. It is an important foodfish in northern California.

The black rockfish has a broad and strongly convex interorbital space; usually 8 anal softrays, rarely 7–9; maxillary to hind border of eye; large eyes; white peritoneum. The body color is very dark, almost black, shading to dirty-white on belly; dark fins; black-spotted lower portion of spinous dorsal membrane.

The flesh of this fish must not be allowed to stand long without refrigeration, for the fats become rancid most rapidly.

BLUE ROCKFISH *Sebastodes mystinus* This species resembles the black rockfish. It is found usually in shallow water from the Bering Sea to southern California. It reaches a length of 20 inches. The blue rockfish has a broad, strongly convex interorbital space; maxillary bone extending to middle of eye; small prefrontal spines; spinous portion of dorsal fin lower than softrays; small eyes; black peritoneum, but sometimes white in specimens exceeding 14 inches. The color is a slaty-blue shading to white on the belly; the lateral and upper portions have light and dark blotches; the fins are blackish. The young are brick-red to about 6 inches in length.

BOCACCIO *Sebastodes paucispinis* This rockfish is common from northern Baja California to central British Columbia in Canada. It reaches a length of 3 feet and a weight of 21 pounds. In the bocaccio the interorbital space is strongly convex; the lower jaw projects greatly; it has a large mouth; a pectoral fin with 15–16 rays; the dorsal fin is deeply notched; normally there are 9 anal softrays. Its color is olivaceous or brown above; orange or reddish laterally; pink to white ventrally; there is a red tinge throughout.

The bocaccio is usually found at depths below 240 feet. It is one of the most important commercially taken rockfishes in California, occurring in greatest numbers on the central and southern coast.

CANARY ROCKFISH *Sebastodes pinniger* The species is probably the most important rockfish on the Pacific coast, dominating the commercial catch of rockfishes in California. It is prized by the angler and the commercial fisherman alike for its palatability. It is found from northern British Columbia to northern Baja California and is common all along the coast.

The canary rockfish has small spines on the top of its head, a lower jaw slightly projecting, a knob on the lower tip, a lower jaw smooth to touch. The general body coloration is orange with 3 bright orange stripes across the head; the lining of mouth is pale red with dusky mottling; the fins are usually bright orange. It reaches a length of 30 inches.

Older fish are usually found in deeper waters to at least 600 feet; young are found inshore.

CHILIPEPPER *Sebastodes goodei* The species is, with the bocaccio, one of the most important rockfishes landed commercially in California. It is found from central lower California to northern California. In the chilipepper the interorbital space is convex, broad; the lower jaw projects but not as much as in the bocaccio; there are scattered small white dots on white peritoneum; it normally has 8 anal softrays. Color, brownish-red above, pink below, with a distinct narrow pink stripe along the lateral line.

CHINA ROCKFISH *Sebastodes nebulosus*   This distinctive rockfish has a broad, irregular bright yellow stripe on each side of a blue-black body, beginning between the third and fourth dorsal spines, dropping to the lateral line, and extending to the base of the tail fin. Except on the stripe, the body is covered with small yellow or white spots sometimes tinged with blue.

The fish is found from northern Baja California to southeastern Alaska. It reaches a length of 16 inches.

COPPER ROCKFISH *Sebastodes caurinus*   This rockfish is found from southern California to southeastern Alaska, and is abundant in and near the Strait of Georgia. It is distinguished by the slightly thickened rays in the long blackish pectoral fins, the coppery-brown coloration, and the 40–48 scales in oblique rows above the lateral line. It reaches a length of 20 inches.

GREENSTRIPED ROCKFISH *Sebastodes elongatus*   This slender rockfish has been taken to depths of about 3,000 feet. It forms only a small part of the commercial catch. The greenstriped rockfish has a slender body; medium-sized eyes; 4 horizontal irregular green bands along the length of the body, joining to form 2 near the tail; a pale pink stripe along the lateral line; a narrow interorbital space, shallowly concave; and strong spines on the head. It reaches a length of 15 inches.

OCEAN PERCH *Sebastes marinus*   Commonly called rosefish, red perch, and sea perch, the ocean perch is a food rather than game species, taken at great depths by commercial trawlers. In recent years the total landings of ocean perch have surpassed those of cod and haddock.

The ocean perch is the only Atlantic member of the rockfish group, although its relatives, the scorpionfishes, are predominantly Atlantic species. The ocean perch is distinguished by 14–15 spines and 13 softrays in the dorsal fin; 3 spines and 7 softrays in the anal fin; red body color; black eyes; irregular dusky patches on the back; a dusky patch on the gill cover. It grows to 3 feet.

The female ocean perch develops mature eggs (37,000–350,000) by February, when fertilization takes place. Subsequently the sexes separate. The young perch are born with almost all of the yolk sac gone. The first year of life is spent in surface waters. The young feed on invertebrates and fry. Larger ocean perch feed mainly on fishes such as herrings, capelins, and cods.

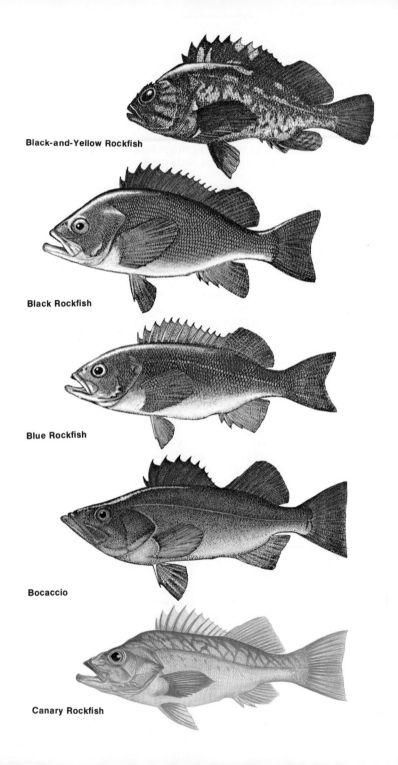

Black-and-Yellow Rockfish

Black Rockfish

Blue Rockfish

Bocaccio

Canary Rockfish

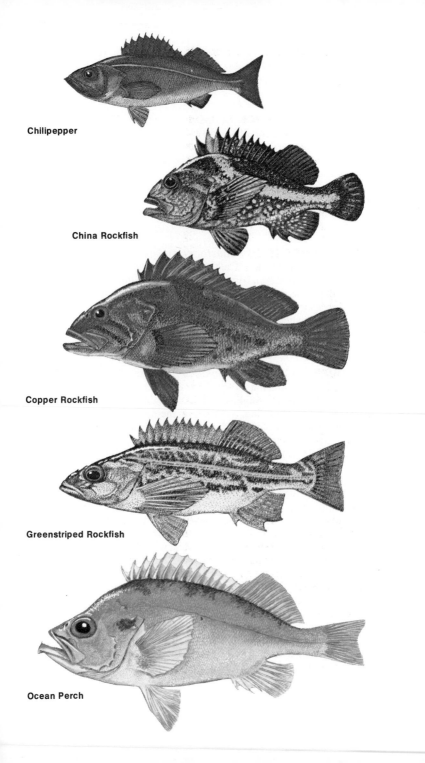

Chilipepper

China Rockfish

Copper Rockfish

Greenstriped Rockfish

Ocean Perch

Ocean perch grow very slowly, maturing at about 10 years of age, but a great many 20-year-olds appear in commercial landings. They have been known to reach 27 years of age. They average about 1 pound, and a 5-pounder is considered large.

PACIFIC OCEAN PERCH *Sebastodes alutus*   This rockfish has been exploited commercially on an extensive basis relatively recently. It is taken all along the coast and occurs in waters of 200–2,000 feet in depth from southern California to the Bering Sea. The interorbital space is slightly convex or flat; the lower jaw is very long but does not extend beyond the upper head profile; there is a large knob on lower side of lower jaw tip; frontal spines medial; no spines under eye; peritoneum dusky to black. This fish is carmine-red with black markings, and grows to 18 inches.

QUILLBACK ROCKFISH *Sebastodes maliger*   Although this rockfish is found from southern California to the Gulf of Alaska, it is best known for the commercial and sport catch in the middle of its range. It readily takes a jig or herring, and is sought at depths of 180–900 feet. It is a fine sport fish because of its fighting ability.

It is distinguished by a high dorsal fin, which is deeply incised, and the yellow to brown coloration with orange or brown spotting. It reaches a length of 24 inches.

REDSTRIPE ROCKFISH *Sebastodes proriger*   The species ranges from southern California to the Bering Sea. It is distinguished from other rockfishes by the shallow notch in the dorsal fin, the distinct red stripe along the lateral line, the knob on the underside of the tip of the lower jaw, the convex interorbital space, and the black peritoneum. Its color is red, mottled with dusky olive-green in the back; the lips are blackened. It has been taken to depths of 600 feet.

ROSY ROCKFISH *Sebastodes rosaceus*   This rockfish is a minor commercial species found from northern Baja California to central British Columbia. It is distinguished by strong spines on top of its head; naked underside of lower jaw; a second spine of the anal fin longer than the third; and a concave interorbital space. Basic color is yellow in the young; orange-red in adults, with dark red or purple bordering 3–5 white blotches. It grows to 12 inches.

SCORPIONFISH *Scorpaena* spp.   When large enough to eat, these rockfishes are excellent foodfishes. The California species is highly prized. There are about 11 species on the East Coast, 1 on the West. Poison glands are to be found at the base of the dorsal fin spines; thus, a wound is extremely painful. The fish periodically sheds its skin, which is replaced. One species sheds about once every 28 days, the time varying with the food intake.

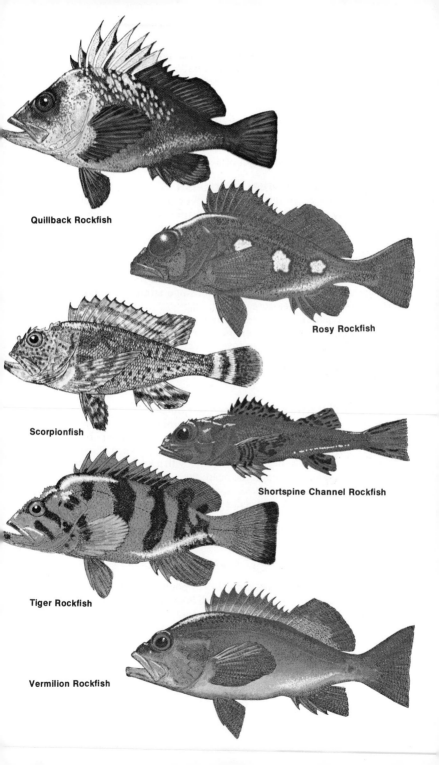

Quillback Rockfish

Rosy Rockfish

Scorpionfish

Shortspine Channel Rockfish

Tiger Rockfish

Vermilion Rockfish

Scorpionfishes are characterized by 12 spines and 13 softrays in the dorsal fin; 3 spines, 5 rays in the anal; 2 spines on top of the head. Body scales are ctenoid or with dermal flaps; head scales are cycloid or absent.

All scorpionfishes feed on crustaceans and fishes, the prey often being one-half as large as the predator. Spawning occurs in the spring. In some species the egg masses form twin hollow balloons that float to the surface to become pelagic. As the eggs hatch, the balloon sinks. Some species reach a length of 17 inches.

SHORTSPINE CHANNEL ROCKFISH *Sebastolobus alascanus*
This rockfish is considered by fishermen to be one of the choicest of the family. The shortspine channel rockfish has a knifelike ridge under the eye; lower rays of pectoral fin thrust out to form a lobe. There are 15–18 spines and 9–10 softrays in the dorsal fin. Fins are black, body bright red.

TIGER ROCKFISH *Sebastodes nigrocinctus* This rockfish is abundant in Juan de Fuca and Johnstone straits. Its range is from California to southeastern Alaska.

The tiger rockfish is typified by high cranial ridges, higher than in any other rockfish, and prominent spinous median frontal ridges. Its color is pink, gray, or pale rose background with 5 vertical carmine bars; or it may have a bright orange-red background with 5 vertical bars. The color pattern can change from one phase to another and back in less than 1 minute.

VERMILION ROCKFISH *Sebastodes miniatus* The species is one of three leading rockfishes in the California commercial markets. It ranges from northern Baja California to Vancouver Island. The vermilion rockfish is similar to the canary rockfish. Lower jaw is rough to the touch; it projects slightly, with a knob on the lower tip; it has small spines on top of the head; the peritoneum is white. Color is vermilion or brick-red above, shading to pink laterally with red belly; black dots on back and sides give a dusky appearance; 3 orange stripes across head radiate from the eye; dorsal fin is gray at base, others vermilion; mouth lining and lips are red; yellow on sides of some large specimens. It grows to a length of 36 inches.

BLUEFISH FAMILY Pomatomidae

BLUEFISH *Pomatomus saltatrix* A popular marine gamefish found in nearly all warm seas, the bluefish is the only member of this family. The bluefish has a moderately stout body, and the belly is flat-sided but blunt-edged on the ventral surface. The snapper, or young bluefish of 7–9 inches, is relatively deeper and more flattened in appearance than the adult fish. The bluefish has a moderately pointed snout and a large oblique mouth with a projecting lower jaw and prominent canine teeth. Its caudal fin is broad and forked, and the first dorsal fin (7–8 spines) originates over the middle of the pectorals; the second dorsal is more than twice as long as the first (23–27 rays) and tapers toward the tail. The coloration is generally a blue-green above shading to silvery-white on the belly. Its fins are of the same general body color, but the pectorals usually have a black blotch at the base.

Bluefish are found along the Atlantic coast of the United States, ranging from Cape Cod Bay off Massachusetts down through Argentina. When a population cycle is at a peak, stragglers may even travel as far east and north as Nova Scotia. Huge specimens swim off the northwest coast of Africa, the Azores, Portugal, and southern Spain. The species is found throughout the Mediterranean and commonly occurs in the Black Sea. Research on bluefish spawning activities, about which very little is known, has been more complete in the Black Sea area than anywhere else in its range. Both coasts of South Africa, the eastern Indian Ocean, the shores of the Malay Peninsula, southern Australia, and New Zealand also support large populations of blues. Although the fish is often found in tidal estuaries, it is basically a deepwater species.

Migrations of bluefish along the coasts of the United States follow a similar general pattern from year to year when the fish are plentiful. Formerly it was believed that the schools worked up along the coast from south to north. From recent investigations, it is apparent that the major movements are from east to west, although there is some south to north migration also as coastal waters warm up.

Individual fish in any given school tend to be of approximately the same size. Their cannibalistic tendencies make the reason for this obvious. Tiny snappers, which are the young of the year, are densely packed and venture well into tidal rivers, although never in entirely freshwater. Larger fish feed in more open waters, and the very large specimens rarely move into the shallows. In general, the bigger the fish, the smaller the school.

Bluefish first appear offshore along the southern Florida coast in midwinter, and by late March catches inshore are good along most of the peninsula. During March and April, schools migrate in quantity past Georgia and the Carolinas to appear off Virginia and Delaware during late April. Some blues break off from the main body and remain in various areas to form what might be termed resident populations. First catches off New Jersey and New York are well offshore at the end of April or in early May, and fishing in that section improves steadily well into September. New England commercial fishermen take the species starting in mid-May, but rod-and-reel angling is not good until June at the earliest. Bluefish leave New England around mid-October, generally after a major northeaster. As elsewhere, just before their departure, fishing is at its peak. Approximately 2 weeks later, blues forsake the coasts of New York and northern New Jersey.

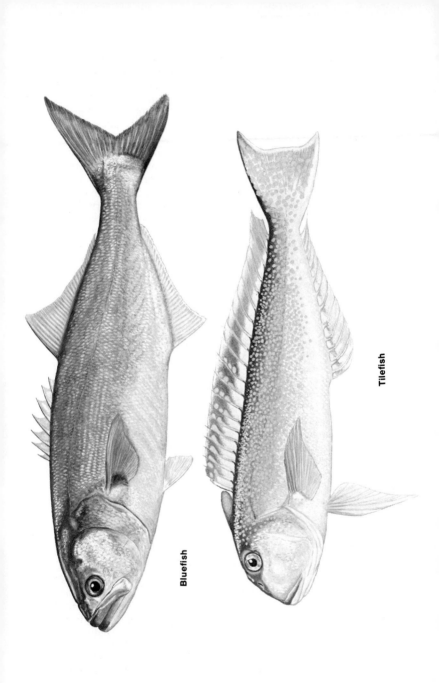

Bluefish

Tilefish

Weather can change this pattern, and a sudden cold storm may speed the fish on their way ahead of schedule. December and early January fishing can be excellent off the Florida shore. Some blues are taken in that state throughout the winter until the spring migrations start again.

Nature equipped the bluefish with a formidable set of teeth, and the fish uses these to great effect from the time it is a tiny snapper a few inches long until it reaches maximum size. This maximum is close to 45 pounds—a specimen recorded off the coast of North Africa. However, the world record on rod and reel is 31 pounds 12 ounces taken at Hatteras Inlet, North Carolina (1972). As many anglers have learned, those teeth can inflict wicked wounds on human flesh. The species is one of the few that apparently can see almost as well out of water as in it, with the result that any bite is accurately aimed. Quite naturally, the bloodthirsty qualities of the blue make it an ideal fighting fish when taken on rod and reel. Although the strike may vary from a gentle nip on a bottom bait to a savage slash at a surface plug, the ensuing battle is remarkable and may include everything from headshaking jumps to powerful, surging runs.

TILEFISH FAMILY Branchiostegidae

There are 4 species of tilefishes, but only *Lopholatilus chamaeleonticeps* and the blackline tilefish *Caulolatilus cyanops* are of angling interest.

TILEFISH *Lopholatilus chamaeleonticeps* The tilefish is found along the outer continental shelf and upper slope from northern Nova Scotia to southern Florida and the Gulf of Mexico.

The tilefish is a colorful fish with bluish to olive-green on the back and upper part of its sides, changing to yellow or rose on lower sides and belly, the latter with white midline. Its head is reddish on sides, white below. The back and sides above lateral line have many irregular yellow spots. Dorsal fin is dusky with larger yellowish spots, its softrayed portion is pale-edged; adipose flap is greenish-yellow; anal fin is pinkish with purple to blue iridescence; pectorals are pale sooty-brown with purplish reflections.

Other distinguishing characteristics of the tilefish are its stout body, which tapers to the caudal peduncle, which is somewhat compressed. A triangular, thin, fleshy flap projects from the upper midline of the head in the nape region. The head is large, strongly convex in dorsal profile, nearly straight in ventral profile; the mouth is moderately large, lower jaw projecting, angle of mouth under front of eye, a small barbellike projection on each side of lower jaw near the angle, canine teeth in both jaws followed by bands of smaller teeth.

Dorsal fin has 7 spines followed by 15 softrays, originating above gill opening and extending to caudal peduncle, nearly twice the length of the head; caudal fin is moderate, lunate, lobes pointed; anal fin has

2 spines and 13 softrays, extending from under middle of dorsal fin to under end of dorsal; pectorals are moderately large.

The tilefish is a benthic species, generally found between 45 and 170 fathoms. It prefers water temperatures of 47°–53°F. Its food is crabs, shrimps, squids, mollusks, marine worms, sea cucumbers, and other invertebrates. Sometimes small fishes are eaten. Spawning takes place in July. The eggs are about $1/20$ inch in diameter and are believed to be pelagic. Tilefish grow to a weight of about 50 pounds.

Owing to the great depths tilefish frequent, the sport fishery is limited. Party boats operating out of New York and New Jersey ports catch tilefish on the slopes of the Hudson Canyon. A similar fishery exists off the east coast of Florida.

WRASSE FAMILY Labridae

Although chiefly found in tropical seas, some species, such as the tautog, cunner, hogfish, and California sheephead, also occur in the temperate zone of North America. All labroid fishes are distinguished by their heavy pharyngeal or throat teeth, which they use to crush their food.

CALIFORNIA SHEEPHEAD *Pimelometopon pulchrum* The unique color and shape distinguish this Pacific member of the wrasse family. A deep body and a slight hump on the head readily separate it from other California wrasses. The head bluntly slopes to the thick lips, and the large canine teeth protrude forward from the heavy jaw. During the breeding season, the male develops a distinct hump over the eyes. The tips of the caudal and spinous dorsal and anal fins are pointed. Coloration of the sexes is distinct. The male has the head, fins, and posterior part of the body purple or black, with the rest of the body red to purple-black; the lower jaw is white. The female is uniformly reddish to rose color, occasionally with black blotches. A weight of 30 pounds and a length of 3 feet are the maximum size.

It ranges from the Gulf of California to Monterey Bay, California, about kelp beds or near rocky bottoms and shores, most commonly in depths of 20–100 feet.

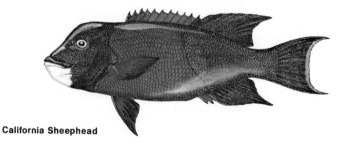

California Sheephead

It is believed to reach an age of at least 20 years, spawning apparently occurring during the summer. Adults defend a given section of territory and are pugnacious, driving away others from the lair. Examination of stomachs of sheephead have revealed lobsters, abalones, and other types of shellfishes. Of some importance to sport fishermen in southern California, the sheephead is taken on cut bait such as abalone, lobster, or fish and is also a chief target for spearfishermen.

CUNNER *Tautogolabrus adsperus* Closely related to the tautog, this wrasse is slender, with a long, low dorsal fin, a pointed snout with thick lips, and protruding canine teeth. The gill cover is scaled, and the body scales are larger than in the tautog, there being about 70 lateral scales in the tautog and about 40 in the cunner. It is highly variable in color, grading from red or a reddish-brown to bluish, depending on the bottom on which it lives. Some individuals are uniform brown, with some mottling; others are olive-green. The young have blotches and dark bars. A small species, the cunner generally grows only to about 10 inches long, although it occasionally reaches 18 inches and a weight of 3 pounds.

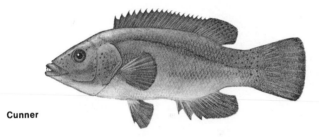

Cunner

It is the northernmost member of the Labridae on the East Coast, occurring from Newfoundland to Chesapeake Bay, being most common north of northern New Jersey. Like the tautog, it is a coastal form, being common in nearshore habitats from a few inches deep down to about 600 feet. But most are taken at 15–100 feet, within 5–6 miles of shore. A bottom dweller, it is very common about rocks, pilings, wharves, ledges, and any place it can find shelter.

Spawning takes place in late spring to early August, in deepwater. Young fish move inshore and grow up in shallow waters. At the end of 2 years they are 3–4 inches long, and a fish 10–11 inches long is 6–7 years old. Females are larger than males. Cunners eat practically anything, including barnacles, mussels, amphipods, shrimps, lobsters, crabs, clams, and worms.

They are taken by anglers using clams, crabs, or worms. Popular sport fish because of their abundance, the small ones are clever bait stealers. The cunner was formerly important commercially, but despite its fine flesh, it has fallen out of favor in recent years.

HOGFISH *Lachnolaimus maximus* Also known as the hog snapper, this member of the wrasse family is distinctive in shape and coloration. It has a pointed, steep snout, thick lips, and well-developed, protruding canine teeth. The first 3–4 dorsal spines are extended into filaments, and the tips of the dorsal and anal fins and the tips of the caudal lobes are pointed. Color is variable from a plain gray-brown phase to red-orange and marbled crimson. There is always a black spot at the base of the posterior rays during these varied phases. Color of the male is more intense than that of the female. The young are mottled red and gray, with bright red eyes. Hogfish are reported to reach 45 pounds, but 25 pounds is very large. The average is about 6 pounds.

This species occurs from Brazil to North Carolina and Bermuda, but it is most common throughout the West Indies, in coral regions.

Hogfish feed on mollusks, crustaceans, and sea urchins. The flesh is excellent, although large specimens are reportedly poisonous in Cuba,

Hogfish

and may be poisonous in certain other areas of the Caribbean, apparently as a result of their eating habits.

The hogfish can be taken by anglers using clams, squids, or small crabs as bait.

SEÑORITA *Oxyjulis californica* A small member of the wrasse family, this common species is one of the few representatives of the family taken off the California coast. It is a slender, elongate fish, with long, low dorsal and anal fins and a convex tail. The snout is somewhat pointed, and the mouth has small, sharp teeth that project forward. The señorita is brown above and cream-colored below; the center of the scales have orange-brown markings. Along the sides of the head are brown and blue streaks, and a large black spot occurs at the caudal fin base. A closely related species, the rock wrasse, is

Señorita

similar to the señorita, but lacks the black spot on the caudal base. The señorita reaches a length of about 10 inches and is found from central California to Baja California. Common around kelp beds and in inshore waters, it has no sport or commercial value. It is seldom taken by anglers since, like other small wrasses, it is a superb bait stealer.

SLIPPERY DICK *Halichoeres bivittatus* This brightly colored member of the wrasse family is recognized by its elongate body, long dorsal fin, small mouth, and protruding canine teeth. Two black lateral bands characterize the species, and these bands occasionally are broken up into squarish blotches. The fins and body are brightly colored; the fins have narrow bands of blue, pink, and yellow, with a row of yellowish spots. The body is olive-buff to pale yellow. The fish reaches a length of about 8 inches.

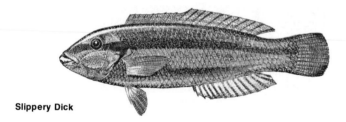

Slippery Dick

Found throughout the West Indies, it ranges from Brazil to North Carolina and Bermuda. It occurs from a few feet deep to at least 100 feet. An extremely common species of the coral reef environment, it also occurs around wharves, pilings, and debris, and over sand, grass, or silt bottom.

SPANISH HOGFISH *Bodianus rufus* This colorful member of the wrasse family has the general body shape of the hogfish. The thick lips reveal the well-developed, protruding teeth. The dorsal, anal, and caudal fins do not possess well-developed rays, as in the hogfish, and there are only 11–12 dorsal spines. The coloration of this beautiful reef fish, as of most other members of the family, is striking. The upper, forward part is violet to violet-red or purple above from about the eyes to the last dorsal spine, grading abruptly to bright yellow to orange beneath, with the anal and soft dorsal fins orange. It reaches a length of about 2 feet and a weight of about 3 pounds.

Found throughout the West Indies and Bermuda northward to Florida, it is a coral reef dweller generally seen in the shallows. It is not a schooling fish, being generally solitary or occurring in small groups. The young are found in somewhat deeper water than the adults.

The hogfish is occasionally taken from coral areas by anglers using small bits of shrimp or squid as bait. Its firm, white flesh makes this species an exceptional foodfish.

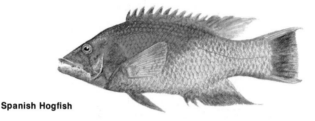

Spanish Hogfish

TAUTOG *Tautoga onitis*   Sometimes called blackfish, this is a fairly large member of the Labridae. This species, in comparison with other Atlantic members of the family, is distinguished by its plain coloration, lack of scales on the gill cover, and a blunt snout with the dorsal profile markedly rounded. The cunner is also plain-colored, but has a scaled gill cover and a more pointed snout. The tautog's body is plump yet elongate, and the long dorsal fin is about the same height throughout. The tautog has thick lips, and the anterior canine teeth are well developed in powerful jaws. The caudal fin is rounded, as are the tips of the soft dorsal and anal fins. It reaches nearly 25 pounds and 3 feet, although about 3 pounds is average.

The tautog is known from Nova Scotia to South Carolina, being most abundant between Cape Cod and Delaware Bay. It is a bottom species and is largely restricted to the coastal environment, around rocky or sheltered areas or around mussel beds. But occasionally tautogs are trawled from over smooth bottom. They are seldom found in more than 60 feet of water.

Spawning occurs in the summer, probably in deepwater. The eggs are floating and drift into shallow water, hatching and development occurring in transit. Young grow up in the shallow protected nursery grounds where seaweed serves as shelter for them and for their food. Their color resembles the bright green sea lettuce in which they hide. During the late fall, they move off into deepwater, where they

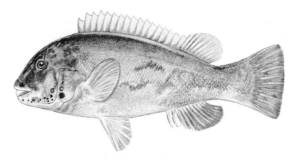

Tautog

overwinter in a state of reduced activity. During the rest of the year, populations of tautogs move about considerably within their own areas, but there is apparently little coastwise movement. Young tautogs eat worms and small crustaceans; the adults, well adapted with their crushing teeth, eat barnacles, mussels, snails, hermit crabs, shrimps, and lobsters.

The tautog is a popular fish with anglers and spearfishermen. Its flesh is good.

SOLE FAMILY Soleidae

Of the 4 true soles found in western Atlantic waters—the hogchoker, lined, naked, and scrawled soles—none attains a size of angling interest. Only the hogchoker is caught with any frequency.

HOGCHOKER *Trinectes maculatus* Also known as the American sole, this common species is easily recognized by the lack of pectoral fins. The upper jaw slightly overhangs the lower jaw, the head is

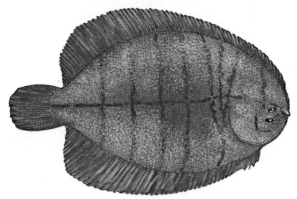

Hogchoker

153

rounded, and there is no snout, as in other flatfishes. The pelvic fin is united with the anal fin, and the dorsal fin begins well forward on the head. The eyes are on the right side, where the color is a dark brown grading to chocolate or gray, with irregular wavy bars of darker color. A dark interrupted stripe is present along the lateral line. Coloration on the blind side varies from creamy to yellow-buff, and dark spots, mottlings, or blotches may occur, the distribution of which is extremely variable from one individual to another and from one geographic area to another, depending to some extent on the bottom type. Often there are no markings at all on the blind side. The hogchoker is a small flounder, seldom exceeding 8 inches long and about $1/3$ pound.

Found from Massachusetts Bay to Panama, it is a shallow-water species occurring on mud or muddy-sand bottom. It is tolerant of a wide salinity range from full-strength seawater to freshwater estuaries. It is most often found in brackish water.

LEFTEYE FLOUNDER FAMILY   Bothidae

CALIFORNIA HALIBUT *Paralichthys californicus* Although a member of the lefteye flounder family, it is right-eyed nearly half the time. The species is somewhat similar in body shape to the Pacific halibut, but the latter's eyes are generally on the right side and its mouth is smaller and armed with numerous sharp teeth. In the California halibut the unbranched lateral line is arched over the pectoral fin, there is a wide flat area between the eyes, and the scales are small. It is greenish to gray-brown and occasionally mottled, the young often with small whitish spots. The species reaches a length of 5 feet and a weight of up to 60 pounds, although unofficially reported to 72 pounds.

Found from central California to within the Gulf of California, these halibut occur generally in water less than 10 fathoms deep. Sandy bottoms are their favorite haunts, although they may be taken in channels or even in heavy surf, along sandy or rocky beaches.

Migrations are not extensive, particularly in the young. Spawning occurs from April through July in rather shallow water. A 30-pound halibut was found to be 15 years old, growth being fairly slow. Maturi-

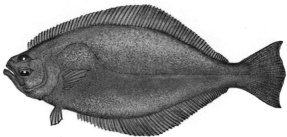

California Halibut

ty occurs at an age of 2–3 years (male) and 4–5 years (female), at a length of about 11–17 inches. Anchovies and other small fishes are eaten in abundance, and halibut themselves are eaten by angel sharks, rays, sea lions, and porpoises.

Important commercially, about a third of the catch is taken in Mexico, the rest in California, most being sold as fresh fillets. The valuable sport fishery is most successful utilizing drift-fishing methods with live anchovies, queenfish, and shrimps, although slow trolling accounts for some of the catch.

GULF FLOUNDER *Paralichthys albigutta* This is a close relative of the summer flounder and can readily be distinguished from the summer flounder by the smaller number of gillrakers. In the Gulf flounder and the southern flounder there are less than 12 gillrakers on the lower limb of the first gill arch; in the summer flounder there are 13–18. The Gulf flounder generally has 11 pectoral rays and a smaller number of dorsal and anal fin rays (71–85 and 53–65, respectively).

This species is a gray-brown in color with a number of round pale blotches, generally in 5 longitudinal rows, with 3 prominent spots forming a triangular pattern. In general, its coloring is similar to that of other closely related species. Although the usual size is less than 10 inches, it has been reported to attain a length of 15 inches.

Common from Cape Lookout, North Carolina, to Corpus Christi, Texas, the Gulf flounder seems to prefer hard or sandy bottoms, being seldom taken over mud bottoms, whereas the southern flounder

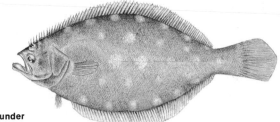

Gulf Flounder

prefers a mud bottom. The Gulf flounder is more common in the South, where it is found together with the southern flounder replacing the summer flounder. It occurs from March to October in the Gulf of Mexico, becoming scarce during the winter.

The Gulf flounder, being a bottom dweller predominantly, lies on the bottom or buried in the mud where it feeds on crustaceans and other invertebrates of small size. Because of its small size, it is of less economic importance than other commercial flounders.

PACIFIC SANDDAB *Citharichthys sordidus*   A lefteye flounder, this dab has a straight lateral line, with no arch as in many flounders. The pelvic fins are dissimilar in shape, that on the eyed side being attached to the belly ridge. The eyes are large, and the left pectoral fin is shorter than the head length, distinguishing this fish from the related longfin sanddab, *C. xanthostigma*. The thin scales fall off more easily than in other flatfishes. The color is tan to brown, variously mottled with dull orange to black. It reaches 2 pounds and 16 inches.

The Pacific sanddab is found from southern California to northwestern Alaska in water of 10–100 fathoms, being commonest at depths of 20–50 fathoms. Like other flatfishes, the sanddab spends most of its time on the bottom, but is capable of swift movement in the capture

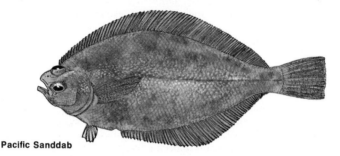

Pacific Sanddab

of small fishes, squids and octopods, shrimps, crabs, sea squirts, and worms. A number of predatory species feed upon the Pacific sanddab.

This species, as well as its relatives, is excellent eating. It is usually sold fresh, although split and dried dabs are prepared in some areas. It is taken primarily in trawls and by hook and line.

SOUTHERN FLOUNDER *Paralichthys lethostigma*   In contrast to its relative, the summer flounder, this species has a white underside and an olive color on the dorsal area. Although it resembles the summer flounder, the gillraker count on the lower limb of the first arch is 10–13 (usually 11–12) in the southern flounder, whereas in the summer flounder it is usually 13–18, generally greater than 15. Where the southern flounder occurs together with the summer flounder, it can be distinguished by the lack of distinct spots. It is also similar to the Gulf flounder, but can be differentiated by its distinctive color; all the spots on the southern flounder are diffused, with no distinct ocelli (spots ringed with lighter distinct areas). The usual size of this species is 12–20 inches, and an individual of 26 inches was reported from North Carolina.

The southern flounder is found in comparatively shallow water over mud bottoms in bays, sounds, and lagoons. Occasionally it occurs in

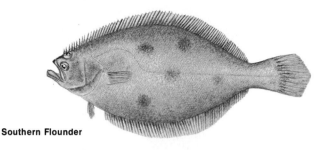

Southern Flounder

large numbers in freshwater throughout its range, which is from North Carolina to Texas. In the Gulf of Mexico, it is taken during all seasons and in bays over a wide salinity range, from brackish water to full-strength seawater, although the greatest numbers occur where freshwater mixes somewhat with the salt.

Spawning takes place during the winter. The southern flounder feeds primarily on mullets, anchovies, and other small fishes, as well as on shrimps.

This species is taken during all seasons in the inshore waters of the Gulf. A considerable volume is harvested by shrimp trawlers offshore during the spring. Another important method is by gigging using a torch or flashlight, the flounders being speared as they come into shallow water at night.

SUMMER FLOUNDER *Paralichthys dentatus* The summer flounder, or fluke, is a popular marine gamefish. Its background color normally appears gray, brown, or olivaceous with tints of orange, pink, and brown nearly to black. Pale to dark mottlings with regularly placed small spots are distinct or pale, depending upon the bottom on which the fish is lying. Although the species is reported to reach 25–30 pounds, 15 pounds and a length of 3 feet are unusual, and the most common weight of the fish is 2–5 pounds.

It is distributed in the continental waters of the eastern United States, from Maine to South Carolina; further south it is replaced by the southern flounder. The summer flounder is found from the shallows to water that is relatively deep, where it spends its life either on the bottom or close to it, as do most flatfishes. It prefers sandy to sandy-mud bottom in bays and harbors as well as the mouths of estuaries. During the summer, it frequents shallow water; during the winter the medium and larger specimens are found at 25–50 fathoms offshore.

It is believed to spawn in late fall, winter, and early spring, depending on the latitude, young fish drifting in during the spring and growing up in the shallow inshore nursery grounds. Although this flounder lies buried in the sand or mud most of the time, it is a rapid swimmer,

157

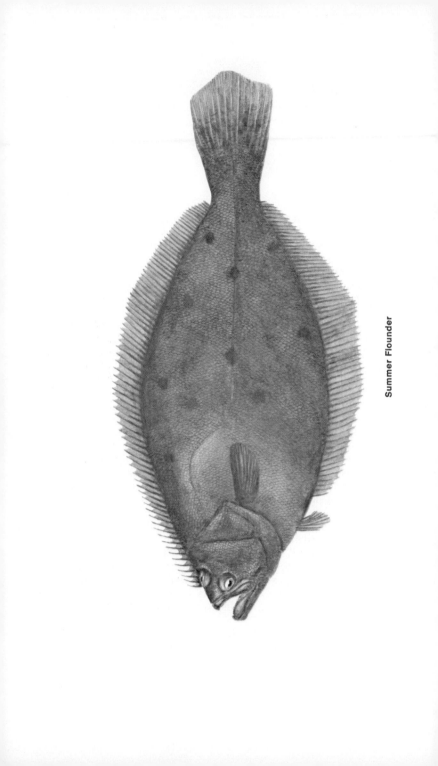

Summer Flounder

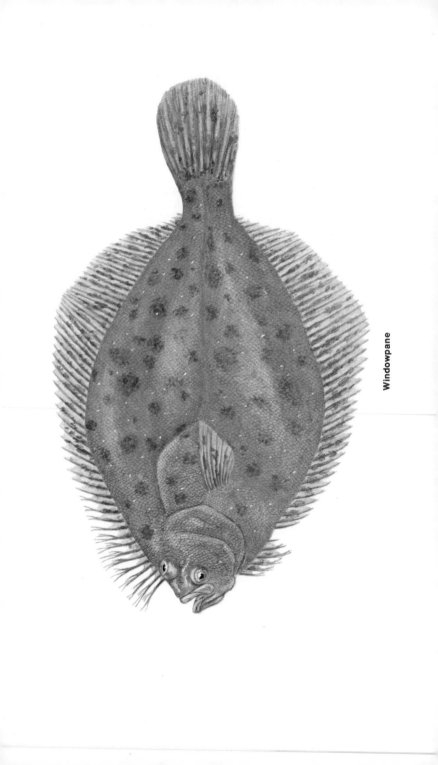

Windowpane

being able to pursue successfully small fishes, squids, crabs, and shrimps.

This valuable fish is a mainstay of the sport fishery along the Middle Atlantic coast, accounting for a proportionately large catch from bridges, jetties and smallboats. The use of live bait consisting of small fishes (killifish) is successful, and summer flounder are also taken on squids, jigs, small spoons, and spinners. Although not as strong a fighter per pound as some other sport fishes, the fluke provides lively action, especially on light tackle.

WINDOWPANE *Scophthalmus aquosus* Also called the brill or spotted flounder, this distinctive flatfish is the only member of its genus. The windowpane is found in the coastal waters of eastern North America from the Gulf of St. Lawrence to South Carolina.

Its color is reddish to grayish-brown with many brown spots, each made up of several sections; there is dark mottling on dorsal, anal, and caudal fins; the right side is usually white, occasionally with some dark blotches.

The growth of this species has been studied in Long Island Sound. There, 2-year-old fish averaged $4^{1}/_{2}$ inches in length, 4-year-old fish averaged $9^{1}/_{2}$ inches, and 7-year-olds 12 inches. Mysids appear to be the preferred food of the young, but individuals over 11 inches long eat sand shrimps and small fishes in about equal amounts. The young fishes eaten are tomcod, smelts, hakes, pollock, striped bass, and herrings. The maximum length of adults is about 18 inches.

Edible but extremely thin (the body transmits light when held to the sun, hence the name windowpane), this flounder has no commercial value.

RIGHTEYE FLOUNDER FAMILY Pleuronectidae

AMERICAN PLAICE *Hippoglossoides platessoides* Also called the Canadian plaice, plaice, dab, sanddab, and blackback, this species, which is broadly distributed on both sides of the North Atlantic, is related to the Bering flounder and the flathead sole of the Pacific coast. It ranges from southern Labrador and the Grand Bank south to Rhode Island. In the eastern Atlantic it is found from west Greenland, Iceland, and Spitzbergen south to the English Channel.

Its color is reddish to grayish-brown on the eyed side, white or bluish-white on the blind side. The tips of the dorsal and anal fins are white. The young are usually marked with dark spots along the edge of the body.

The plaice lives at various depths from 20 to 390 fathoms on bottoms with fine sand or soft mud. It prefers cool to cold water, not over 55°F. The males become mature at about 10 inches in length and the females at about 18 inches. The females produce 30,000–60,000 eggs, spherical in shape. The eggs have a large perivitelline space and float

160

near the surface. Spawning takes place in the spring in the southern part of the range and about midsummer in the northern part.

The growth rate varies depending on water temperature. On the Grand Bank plaice reach a length of 12 inches in 5 years. Growth is slower in later years, and 20-inch fish from the Grand Bank may be up to 26 years old. One plaice $32^1/_2$ inches long and weighing 14 pounds was caught at Sable Island. The pelagic fry eat diatoms and small copepods. Young on the bottom eat amphipods, caprellids, mysids, decapods, and other small crustaceans. Adults eat sand dollars, sea urchins, brittle stars, mollusks, shrimps, and worms.

ATLANTIC HALIBUT *Hippoglossus hippoglossus* Similar in general shape to the Pacific halibut, this large member of the righteye flounder family has a concave tail, and the dorsal and anal fins have their middle rays pointed. The large mouth extends to the middle of the eyes, and a distinct arch occurs over the pectoral fin. The color on the eyed side is chocolate to olive to grayish-brown, occasionally becoming almost black in large fish. Irregular dark markings sometimes enclose a lighter center region. The blind side is white in small individuals, but may be blotched in large specimens. One of the largest of marine bony fishes, the Atlantic halibut grows to a weight of 600–700 pounds and a length in excess of 9 feet, although fish over 300 pounds are rare. Females are generally larger; males run 50–200 pounds. Growth is slow; a 3-year-old fish is only 13 inches long. Females grow more rapidly; a 400-pound halibut measuring about 68 inches long was 20 years old.

This halibut occurs in the cooler waters of the North Atlantic from New Jersey, and occasionally to Virginia, to Greenland and along the northern European coast southward to the English Channel. A cold-water species, it is found in relatively deepwater over sand, gravel, or clay, rather than on soft mud or on rock. It is not an Arctic form, generally being taken in waters from about 40° to 50°F, although it may be found either in cooler or somewhat warmer waters. A deepwater species, it seldom enters water shallower than about 200 feet and frequents waters as deep as 3,000 feet. It feeds primarily on fishes, including cods and their relatives, ocean perches, herrings, skates, mackerels, and other flounders. Crabs, mussels, lobsters, and clams are also eaten; in turn, halibut are eaten by seals and the Greenland shark.

Formerly, the Atlantic halibut was an extremely important commercial species, but overfishing and perhaps other factors have reduced it from its former strength. A few are taken in trawls, but the commonest method is by longline fishing on the bottom. Some are taken by anglers drift-fishing, and the species is an excellent fighter. Its flesh is highly desirable, particularly the specimens less than 20 pounds, called chicken halibut. The liver produces a vitamin-rich oil.

BUTTER SOLE *Isopsetta isolepis*   Rough scales and, usually, yellow-edged dorsal and anal fins distinguish this Pacific member of the righteye flounder family. A slight arch of the lateral line over the pectoral fin, an accessory dorsal branch to the lateral line, and scales that extend onto the fins also help to identify this species. It is brownish to gray, irregularly blotched with yellow or light green spots on the eyed side, occasionally with darker markings. It reaches a length of 18 inches and is found from southern California to northwestern Alaska, being more common in its northern range. Found usually over a soft, silty bottom, it is a shallow-water form. A spring spawner, it is of importance to both commercial and sport fisheries.

CURLFIN SOLE *Pleuronichthys decurrens*   This species is characterized by having the anterior edge of the dorsal fin overlapping onto the blind (eyeless) side extending past the mouth, at least 9 rays of the fin occurring on the blind side. The eyes are large and protruding. The body is deep and somewhat diamond-shaped, but less so than the body of the diamond turbot. The small mouth has the teeth chiefly on the blind side, and there is a dorsal accessory branch to the lateral line which extends posteriorly to about the midpoint of the body. The body is black to yellowish-brown, mottled and with fine spots, and the fins are dark. The curlfin reaches a length of 13 inches and is found from southern California to northwestern Alaska in depths of from 60 to nearly 1,800 feet.

DIAMOND TURBOT *Hypsopsetta guttulata*   Occasionally called diamond flounder, this Pacific species is one of the most common flatfish in southern California. A righteye flounder, it has a yellowish patch on the eyeless side that readily distinguishes it from other California flounders; the colored side is green to green-brown with pale blue spots to mottled greenish-brown. The accessory branch of the lateral line found along the anterior base of the dorsal fin is held in common with the English sole; however, the English sole lacks the characteristic diamond shape and has a straight edge to the tail. The rhomboid (diamond) shape of the fish is also somewhat similar to that of the curlfin sole, but the turbot lacks an extension of the dorsal fin onto the blind side. Reaching a length of 18 inches and a weight of 4 pounds, it is found from northern California to the Gulf of California.

Taken throughout the year on hook and line and by trawls, it is of minor importance commercially, although the flesh is excellent. Anglers take the diamond turbot using shrimps, clams, and cut bait.

DOVER SOLE *Microstomus pacificus*   Large eyes and a small mouth characterize this righteye flounder. It has a straight, unbranched lateral line and a small gill cover opening. The slender body has numerous small scales, and a heavy slime covers the body. Its teeth are found only on the blind side. It is uniformly light to dark

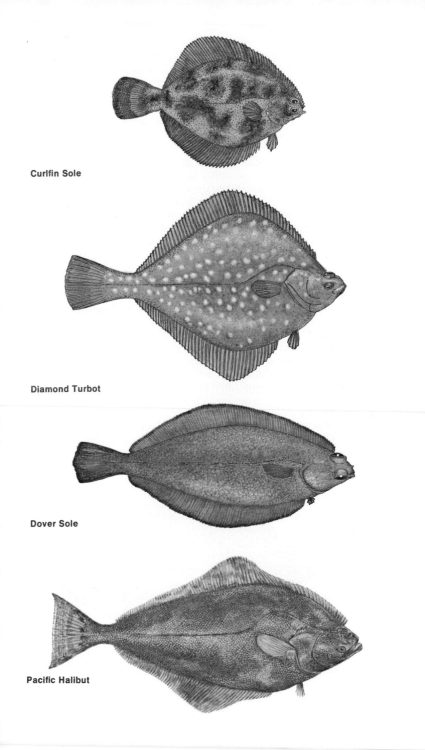

Curlfin Sole

Diamond Turbot

Dover Sole

Pacific Halibut

brown on the eyed side, sometimes with vague blotches. The dark fins are blackish at the tips of their rays. It reaches 10 pounds and 30 inches. This sole occurs from 100 to more than 3,000 feet, often over mud bottom, being more common in the northern part of its range, which is from southern California to northwestern Alaska.

In spite of the heavy slime cover, the flesh is delicious, and recently the Dover has become a major part of the commercial sole catch.

PACIFIC HALIBUT *Hippoglossus stenolepis* The largest flatfish of the Pacific coast and a member of the righteye flounder family, it has a high arch of the lateral line over the pectoral fin, with no accessory dorsal branch. A lunate caudal fin and the middle rays of the dorsal and anal fins, which form a peak, help to identify the species. The scales are smooth, and the small mouth, which does not extend past the middle of the lower eye, contains well-developed teeth on both sides of the jaws. This halibut is dark brown with irregular blotches and is uniformly white on the pale side. Reaching nearly 500 pounds and 9 feet, it is found from central California to the Bering Sea and northern Japan in depths of 60–3,600 feet.

It spawns in the winter, in deepwater, and a 140-pound female may contain about 2,700,000 eggs. The young fish settle to the bottom of the inshore waters by spring, where they live in sandy bays and inshore banks, eventually returning to deeper waters with age. Females grow faster and reach a larger size, attaining an age of at least 35 years. Immature fish do not migrate extensively, but the mature adults may migrate at least 2,000 miles. They eat fishes, crabs, clams, worms, and squids.

PETRALE SOLE *Eopsetta jordani* Also known as brill, this rough-scaled righteye flounder has a pointed tail and a rather broadly rounded snout. The unbranched lateral line curves gradually upward anteriorly. The eyes and mouth are of moderate size; there are well-

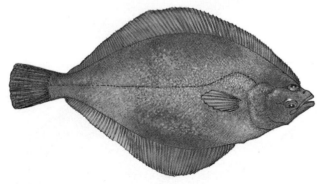

Petrale Sole

164

developed teeth on both sides of the jaws, the teeth in the upper jaw occurring in 2 rows on each side. The fish is a uniform olive-brown on the eyed side, with indistinct pale blotches on the body and fins. It grows to 24 inches and 6–8 pounds. Found from the Mexican border to northwestern Alaska, it occurs in depths of from 60 to 1,300 feet. It eats crustaceans and small fishes, such as anchovies.

REX SOLE *Glyptocephalus zachirus* The long pectoral fin on the eyed side and the thin, slender, and tapering body help distinguish this righteye flounder from its relatives. The mouth is small, the eyes are relatively large, and the straight lateral line lacks a dorsal branch. The color is uniformly light brown on the eyed side and white to dusky on the blind side. Reaching a length of 20 inches, the rex sole occurs from southern California to the Bering Sea. Although a few are taken in relatively shallow water, they generally are taken in trawls at 60–800 feet, the greatest depth (in Alaska) being about 2,100 feet.

Although the rex constitutes only a small percentage of the commercial catch, the flesh of this superior table fish is exceedingly delicate.

ROCK SOLE *Lepidopsetta bilineata* Belonging to the flounders with a short, accessory branch to the lateral line, this righteye flounder is readily identified by the added presence of a high arch over the pectoral fin. The deeply oval body is dark brown, mottled with dark markings, sometimes with red spots or pale blotches. The fins are marked with dark broken lines. It grows to 20 inches and 5 pounds. Found from southern California to the Bering Sea, it is also taken south to Japan. Along the American Pacific coast, it is most abundant in the central California region. A fairly common species in the cooler waters, it occurs from depths of about 400 feet to shallow waters of a few feet deep over sand and gravel bottom. Spawning occurs from late winter to early spring. Crabs, worms, clams, and shrimps are eaten.

SAND SOLE *Psettichthys melanosticus* In North America this righteye flounder is found from southern California to southeastern Alaska.

The sand sole has a lateral line curving only slightly over the pectoral fin and a dorsal branch. The first 8 or more rays of the dorsal fin are elongated and not connected by membrane for about half their length. The teeth and jaws are developed about equally on each side. The maxillary extends to a point below the pupil of the eye. The eyes are small and are on the right side, widely spaced. The fish has a rounded caudal fin and a pectoral fin shorter than the head. The color is light green or brown obscurely mottled with dark spots, and a light brown tinge finely speckled with black or brown.

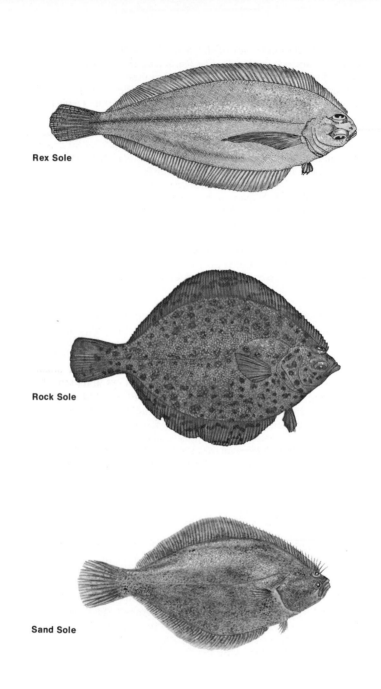

Rex Sole

Rock Sole

Sand Sole

STARRY FLOUNDER *Platichthys stellatus* Easily recognized by the alternating pattern of orange-white and dark bars on the fins, the species has a small mouth and a nearly straight lateral line. Although usually a left-eyed form it may have the eyes on the right side. The body is rough, being covered with scattered spinous plates on the eyed side. It is dark brown to black, with mottlings on the eyed side. Reaching a weight of 20 pounds and a length of 3 feet, it occurs from central California to Alaska and south from the Bering Sea to Japan and Korea. It is most abundant in shallow water, but also occurs to depths of at least 900 feet, generally over sandy bottoms.

The species, particularly the young, sometimes enters brackish water and the mouths of rivers. Males mature sexually in their second year (about 1 foot long); the females mature during their third year (about 14 inches). Spawning occurs in late winter and early spring, taking place in California waters in depths of less than 25 fathoms. The starry flounder eats crabs, shrimps, worms, clams, and their relatives, and small fishes.

Most starry flounders are taken by still-fishing throughout the year, chiefly on clams, shrimps, and small live fishes.

WINTER FLOUNDER *Pseudopleuronectes americanus* One of the best-known flounders to anglers, this important species is a right-eyed fish, although a few specimens have pigment on the left side and occasionally on both sides. It is also known regionally as flatfish, blackback, blueback, black flounder, and muddab. It has a small mouth like the yellowtail flounder, from which it differs in its straight lateral line with no arch over the pectoral fin, its thicker body, and its widely spaced eyes. The color varies from reddish-brown to dark slate, occasionally with hues of dark green. During the brown phase, small dark spots are usually visible.

It occurs from Labrador to Georgia, commonly from the Gulf of St. Lawrence to Chesapeake Bay. This is a shallow-water flounder, found from well up into the high-tide mark to depths of at least about 400 feet. Generally, smaller fish are found in shallow water and large fish in deeper water, although large fish will enter water less than 1 foot deep. They prefer muddy sand but may occur on sand, clay, or fine gravel. Offshore, they may be found on hard bottom as well as soft. They enter mouths of estuaries and occasionally are taken in water that is nearly fresh.

Spawning occurs usually from January to May, with a peak of from March to April over sandy bottom. The spawning depth is 1–40 fathoms, and the eggs, unlike those of other flatfishes, sink to the bottom and stick together. This common species moves about considerably in search of food, but does not generally migrate far from its home territory. There is a distinct movement from deepwater toward shallow water during the fall and an offshore movement in the spring.

Starry Flounder

Winter Flounder

Yellowtail Flounder

The size of winter flounder is generally 12–15 inches and 1–2 pounds, sometimes reaching 20 inches and 5 pounds. The larger fish are sometimes called sea flounders to distinguish them from the smaller bay fish. In waters off Montauk Point, New York, and around Block Island, Rhode Island, there exist populations of extra large flounders, locally known as snowshoes because of their shape and size. These fish can weigh up to 6 pounds, and a winter flounder of 8 pounds has been caught.

YELLOWTAIL FLOUNDER *Limanda ferruginea* Also known as the rusty dab, this righteye flounder is characterized by its small mouth, pointed snout, and thin body, which has a definite arch in the lateral line over the pectoral fin. The top of the head is slightly concave, and the general body shape is nearly oval, its depth being about half its length. This flounder varies from grayish-olive-green to reddish-brown, with large, irregular rusty spots. The tail fin and the edges of the dorsal and anal fins are yellow. Yellow markings are also seen on the caudal peduncle on the blind side, the rest of which is white. A medium-sized species, its maximum size is about 22 inches and a little over 2 pounds.

Found along the Atlantic coast from Labrador to Virginia, it is most common in the northern part of its range. It occurs at about 30–300 feet, although occasionally it is in shoaler water and has been taken in nearly 600 feet of water. It shows a preference for sand or sand-mud bottom. Small crustaceans such as shrimps, amphipods, and mysids are eaten, as are small shellfishes and worms. Apparently it does not feed during the spawning period.

Spawning occurs from late March to August, and the pelagic eggs have been taken in the Gulf of Maine between the 20- and 50-fathom curves. The eggs hatch in approximately 5 days. The young assume a bottom existence when they reach a little over $^1/_2$ inch long. Tagging studies have shown that this species moves about considerably. Formerly of little commercial value, it is now one of the most important flatfishes. It is taken commercially in otter trawls and occasionally by anglers drift-fishing from party boats.

MACKEREL AND TUNA FAMILY Scombridae

Although members of the same family, for purposes of identification the mackerels and tunas are divided here and species arranged alphabetically within each group.

ATLANTIC MACKEREL *Scomber scombrusa* The Atlantic mackerel occurs in the Atlantic Ocean and the Mediterranean Sea. In the western Atlantic it is found roughly from the Gulf of St. Lawrence to Cape Hatteras. It has 2 dorsal fins, separated by a space the length of the first. There are 11–13 spines in the first dorsal. Both the second dorsal and the anal fins are followed by 4–6 finlets. The caudal penducle bears 2 small keels on either side but lacks a median lateral keel. The scales are so minute that the mackerel feels velvety to the fingers. In color, the fish merges from steel-blue into greenish-blue, which darkens almost to black anteriorly. From 23 to 33 dark transverse bars extend in an irregular wavy course to the middle level of the body. Below the midline the sides glint silvery, without spots. (In the related chub mackerel, dusky spots mottle the sides below the midline.) Maximum size is about 25 inches and 36 pounds. Most adults range from 13 to 18 inches. A 1-foot mackerel weighs 12–16 ounces.

The Atlantic mackerel spawns off the Atlantic coast from Cape Hatteras to the Gulf of St. Lawrence in spring or early summer. The peak of the spawning season in Massachusetts Bay arrives during the latter half of May and in June. The fish do not seek out a particular ground, but shed their eggs when ripe, wherever a school happens to be. A moderately prolific medium-sized female produces 360,000–450,000 eggs. The eggs float, being about 1 millimeter in diameter, with a large oil globule. At 60°F incubation takes about 96 hours. The mackerel grows rapidly and reaches a length of 12–16 inches when 2 years old. At this age, it reproduces for the first time. It schools according to size groups.

During the fishing season it appears most abundant in waters over the inner third or half of the continental shelf. Smaller and younger specimens usually stray closer to the shoreline than do the adults. During the winter mackerel cluster in a narrow band of relatively warm water flanking the edge of the continental shelf from Cape Hatteras to the easterly end of George Bank. In this zone the mackerel probably occupy middepths and feed on plankton concentrations. During spring, summer, and fall, mackerel stay in the warm layer of water above the thermocline, which lies about 50–65 feet deep inshore to 130–165 feet deep offshore. Variations in availability of schools to fishermen depend partly upon the variable depth of the thermocline. Southern and northern contingents of the fish perform different spring migrations, occupy different areas in the summer, and leave the coastal waters by different routes in the fall.

Young mackerel feed on small plankton, such as copepods, and on fish eggs. Later they eat shrimps, crab larvae, and similar small organisms. Mackerel feed either by filtering out the smaller pelagic plankton organisms from the water, using their long, thin gillrakers, or by gulping down their prey on sight. Larger mackerel consume larger copepods, squids, and fishes such as herrings, silversides, and lances. Apparently they eat very little in the winter, since they usually seem thin when they reappear in the spring.

CERO *Scomberomorus regalis* Also called cero mackerel and pintada, this fish differs from the king mackerel and Spanish mackerel in having a pattern of both spots and stripes on the sides of the body.

The first dorsal fin is black anteriorly, and there are 17–18 spines in the first dorsal fin, as in the Spanish mackerel. The pectoral fin is covered with scales, as in the king mackerel. There are 11–14 gillrakers on the first branchial arch. Cero may reach a weight of as much as 35 pounds, but the average is 5–10 pounds.

Cero are found from Cape Cod to Brazil and are abundant around southern Florida and the West Indies.

CHUB MACKEREL *Scomber japonicus* Also known as tinker mackerel, chub mackerel have a distribution somewhat similar to that of the Atlantic mackerel, but are found farther south, at least to Cuba in the western Atlantic Ocean. Chub mackerel are known from the Gulf of Alaska to southern Baja California and the Gulf of California. They are also found through much of the Pacific and Indian oceans.

The chub mackerel differs from the Atlantic mackerel in that the Atlantic lacks spots on the sides below the midline and has no swimbladder, whereas the chub has spots or blotches on the sides below the midline and has a swimbladder. Chub mackerel are also smaller, reaching a length of 8–14 inches.

FRIGATE MACKERELS *Auxis thazard* and *A. rochei* Both species have the 2 dorsal fins separated by a wide space, with 8 free finlets behind the second dorsal fin and 7 behind the anal fin. In both, the body has scales that form a corselet on the anterior portion and has no scales on the posterior portion. Between the pelvic fins there is a fleshy flap (the interpelvic process) that is about as long as the pelvic fins.

The species are difficult to distinguish. In both an extension of the corselet follows the lateral line posteriorly. In *A. thazard,* this extension is not more than 5 scale rows wide under the second dorsal fin; while in *A. rochei* it is 6–28 scale rows wide.

Frigate mackerels are generally small, seldom reaching a length of 2 feet.

A. rochei is found worldwide in tropical and subtropical waters. *A. thazard,* also known as the bullet mackerel, is found in the Indian and Pacific oceans and from Florida to the Carolinas in the Atlantic Ocean. They form dense schools of hundreds of individuals.

The food of frigate mackerels consists mainly of fishes, crustaceans, and occasionally squids. They are themselves eaten by larger fishes such as marlins and tunas.

KING MACKEREL *Scomberomorus cavalla* Also called kingfish and cavalla, this mackerel differs from the other western Atlantic species of Spanish mackerels in lacking any black pigment in the anterior part of the first dorsal fin and in having fewer (15–16) spines in the first dorsal fin. Like the cero, the king mackerel has the pectoral fin covered with scales. There are 6–10 gillrakers on the first

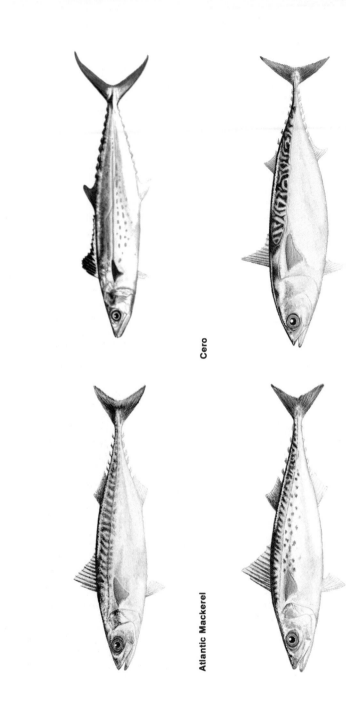

Cero

Frigate Mackerel

Atlantic Mackerel

Chub Mackerel

King Mackerel

Spanish Mackerel

Wahoo

branchial arch. King mackerel reach a large size, to 5 feet and 100 pounds. In the summer, they are found regularly from Brazil north to North Carolina and occasionally to Cape Cod.

MONTEREY SPANISH MACKEREL *Scomberomorus concolor*
This member of the mackerel family is related to the other Spanish mackerels. It lacks the golden spots present on the sides of the sierra and has a greater number of gillrakers (20–29 on the first arch).

This species is now found from Panama Bay to the Gulf of California. It was once common in Monterey Bay, California, but in the late 1880s it disappeared from the California coast, and only a few specimens have been taken in that area since then. The flesh was considered a great delicacy and brought a high price on the market.

SIERRA *Scomberomorus sierra* A fish closely related to the Spanish mackerel, it differs from its only close Pacific coast relative, the Monterey Spanish mackerel, in having several rows of prominent golden spots along the sides of the body and fewer gillrakers (14–16) on the first arch. It attains a weight of about 12 pounds.

The sierra is found along the Pacific coast of North America from San Diego south.

SPANISH MACKEREL *Scomberomorus maculatus* This species differs from the king mackerel and cero in having spots on the sides and no stripes and in lacking scales on the pectoral fins. There are 17–18 spines in the first dorsal fin, as in the cero, and 11–16 gillrakers on the first gill arch. Spanish mackerel reach a maximum weight of about 20 pounds, but 9–10 pounds and a length of about 3 feet are generally considered large.

Spanish mackerel are found south to Brazil and north commonly to the Chesapeake Bay, occasionally to Cape Cod. Generally, they are abundant in Florida from October through February or March, appearing off the Carolinas by April, off Chesapeake Bay by May, and off Narragansett Bay by July. They remain in the north until September.

WAHOO *Acanthocybium solandri* Similar to the Spanish mackerel, the wahoo has a long and slender body. The snout is long and tubular, and the teeth are strong and flattened laterally. There are 21–27 spines in the dorsal fin, and gillrakers are absent. Its sides are usually marked with narrow vertical bars. Among the largest fish known is a wahoo caught off Freeport, Grand Bahama, 6 feet 9 inches long and weighing 180 pounds.

Wahoos are found around the world in tropical and subtropical seas. Unlike most other mackerellike fishes, they do not ordinarily occur in schools. Their food consists of fishes and squids. They may spawn over an extended period of time, and a single female may shed several million eggs.

Wahoos are excellent gamefish, usually caught by trolling. The flesh is white and tasty.

ALBACORE *Thunnus alalunga*   Also called longfin tuna, this fish has longer pectoral fins than other tunas, although it may be difficult to distinguish from small individuals of bigeye tuna. There is a narrow white margin on the caudal fin that is absent in the other tunas. The deepest part of the albacore's body is near the second dorsal fin, rather than near the middle of the first dorsal fin as in other species of tunas. There are 25–32 gillrakers on the first branchial arch, and the ventral surface of the liver is covered with fine striations. The hook-and-line record is a fish taken from the Canary Islands that was 4 feet long and weighed 74³/₄ pounds. Commercially caught fish from near Hawaii have weighed as much as 93 pounds.

The Atlantic and Pacific forms of albacores, once believed to be separate species, are now known to be a single species, found in tropical, subtropical, and temperate waters around the world. Tagging has shown that the albacores in the North Pacific migrate annually between the American and Japanese fisheries. Their food consists of fishes, squids, and crustaceans. Spawning occurs in the summer in the North Pacific and in the southern summer in the South Pacific. A single female may shed 1–3 million eggs.

Albacores are strong gamefish and are eagerly sought by anglers when the runs occur (from July through October along the west coast of North America). Water temperature plays a key role in locating albacores, with the fish commonly found at 60°–66°F. Colder or warmer currents tend to divert the schools farther offshore, and both sportfishing boats and commercials may operate from several up to 100 miles from land in clear bluewater at various points along the coast. When the schools are beyond a practical distance for a 1-day trip, some large party boats go out for 2–3 days. A standard procedure on the fishing grounds is to locate the albacores by fast trolling with feathered jigs; when contact is made, these tuna are more readily caught with live bait such as anchovies, herrings, sauries, and sardines. They are the most valuable of the tunas for canning and the only species that can be labeled as "white-meat tuna."

BIGEYE TUNA *Thunnus obesus*   This species is difficult to distinguish from some individuals of the 4 other tunas in American waters. The length of its pectoral fin is greater than 80 percent of the head length; the dorsal and anal fins are never greatly elongated; the finlets behind the dorsal and anal fins are yellow with black margins; and there is no white margin on the caudal fin. There are 23–31 gillrakers, and the ventral surface of the liver is striated. The largest fish taken by

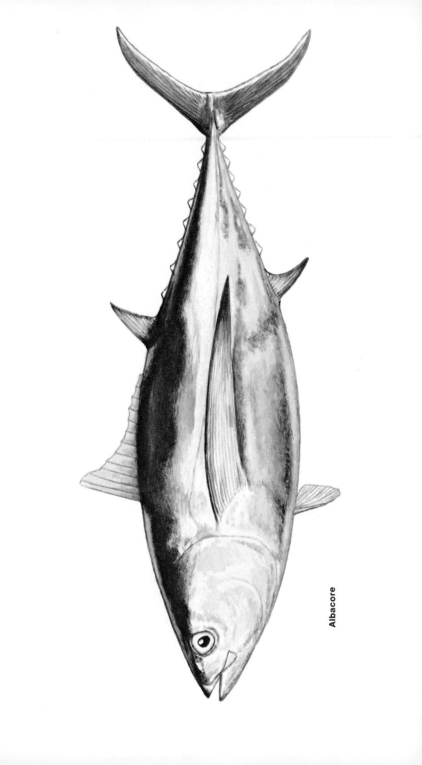

Albacore

Bigeye Tuna

hook and line, from the Hudson Canyon, off New York, weighed 321 pounds, 12 ounces.

BLACKFIN TUNA *Thunnas atlanticus* This is a small, dark-colored species, with fewer gillrakers (20–24) than any other tuna. The finlets behind the second dorsal and anal fins are uniformly dark, not partly yellow. When freshly caught, the blackfin has prominent gold bars, but these fade quickly after death. An occasional fish may reach 35 pounds, but most are less than 10 pounds. Large blackfin (20–30 pounds) occur with some frequency around Bermuda.

This species is found only in the western Atlantic from Cape Cod to Brazil. Its food includes fishes, squids, and crustaceans. It is one of the commonest items in the diet of blue marlin. Spawning occurs off southern Florida from April to November.

BLUEFIN TUNA *Thunnus thynnus* One of the largest marine game-fishes, the bluefin tuna has shorter pectoral fins (less than 80 percent of head length) than the other American tunas. It also has more gillrakers on the first branchial arch (31–43) than any other species of *Thunnus*. The ventral surface of the liver is covered with striations, as in the albacore and bigeye tuna. The body of the bluefin is robust, tapering to a pointed snout. Its color is generally dark steel-blue above with green reflections, blending to a silvery-gray on the ventral surface. Small bluefins have white spots and streaks forming vertical lines on the lower sides. The bluefin has 2 dorsal fins, the first retractable and the second fixed. There are 9–10 yellow finlets with black edges behind the second dorsal fin, and 8–10 finlets behind the anal fin. The tail is lunate.

Bluefin tuna are worldwide in distribution, being caught chiefly in temperate and subtropical waters. In the western Atlantic concentrations of tuna appear inshore seasonally in the Bahamas and as far north as the Labrador Current. For a number of years, the late spring run of large bluefins in the Bahamas was thought to be part of a yearly migration to New England and as far north as Newfoundland. However, fish tagged in the Bahamas have been recaptured off Norway, proving that at least some individuals undertake a transatlantic migration. Other smaller fish have been tagged off New England and recaptured in various European areas.

Their summer habitat extends from Cape Hatteras to southern Labrador, including the continental shelf at least as far northeast as the Nova Scotia banks. In this area, the first bluefins are usually taken in late May or early June, frequently in Cape Cod Bay or near Gloucester, and they are generally large fish. The small individuals usually appear next, in late June or early July, anywhere from Cape Cod to just north of Cape Hatteras. The medium-sized bluefins generally enter the coastal fishery last. They are sometimes numerous off northern New Jersey or eastern Long Island in July, but do not ordinarily appear in the Gulf of Maine, where they are more usually abundant, until August, or in Nova Scotia waters until September. This size group also tends to be the last to depart in the fall, being available to the fishery well into October and sometimes into November, after the larger and smaller individuals have disappeared.

There are three major size groups in the fishery, each with a distinct distributional pattern. These are small (5−69 pounds, 1−4 years old), medium (70−269 pounds, 4−9 years old), and large or giant (270 pounds and over, 9 years old or older). The cycles of these groups overlap during parts of the year, and, of course, individuals of nearly marginal sizes may be found with one group or the other. There are also some differences in the cycles of the respective ages constituting the small group and possibly of those constituting the medium group also, but the major changes usually occur at about the sizes indicated.

Bluefin tuna feed on a variety of fishes, squids, and crustaceans. Whatever is available seems to be eaten. Thus stomachs of bluefins feeding near land may be filled with herrings, sand lances, or hakes, while those offshore will often contain, among other items, luminous deepsea fishes.

Bluefin tuna grow to a large size; although the rod-caught record is a 1,120-pound fish, taken off Prince Edward Island, they are known to exceed 1,500 pounds.

BONITO Three species of the genus *Sarda* are likely to be taken by the American angler. These are *S. sarda,* the Atlantic bonito; *S. chiliensis,* the Pacific or California bonito; and *S. orientalis,* the striped bonito. These fishes have prominent longitudinal or oblique stripes on the back, large conical teeth, and numerous spines in the first dorsal fin (17−22).

The species are somewhat difficult to distinguish. *S. sarda* is found only in the Atlantic Ocean and Mediterranean and Black seas. It differs from the other species in having 20−23 spines in the first dorsal fin (compared with 17−19 in the others). It has 17−23 gillrakers on the first branchial arch, overlapping *S. chiliensis,* which has 20−27, while *S. orientalis* has only 8−13. *S. chiliensis* is found along the Pacific coast of the Americas, but its range is divided into a northern portion, from British Columbia to southern Baja California, and a southern portion, from Peru to Chile. Between these two areas, *S. orientalis* occurs from Baja California to Peru. All are medium-sized fishes. *S. sarda* may reach a length of 3 feet and a weight of 12 pounds; *S. orientalis* attains at least 2 feet 8 inches and 7 pounds.

LITTLE TUNNY *Euthynnus alletteratus* Until 1970, three scombrids and sometimes a fourth of the genus *Euthynnus* were loosely regarded as little tunas: *E. alletteratus,* also called false albacore or bonito; *E. affinis,* also called wavyback skipjack or kawakawa

Blackfin Tuna

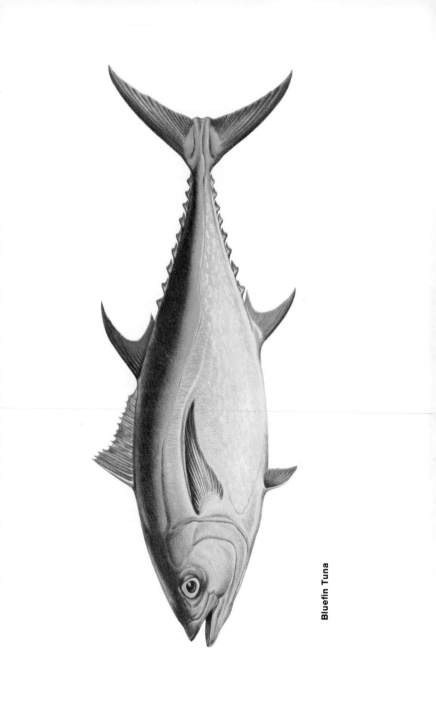

Bluefin Tuna

(Hawaii); *E. lineatus*, also called black skipjack; and *E. pelamis*, also called skipjack tuna. The common name, little tunny, applies only to *E. alletteratus*.

The species are difficult to distinguish. *E. alletteratus* is found only in the Atlantic Ocean and Mediterranean Sea. It differs from the other species in lacking teeth on the vomer, a small bone in the roof of the mouth. *E. lineatus* occurs only off the west coast of America from California to Peru. It typically has 3–5 horizontal black lines on the back, while the others have wormlike or oblique wavy lines. *E. affinis* is rare off the American west coast but is common from Hawaii through the western Pacific and Indian oceans; it has teeth on the vomer and has wavy lines on the back. All are medium-sized fishes. *E. lineatus* attains a weight of about 10 pounds and a length of about 2 feet; *E. affinis* and *E. alletteratus* both become larger, reaching 20 pounds or more and over $2^1/_2$ feet.

SKIPJACK TUNA *Katsuwonus pelamis*   Also called oceanic skipjack, striped tuna, and many other names, it is a fish of the mackerel family with prominent dark longitudinal stripes on the lower half of the body. It has more gillrakers (53–63) than any other mackerellike fish in the Americas. The largest fish caught by hook and line, taken in the Bahamas, was 3 feet 3 inches long and weighed 39 pounds 15 ounces.

This species is found around the world in tropical and subtropical seas. It forms schools that at times may include 50,000 fish. The food consists mainly of fishes, squids, and crustaceans. Spawning probably occurs throughout the year in equatorial waters, but tends to be restricted to the summer months as distance from the equator increases.

This is one of the most important commercial fishes, particularly in the Pacific, where many are taken near Japan, Hawaii, and the Central American coast.

YELLOWFIN TUNA *Thunnus albacares*   The yellowfin tuna is not difficult to distinguish from the other species of tunas in American waters. The length of its pectoral fin is greater than 80 percent of the head length, the finlets behind the second dorsal and anal fins are yellow with black margins, and there is no white margin on the caudal fin. In large individuals the second dorsal and anal fins become very long, and such individuals cannot be mistaken for any other species. There are 25–34 gillrakers, and the ventral surface of the liver has no striations.

The yellowfin is the most brilliantly colored of the tunas, with a poorly defined stripe of golden-yellow on its upper sides and much bright yellow in most of the fins. The lower sides commonly have white spots and vertical streaks, even in quite large fish.

The Atlantic and Pacific forms of yellowfins have been called separate species, but all yellowfins are now considered to be a single species, found in tropical and subtropical waters around the world. Individuals with exceptionally long second dorsal and anal fins have been called Allison tuna, but these are merely variations.

Yellowfin tuna grow to a fairly large size. Most fish caught weigh 20–120 pounds, but the largest yellowfin ever taken with rod and reel, caught in Mexico, was 308 pounds.

Yellowfin tuna are found in tropical and subtropical waters around the world. In the western Atlantic, they are found regularly as far north as New Jersey, where the Gulf Stream makes its influence felt, especially in late summer and fall. Exploratory fishing has shown them to be found in the Gulf Stream throughout the year. Very rarely is a yellowfin caught inshore in the New England states and Canada, unlike the bluefin tuna, which becomes common there during the summer and early fall.

Atlantic yellowfins have been little studied. Most of the information on yellowfin biology comes from the Pacific. Spawning takes place throughout much of the year in tropical waters, but tends to be restricted to late spring and summer in subtropical regions. Each female is believed to spawn at least two batches of one to several million eggs each year. The young grow rapidly, averaging $7^{1}/_{2}$ pounds at 18 months of age. A 4-year-old fish weighs about 140 pounds.

Yellowfins seem to be nonselective in their feeding habits, and a great variety of fishes, crustaceans, and squids has been found in their stomachs. The abundance of organisms in a given area determines what the yellowfins eat.

Yellowfin tuna are taken commercially in great abundance in all tropical regions of the world. The species is the mainstay of the California-based tuna fleet. Japanese fishermen are now operating over virtually the entire world range of yellowfin tuna and deliver their catch to the market or to canneries in North and South America as well as Europe, Africa, and Asia. Of the world catch of about 800,000 tons of mackerellike fishes in 1960, over 250,000 tons were yellowfins.

Live-bait fishing, using feathered jigs or baited hooks attached by short lines to bamboo poles, accounts for the capture of most yellowfins. In recent years, most American fishermen have switched from live bait to purse seine, and most of the eastern Pacific catch is made by this method. The longline technique is also used to a considerable extent, particularly by the Japanese high seas fishery.

The flesh of yellowfin tuna is light, neither so dark as that of the bluefin nor so white as that of the albacore.

Yellowfins are commonly caught by sport fishermen in the West Indies and Gulf of Mexico and as far north as Maryland and New Jersey. On the American Pacific coast, they are caught in small numbers in California, but most are caught south of that area.

Bonito

Little Tunny

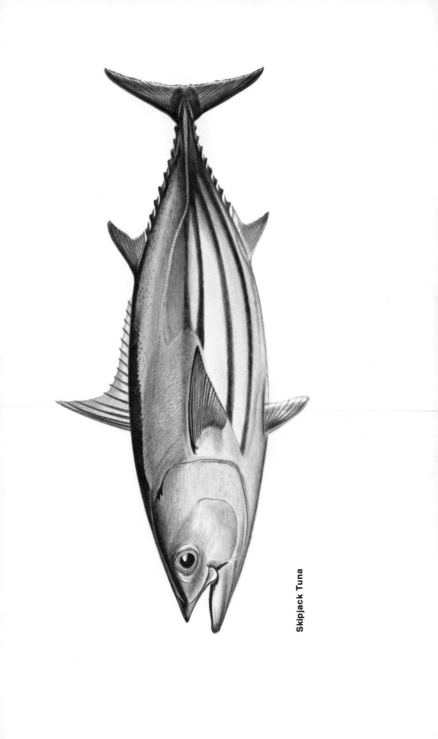

Skipjack Tuna

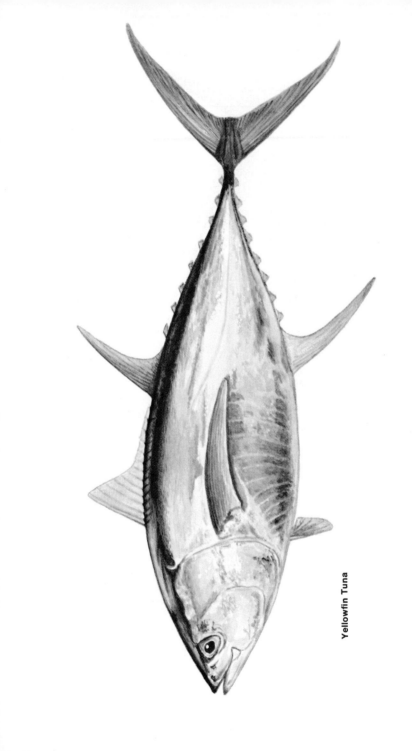

Yellowfin Tuna

DOLPHIN FAMILY Coryphaenidae

DOLPHIN *Coryphaena hippurus* Also called dorado. One of two members of its family, the dolphin may usually be distinguished from the pompano dolphin by its slender body; in the dolphin, the greatest depth of the body goes 4 or more times into the length from snout to fork of tail. It differs further in usually having more than 240 scales in the lateral line and 56 or more rays in the dorsal fin. Certain porpoises are also known as dolphins, but these are mammals, not fishes.

In large male dolphins, the front of the head becomes very high and almost vertical, but until this happens, males and females are similar in appearance. In the water, the dolphin is usually a vivid greenish-blue with dark vertical bands that may appear and disappear. When the fish is caught, the color fluctuates rapidly, so that within a few minutes, it may be blue, green, or yellow. After death, these colors fade rapidly to a uniform yellowish or silver.

The usual angler catch is a 5- to 15-pound dolphin. The largest dolphin on record was caught off Spanish Wells, Bahamas, and weighed 85 pounds.

The dolphin is cosmopolitan in tropical and subtropical waters. On the Atlantic coast of North America, it is found in areas influenced by the warmwaters of the Gulf Stream and has been caught as far north as Prince Edward Island. Throughout much of its range, it is a favorite gamefish, and the flesh is a gourmet's delight, often being sold in restaurants under its Hawaiian name, *mahi-mahi.*

In warmer waters, the spawning season appears to be rather long, extending from April to August; further north, as in the Gulf Stream, spawning is concentrated in early summer. The young are commonly found in warm offshore waters, frequently in or near patches of sargassum weed, and are occasionally found inshore. They, like the young of many other fishes, are attracted to lights at night and are easily caught with a dipnet.

The food of the dolphin consists of a variety of fishes, squids, and crustaceans. Flyingfishes are said to form a large portion of the diet in some areas. Well offshore in the Gulf Stream, where flyingfishes are plentiful, dolphins feed mainly on juvenile fishes associated with sargassum, such as filefishes, triggerfishes, and jacks.

The riotously colored dolphin follows only the sailfish, marlins, and tunas as a desirable offshore gamefish; it is a spectacular gamefish in many ways. In addition to its brilliant coloration, the dolphin strikes explosively, fights frantically, and performs beautifully in the air. The attack of a dolphin school at a trolled bait is one of the top thrills of Gulf Stream fishing. Often they will streak toward the bait from several hundred feet out, their stubby dorsals knifing through the surface of the water. It is not unusual when two or more baits are being trolled to have a single dolphin hit them all in a racing strike that seems to occur almost instantly.

Dolphin (Male)

Dolphin (Female)

Pompano Dolphin

There are times during the spring and summer when school dolphins may be found concentrated by the thousands in the blue-water off the coast. Seaweed rips are their favorite haunts, but they may also be found hovering about almost any drifting object.

POMPANO DOLPHIN *Coryphaena equiselis*   This smaller relative of the dolphin is probably more common than records indicate, but it is easily confused with females and smaller males of the other species, which lack the high vertical forehead of larger males. Pompano dolphins are most easily distinguished from dolphins by their greater body depth; the greatest body depth goes into the length from tip of snout to fork of tail fewer than 4 times, and this greatest depth occurs near the middle of the body, rather than just behind the head, as in the dolphin. There are usually fewer than 200 lateral line scales and fewer than 56 dorsal rays. The color of the pompano dolphin is similar to that of the dolphin. A pompano dolphin may reach a length of 2 feet and a weight of 5 pounds.

Because of the difficulty in distinguishing between the species of dolphins, the published information does not accurately depict the range of the pompano dolphin. It is probably found around the world in warm seas, but the pompano dolphin generally appears to be a more oceanic species than the dolphin.

SEA CHUB FAMILY   Kyphosidae

BERMUDA CHUB *Kyphosus sectatrix*   The sea chubs or rudder-fishes are ovate fishes with somewhat compressed bodies, forked tails, small heads, and relatively small mouths with incisiform outer teeth but no molariform teeth. They are herbivorous, in general, and have long digestive tracts. Two species are recognized in the western Atlantic, the Bermuda chub (*K. sectatrix*) and the closely related *K. incisor*. The dorsal fins of both nearly always have 11 dorsal spines, but the number of softrays differs. *K. sectatrix* has 12 dorsal rays (rarely 11–13), and *K. incisor* usually has 14 (sometimes 13 and rarely 15). Similarly, *K. sectatrix* has 11 (rarely 12) anal softrays and *K. incisor* 13 (sometimes 12). Specimens falling within the small zone of overlap in fin ray counts may be differentiated by gillarker counts. *K. sectatrix* usually has 17–18 rakers on the lower limb of the first gill arch; *K. incisor,* 19–22.

At first glance the Bermuda chub seems to be a drab gray fish, but closer inspection reveals that it has lengthwise brassy bands on the body following the scale rows and 2 horizontal yellowish bands on the head that are confluent on the snout. One color phase shows pale spots on the body as large as the eye.

The Bermuda chub is known from Brazil to Cape Cod, the West Indies, and Bermuda. It is also reported from the Mediterranean, the Canary Islands, Madeira Islands, and Azores. Fully grown adults are not known along the Atlantic coast of the United States north of Florida. The occurrence of the species in the more northern localities is probably the result of transport of the young in the Gulf Stream.

The Bermuda chub reaches a length of nearly 30 inches and has been reported to a weight of 20 pounds. It is a powerful fish and fights vigorously on hook and line.

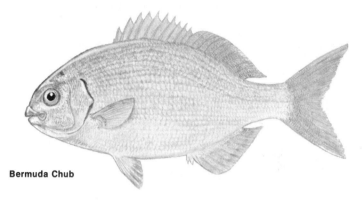

Bermuda Chub

OPALEYE *Girella nigricans* Also known as the green fish, blue bass, blue-eyed perch, button perch, and Catalina perch, the opaleye is known from Monterey, California, southward to Magdalena Bay, Baja California, but is uncommon in the extremes of its range. This sea chub is found over rocky bottoms and around kelp beds. It is common in 5–50 feet of water and is often caught from shore.

The opaleye is perchlike in general shape, but is easily distinguished from other fishes of this general appearance that occur within its range by its higher number of dorsal fin spines, 14. The surfperch family, Embiotocidae, with 19 marine species off California, has 11 dorsal spines. The halfmoon, *Medialuna californiensis*, of the family Scorpidae might be confused with the opaleye, but it has 11 or fewer

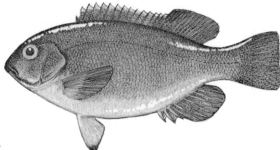

Opaleye

dorsal spines. The only other fish that might cause confusion is the blacksmith, *Chromis punctipinnis,* of the damselfish family (Pomacentridae), and it has 13 dorsal spines. The body of the opaleye is laterally compressed and moderate in depth. The head profile is evenly convex. The angle of the preopercle is minutely serrate. The dorsal fin has 14 spines and 12–14 relatively longer softrays, giving the posterior portion of the fin a lobed appearance. The eyes are a beautiful opalescent blue. The largest fish on record weighed $13^1/_2$ pounds; however, individuals larger than 15 inches are uncommon.

Despite its moderately small size, the opaleye affords considerable sport to the California fisherman, particularly during the winter months, when certain of the other surf fishes are scarce and the larger opaleyes seem to move inshore. Effective baits are redrock shrimps, mussels, razor clams, and moss.

SURFPERCH FAMILY   Embiotocidae

Most members of this Pacific marine family live in the surf, in the ocean proper, in tidepools, or in bays. Exceptions are a species that is found in freshwater streams of northern California and one that inhabits deepwater.

The common names indicate various habitats: fish that dwell in the ocean but not primarily in the surf are seaperch; those in the surf are surfperch; those with varying habitats are perch.

BARRED SURFPERCH *Amphistichus argenteus*   This is the most important surf fish taken by anglers in California.

There is a row of scales along the posterior half of the base of the anal fin; a broad frenum interrupts the posterior groove of the lower lip; the lower jaw is somewhat shorter than the general height of the soft dorsal; a series of olivaceous brassy vertical bars alternating with spots usually on sides, softrays in dorsal 23–27, in anal 25–28; length to 16 inches; weight $4^1/_4$ pounds. Its color is silvery to white, with blue or gray above and plain white along the belly and sides. Sometimes it is brassy-olive above and silvery below. Taken in the surf and to depths of 40 fathoms, its range is from central Baja California to central California.

The California Department of Fish and Game conducted an intensive study of the species, determining that the young at birth were about $1^5/_8$–$2^1/_8$ inches long; the number of embryos per female was 4–113, with an average of 33.4; the young are dropped from mid-March at least through July; they mature at the end of their second year at about $5^1/_8$ inches; females reached 9 years of age, and no males were found older than 6 years. Sandcrabs were found in 90 percent of 479 stomachs examined and made up over 90 percent of the food by volume. The December–January period usually provided the best fishing, and in that period the best return to the angler was found in the Oceanside region, where fishermen averaged 20 minutes per perch. Tag-recovery data indicated that some mixing occurs between areas studied. The longest distance traveled was 31 miles in 48 days out; the longest time at liberty was 242 days, and the fish was recaptured 2 miles from the release point.

There is no commercial season for the species in California.

BLACK PERCH *Embiotoca jacksoni* This fish is often taken by sportsmen around pilings, in bays, and along rocky coasts. The overall color varies from brown to being tinged with blue, yellow, orange, green, or red; anal and pelvic fins may be orange to red; anal sometimes barred with blue; lips vary from brown to orange and yellow. Its range is from Bodega Lagoon, California, to Abreojos Point in Baja California. A cluster of large scales occurs between pectoral and pelvic fins; a broad frenum interrupts the posterior groove of the lower lip; a row of small scales along the anal fin base; softrays in anal 24–27; softrays in dorsal 19–22; dorsal softrays longer than dorsal spines; lips somewhat thick. Length to 14 inches.

CALICO SURFPERCH *Amphistichus koelzi* This species is similar to the redtail and barred surfperches; the frenum is usually absent but is narrow when present; the lower jaw projects slightly; dorsal spines are similar in height to softrayed portion; 17–20 scales between lateral line and anterior end of vent; 24–48 dorsal softrays, 26–32 softrays in the anal fin. It is found in the surf from northern California to northern Baja California.

GUADALUPE PERCH *Micrometrus aletes* This surfperch is confined to Guadalupe Island in the Pacific off the coast of Baja California. Little is known of its habits or appearance in nature, since it is a comparatively newly identified species and described from specimens preserved in alcohol. Length of preserved specimens is approximately $2^1/_2$–4 inches. Dorsal softrays 13–14, anal softrays 21–23.

ISLAND SEAPERCH *Cymatogaster gracilis* This fish is similar to the shiner perch, but more slender and confined to some of the Santa Barbara Channel islands.

KELP PERCH *Brachyistius frenatus* This handsome surfperch, usually found along rocky coasts in kelp, is colored rosy to copper-brown overlaid with olive above, becoming copper-red below. Fins are plain to reddish. A frenum interrupts the posterior groove to the lower lip; the upper jaw is slightly shorter; no black triangle in axilla; soft portion of dorsal slightly lower than spinous; 13–16 soft dorsal rays; 21–14 soft anal rays. Length to about 8 inches. The kelp perch is of little importance to the angler.

PILE PERCH *Rhacochilus vacca* This common shore-dwelling surfperch is dusky-brown or blackish on the back; silver ventrally; it may have 3-4 darker blotches on upper body; a black spot on preopercle just behind posterior tip of maxillary; fins dusky except for clear pectorals; pelvics may be pale yellow or orange tipped with black. A broad frenum interrupts the posterior groove of the lower lip. The tail is deeply forked; first softrays of dorsal sharply elevated above spiny portion. Length to 16 inches. Its range is from Baja California to Alaska.

The life history, food, and angling value are the same as for surfperch in general.

RAINBOW SEAPERCH *Hypsurus caryi* Striking and beautiful colors make the species an outstanding surfperch. The body is marked by horizontal stripes of red, orange, and blue; streaks of sky-blue and orange on head; orange on fins; a black blotch anteriorly on the dorsal. The lower body margin is long and straight; the vent is behind origin of soft dorsal; a frenum interrupts posterior groove of lower lip; 21-24 dorsal softrays; 21-23 anal softrays. Its range is from northern California to northern Baja California. Length to 12 inches.

REDTAIL SURFPERCH *Amphistichus rhodoterus* This species is much like the barred surfperch, but a frenum does not interrupt the posterior groove of the lower lip; the lower jaw projects slightly; the dorsal spines are higher than the contour of the softrays; there are 20-22 scales between the lateral line and the anterior end of the vent; softrays of the dorsal 25-28; anal softrays 28-31. There are 9-11 vertical, reddish-brown or brassy bars on the sides; the pelvic and caudal fins are usually reddish. Called porgy north of California. Common in surf along sandy beaches. Found from Washington to central California.

RUBBERLIP SEAPERCH *Rhacochilus toxotes* This is considered to be the best foodfish of the many surfperches. It has very thick lips; a frenum does not interrupt the posterior groove of the lower lip; the soft portion of the dorsal fin is higher than the spinous part; 22-24 dorsal soft rays; 27-30 anal soft rays. Color usually whitish with brassy or bluish-black tinge; overlaid with blackish on belly and sides; yellowish pectorals; black or dusky tips on anal, dorsal, and pelvic fins; white or pink lips; 1-2 dusky vertical bars on juveniles only. Central to southern California. Length to 18 inches.

SHINER PERCH *Cymatogaster aggregata* This is an abundant surfperch found in shallow and deepwater (to 240 feet) from northern Baja California to northwestern Alaska. It is silvery; greenish upper body; about 8 longitudinal, partially interrupted, horizontal lines on body; 3 vertical yellow bars on body; males nearly black in winter and spring. The posterior groove of lower lip is not interrupted by a frenum; scales are large, caudal peduncle short and slender, 18–23 rays in dorsal fin. Length to 8 inches.

SILVER SURFPERCH *Hyperprosopon ellipticum*   This species does not have the black-tipped pelvics of the walleye surfperch; otherwise it is similar in appearance. Both species have 25–28 softrays in the dorsal fin, but the walleye has 30–35 anal softrays and the silver has 29–34 anal softrays. The silver surfperch has no commercial value, but is taken in the surf by sportsmen. It is found from Washington to southern California.

TULE PERCH *Hysterocarpus traski*   This unique surfperch inhabits freshwater in central California from Lassen to San Luis Obispo counties. There are two pattern phases: a slender form in Clear Lake, and a more robust form in rivers. The former has gray overlaying a brassy color, dark gray dorsally thinning to white on the belly; the latter has about 8 slate-gray bars which run across the body, fading just above the belly. The dorsal and anal fins are dusky, the pectorals and pelvics plain. Dorsal softrays 9–13; the unique count of 15–18 dorsal spines characterizes the genus.

WALLEYE SURFPERCH *Hyperprosopon argenteum*   The walleye is a handsome fish, steely-blue above and silver ventrally, with black-tipped pelvic and caudal fins and about 5 obscure dusky bars on the sides. No frenum between lower lip and symphysis of lower jaw; eye about one-third of head length; longest dorsal spine longer than softrays; closed mouth outline parallels lower edge of head. Length to 12 inches.
It is the second most important surfperch in California.

WHITE SEAPERCH *Phanerodon furcatus*   An important sport fish, the white seaperch ranges from northern Baja California to Vancouver Island along sandy coasts.
It is silver; darker dorsally; anal fin often has dusky anterior spot; ventrals plain; dusky caudal fin margin; a continuous dorsal margin; last spine of dorsal as long or nearly as long as first softray; deeply forked tail; peduncle slender; posterior groove of lower lip interrupted by a frenum; 4–5 rows of large scales between lower edge of scale sheath at junction of spiny and soft portions of dorsal fin and lateral line (one small scale may be present above larger ones). Length to about 12 inches.

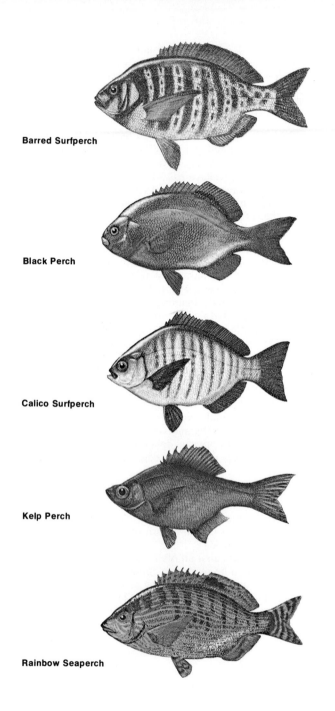

Barred Surfperch

Black Perch

Calico Surfperch

Kelp Perch

Rainbow Seaperch

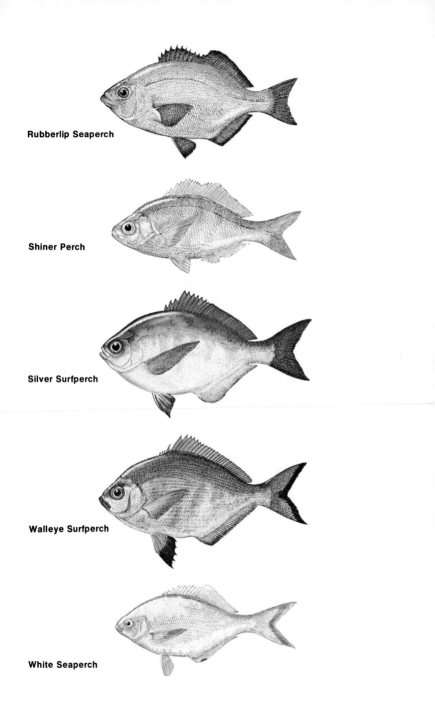

Rubberlip Seaperch

Shiner Perch

Silver Surfperch

Walleye Surfperch

White Seaperch

SNAPPER FAMILY Lutjanidae

BLACK SNAPPER *Apsilus dentatus* This distinctive, deepwater snapper is placed in a genus of its own. It belongs to the family Lutjanidae, a huge group consisting of about 25 genera and 250 species. The family is worldwide in distribution, and most of the species inhabit the shallow waters of the tropics. The black snapper is found only in the western Atlantic from southern Florida to the West Indies. It is quite rare in most of its range, but is reported to be common in Cuban waters.

The color of the black snapper is dusky-violet above and paler on the sides. The inside of the mouth and the fins are the same violet or brownish color, except that the anal and ventral fins have blackish tips and the soft dorsal has some olive shades.

Other distinguishing characters of the black snapper are dorsal fin spines 10, softrays 10; anal fin spines 3, softrays 8; scales above lateral line 7, along lateral line 60, below 16; other scales in rows running parallel to lateral line, 7 rows on cheek, 2 rows on interopercle. Mouth small; maxillary broad, almost reaching pupil. Upper jaw has a narrow band of villiform teeth, outside of which is a series of larger, caninelike teeth; lower jaw has a single series of small teeth, about 6 of those in front larger, similar to the larger teeth of upper jaw; inside this series is a comparatively wide band of villiform teeth in front of jaw only; tongue without teeth; vomer has an A-shaped patch of teeth.

Nothing is known of the life history of the black snapper. It attains a length of at least 18 inches and prefers a depth of 100 feet or more. It is sometimes caught by hand lines incidental to some other commercial fishery.

BLACKFIN SNAPPER *Lutjanus buccanella* This species occurs around southern Florida and throughout the tropical American Atlantic. A medium-sized snapper, it may reach a weight of 30 pounds and a total length of over 2 feet.

The blackfin snapper has 10 dorsal spines, 14 dorsal rays, and 8 anal rays. Pectoral rays normally number 17. There are 11–13 gillrakers on the lower limb of the first arch, not counting rudiments. Rows of scales around caudal peduncle 24–27, usually 25–26. Cheek scales in 6, rarely 7, rows. Upper jaw reaching to or beyond vertical from anterior margin of orbit. Pectoral fin not reaching to vertical from origin of anal fin. Anal fin rounded, not angulate posteriorly. General coloration crimson-red, silver below. Pelvic and anal fins yellow. Dorsal fin crimson-red, margined with scarlet. Pectoral fin pink, its base and axil jet-black. Caudal fin orange-yellow. Black spot on sides of body absent. Eyes orange.

The jet-black base and axil of the pectoral fins distinguish this species from all the other snappers.

A bottom feeder occurring in waters of medium depth, usually at 20–60 fathoms, small individuals may occur in shallower water. It takes live or dead bait but is not known to have been taken on artificial lures.

Although this snapper is a good fighter, specimens taken on rod and reel in shallow water are usually small. As is true of the silk snapper, larger individuals may be taken in deepwater with electric reels and wire lines.

Good eating, this commercial snapper is usually marketed as red snapper.

CUBERA SNAPPER *Lutjanus cyanopterus* This fish, also called Cuban snapper, is by far the largest of the snappers. It may exceed a weight of about 100 pounds, and specimens weighing up to 80 pounds have been caught by anglers along the coast of southern Florida. It occurs throughout the tropical American Atlantic.

The cubera snapper has 10 dorsal spines, 14 dorsal rays, and 8 anal rays. Pectoral rays 16–17. Gillrakers 5–7 on lower limb of first arch, not counting rudiments. Rows of scales around caudal peduncle 25–26. Cheek scales in 9–10 rows. Upper jaw reaching to vertical from center of eye (young) or from posterior margin of orbit (large adult). Pectoral fin not reaching to vertical from origin of anal fin. Anal fin rounded, not angulate, posteriorly. General coloration greenish or dusky-gray; paler below; sometimes tinged with red on sides. Black spot on sides of body absent. Eyes dark red.

In addition to its large size, this snapper is distinguished from the others by the low number of gillrakers. Anglers sometimes confuse this species with the gray snapper.

This shallow-water snapper is usually found along ledges in depths of from a few feet to about 20 fathoms. Small- to medium-sized individuals are also known to occur in estuaries and in the tidal zone of the lower course of streams and canals. It takes live or dead bait and artificial lures. A very strong fighter, large individuals afford quite a challenge even on fairly heavy tackle. The cubera may be taken by trolling close to the bottom.

DOG SNAPPER *Lutjanus jocu* This medium-sized snapper is fairly common throughout its range. It occurs arround southern Florida and southward throughout the tropical American Atlantic. It may reach a weight of 20 pounds or more, but most of the individuals seen weigh less than 5 pounds. The common name refers to the large anterior fangs.

The dog snapper has 10 dorsal spines, 14 dorsal rays, and 8 anal rays. Pectoral rays normally 17. Gillrakers 7–9 on lower limb of first arch, not counting rudiments. Rows of scales around caudal peduncle normally 25. Cheek scales in 7–8, usually 8, rows. Upper jaw reaching to or somewhat beyond vertical from anterior margin of

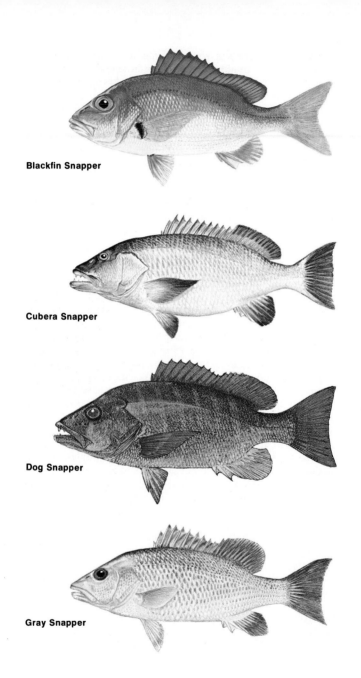

Blackfin Snapper

Cubera Snapper

Dog Snapper

Gray Snapper

orbit. Pectoral fin not reaching to vertical from origin of anal fin. Anal fin rounded, not angulate, posteriorly. General coloration olivaceous above, paler below with a reddish tinge. Dorsal, pectoral, and caudal fins orange. Pelvic and anal fins yellow. Black spot on sides of body absent. Eyes red.

The large fangs and the color pattern distinguish this snapper from the others.

A shallow-water snapper most frequently found along the shore in rocky areas, it takes live or dead bait and artificial lures.

GRAY SNAPPER *Lutjanus griseus* This is the most common snapper in the western Atlantic. Its range extends from the middle Atlantic and Gulf coasts of the United States southward to Brazil. It is very common around southern Florida, the Bahamas, and the Caribbean area. Known as gray snapper in the northernmost parts of its range, the common name mangrove snapper is used elsewhere and refers to its shallow-water habitat. It seldom reaches a weight of much over 10 pounds.

The gray snapper has 10 dorsal spines, 14 dorsal rays, and 8 anal rays. Pectoral rays 15–17, usually 16. Gillrakers 7–9 on lower limb of first arch, not counting rudiments. Rows of scales around caudal peduncle 21–23, usually 22. Cheek scales in 7–8, usually 8, rows. Upper jaw reaching to or somewhat beyond vertical from anterior margin of orbit. Pectoral fin not reaching to vertical from origin of anal fin. Anal fin rounded, not angulate, posteriorly. General coloration grayish above, paler below, with a red tinge on sides. Dorsal and caudal fins grayish. Pectoral, pelvic, and anal fins reddish. Black spot on sides of body absent. Eyes red.

In this species, the pectoral fin is shorter than in the other snappers, and it usually does not reach to a vertical from the anus.

A shallow-water snapper, the gray is most abundant along the shore in mangrove habitats. It is extremely cunning. Large individuals are very difficult to catch because of their reluctance to take a baited hook or artificial lure. Only the most enticing of bait (live shrimps), the smallest possible hook, and the most transparent of leaders will induce the big ones to strike. Its accessibility, abundance, and good fighting qualities make this snapper a favorite in the very light tackle class.

The gray snapper is very good eating. Its small size makes it suitable for panfrying. It is a common commercial snapper in the southern United States and in the Caribbean.

LANE SNAPPER *Lutjanus synagris* This is one of the smallest and most common snappers. It is fairly abundant around southern Florida and throughout the tropical American Atlantic. The usual total length is less than 12 inches.

The lane snapper has 10 dorsal spines, 12 dorsal rays, and 8 anal rays. Pectoral rays 15–16, usually 16. Gillrakers 8–10 on lower limb of first arch, not counting rudiments. Rows of scales around caudal peduncle 25–27, usually 26. Cheek scales normally in 6 rows. Upper jaw reaching to or beyond vertical from anterior margin of orbit. Pectoral fin not reaching to vertical from origin of anal fin. Anal fin rounded, not angulate, posteriorly. General coloration rosy-red with longitudinal yellow stripes; paler below. Black spot on sides of body present. Pectoral and caudal fins reddish. Dorsal fin pale, margined with orange-yellow. Pelvic and anal fins tinged with orange-yellow. Eyes scarlet.

This snapper is distinguished from the others by the color pattern and the fewer dorsal rays. The mahogany snapper also has 12 dorsal rays, but fewer pectoral rays and cheek scales.

A bottom-feeding, shallow-water species, the lane snapper takes live or dead bait and, occasionally, artificial lures. It is accessible from shore, piers, or bridges and is one of the best eating snappers. Its small size makes it suitable for panfrying.

MAHOGANY SNAPPER *Lutjanus mahogoni* This rather uncommon snapper is occasionally taken around southern Florida. It occurs throughout the tropical American Atlantic. Not known to reach a large size, most of the specimens taken by anglers or seen in Caribbean markets measure less than 20 inches in total length. The Spanish name, *ojanco,* refers to the large eyes.

The mahogany snapper has 10 dorsal spines, 12 dorsal rays, and 8 anal rays. There are normally 15 pectoral rays. Gillrakers 8–10 on lower limb of first arch, not counting rudiments. Rows of scales around caudal peduncle 24–26, usually 25. Cheek scales in 5, rarely 6 rows. Upper jaw reaching beyond vertical from anterior margin of orbit. Pectoral fin not reaching to vertical from origin of anal fin. Anal fin rounded, not angulate, posteriorly. General coloration reddish-brown with bronze streaks; silvery below. Black spot on sides of body present. Caudal fin red. Dorsal fin pale, edged with red. Pectoral, pelvic, and anal fins scarlet. Eyes scarlet.

The large eyes and color pattern distinguish this species from the other snappers.

MUTTON SNAPPER *Lutjanus analis* This is one of the most common snappers. It occurs along the lower east and west coasts of Florida southward throughout the tropical American Atlantic. A medium-sized snapper, it may reach a weight of 25 pounds or more.

The mutton snapper is a brightly colored fish: olive-green dorsally, reddish on the sides, and paler below. The pectoral, pelvic, anal, and caudal fins are brick-red. A black spot is present on both sides of the body. The eyes are red.

When small, the mutton snapper is sometimes confused with the lane snapper, while the larger individuals may resemble the red snapper. However, the mutton snapper can be separated from these by the following characteristics: It has 10 dorsal spines, 14 dorsal rays, and 8 rays in the anal fin. The pectoral rays usually number 16. There are 7–9 gillrakers on the lower limb of the first arch, not including rudiments. There are generally 26 rows of scales around the caudal peduncle, and 7 rows of scales on the cheeks. The upper jaw does not reach to a vertical from the anterior margin of the orbit (large adults); it reaches to or somewhat beyond the orbit in the young. The pectoral fins do not reach to a vertical from the origin of the anal fin. The anal fin is angulate, and not rounded, posteriorly.

Although mutton snappers are most frequently caught in blue holes, around coral heads, in channels, and in creeks, at depths of 10–30 feet, they sometimes appear on bonefish flats where a variety of spinning and fly-rod lures are successful.

The mutton snapper is one of the best saltwater fishes to eat. The flesh is firm and white, and ideally suited to baking or broiling. Do not neglect the cheek and throat meats, which are considered gourmet items when taken from the larger fish.

RED SNAPPER *Lutjanus campechanus* The species occurs along the Middle Atlantic and Gulf coasts of the United States southward throughout the tropical American Atlantic. A medium-sized snapper, it may reach 35 pounds and over 30 inches in total length.

The red snapper has 10 dorsal spines, 14 dorsal rays, and 9 anal rays. Normally 17 pectoral rays. There are 8–10 gillrakers on lower limb of first arch, not counting rudiments. Rows of scales around caudal peduncle 25–27, usually 26. Cheek scales in 6, rarely 5, rows. Upper jaw reaching to or beyond vertical from anterior margin of orbit. Pectoral fin reaching to or beyond vertical from origin of anal fin, except in large specimens. Anal fin angulate, not rounded, posteriorly. General coloration rose-red, paler below. Fins red, the dorsal margined with orange. Black spot on sides of body present; faint to obsolete in large individuals. Eyes red.

This snapper is distinguished from the others by the color pattern, the longer pectoral fin, and the more numerous anal rays.

The red snapper usually occurs in schools, a few feet above hard bottom. This fish may frequent depths of about 100 fathoms, but it is usually found at 20–60 fathoms. Smaller individuals also occur in shallow water. It is usually taken on dead bait. A good fighter frequently caught by anglers on rod and reel, it is seldom caught on artificial lures.

This excellent eating fish is the most important commercial snapper in the United States and in many tropical American countries.

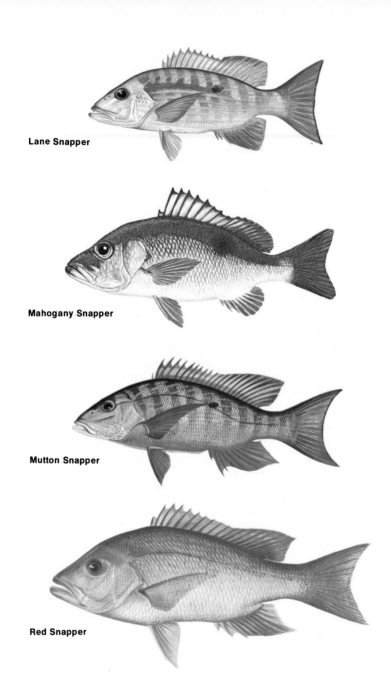

Lane Snapper

Mahogany Snapper

Mutton Snapper

Red Snapper

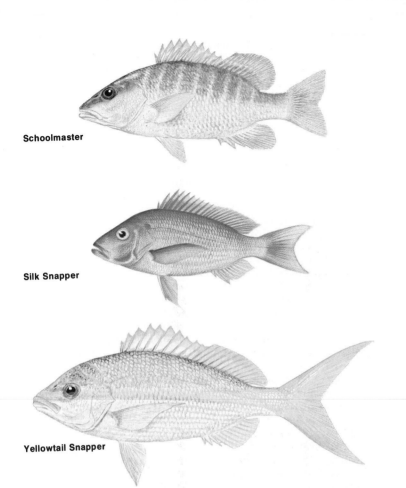

Schoolmaster

Silk Snapper

Yellowtail Snapper

SCHOOLMASTER *Lutjanus apodus* This is one of the smallest snappers. It is fairly common around southern Florida and throughout the tropical American Atlantic. It seldom reaches a weight of 5 pounds, and most of the individuals seen weigh less than 1 pound.

The schoolmaster snapper has 10 dorsal spines, 14 dorsal rays, and 8 anal rays. Pectoral rays 16–17, usually 17. Gillrakers 7–9 on lower limb of first arch, not counting rudiments. Rows of scales around caudal peduncle 21–22. Cheek scales in 7, rarely 6, rows. Upper jaw reaching to or somewhat beyond vertical from anterior margin of orbit. Pectoral fin not reaching to vertical from origin of anal fin. Anal fin rounded, not angulate, posteriorly. General coloration brassy-yellow, paler below; sides of body usually with vertical bars. Fins yellow or orange-yellow. No black spot on sides of body.

This species differs conspicuously from the other snappers in the color pattern. The schoolmaster occurs in shallow water along the shore. It is most frequently found among rocks and takes live or dead bait and artificial lures.

SILK SNAPPER *Lutjanus vivanus* This snapper occurs around southern Florida and throughout the tropical American Atlantic. It does not reach a large size, and most of the specimens captured weigh less than 10 pounds.

The silk snapper has 10 dorsal spines, 14 dorsal rays, and 8 anal rays. Pectoral rays normally 17. Gillrakers 11-12 on lower limb of first arch, not counting rudiments. Rows of scales around caudal peduncle 27-29. Cheek scales in 7, rarely 6, rows. Upper jaw reaching to or beyond vertical from anterior margin of orbit. Pectoral fin not reaching to vertical from origin of anal fin. Anal fin angulate, not rounded, posteriorly. General coloration rose-red, paler below. Dorsal, pelvic, and anal fins pale rose; dorsal fin edged with yellow. Black spot on sides of body present, faint to obsolete in large individuals. Eyes bright yellow.

The color pattern, especially the bright yellow eyes and the black-margined caudal fin, distinguishes this snapper from the others.

A deepwater species, it occurs on the bottom and is most abundant at depths of 60-120 fathoms. Small individuals may occur in shallower water (20-60 fathoms). It is usually taken on live bait.

YELLOWTAIL SNAPPER *Ocyurus chrysurus* A rather small, fairly common snapper occurring around southern Florida and throughout the tropical American Atlantic, it seldom reaches a weight of over 5-6 pounds, and most of the individuals seen weigh less than 2 pounds.

The yellowtail snapper is distinguished by its 10 dorsal spines, 13 dorsal rays, and 9 anal rays. Pectoral rays normally 16. Gillrakers 19-21 on lower limb of first arch, not counting rudiments. Rows of scales around caudal peduncle 25-26. Cheek scales in 5-6 rows. Upper jaw reaching to or somewhat beyond vertical from anterior margin of orbit. Pectoral fin not reaching beyond vertical from origin of anal fin. Anal fin broadly rounded, not angulate, posteriorly. General coloration pale olivaceous with yellow spots above, paler and tinged with violet below. A yellow stripe from snout to caudal fin, which is deep yellow. Dorsal, pectoral, and anal fins yellow.

This snapper usually occurs offshore in schools and seems to feed better at night. Cut bait (pilchard) is a favorite bait for this species. A good catch can be obtained by chumming. The yellowtail snapper fights well but has a small mouth; the hook size must be selected accordingly. It is for this reason that this species is not caught more frequently by anglers trying for snappers in offshore grounds.

BIGEYE FAMILY Piacanthidae

The bigeyes superficially resemble some small snappers and of the 5 known species around our shores, the glasseye misleadingly bears the common name glasseye snapper (*American Fisheries Society,* 1970). These priacanthids, the bulleye (*Cookeolus boops*), bigeye (*Priacanthus arenatus*), short bigeye (*Pristigenys alta*), one Pacific species—the popeye catalufa (*Pristigenys serrula*)—and the glasseye snapper (*Priacanthus cruentatus*) are similar in appearance; they have large eyes, an oblique mouth, and small rough scales. Found over reefs, usually in deepwater, they are of no angling importance. Only the glasseye snapper, which occurs on shallow reefs, enters the angler's catch.

GLASSEYE SNAPPER *Priacanthus cruentatus* This wide-ranging species is believed to occur in the eastern and western Pacific Ocean as well as the Atlantic. In the western Atlantic, it ranges from New Jersey south to Rio de Janeiro and in the Gulf of Mexico. Its close relative in the western Atlantic, *P. arenatus*, has a similar range.

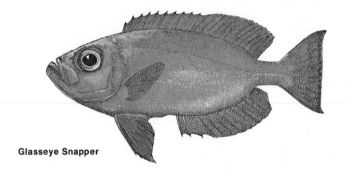

Glasseye Snapper

An adult *P. cruentatus* can be distinguished from *P. arenatus* by its truncate instead of forked caudal fin; by its 13 soft dorsal and 14 soft anal fin rays, instead of the usual 14 and 15, respectively, of *P. arenatus;* and by its lower number (54–62 versus 61–72) of lateral line scales. The adult glasseye snapper is bright red. Pelagic postlarvae are silver with deep blue markings. Both species have large, lustrous eyes, which may be 1 inch in diameter in a specimen 8 inches long. Like those of the short bigeye, the larvae of this species are pelagic, and the carnivorous adults are bottom living, usually over rocks.

Although they are relatively common over shallow reefs, glasseye snappers usually enter the sport fishery as a deepwater (about 50–100 fathoms) catch. Owing to their small size, they are not widely sought.

GRUNT FAMILY   Pomadasyidae

This is a large family of shallow-water, tropical bottomfishes. Many of the species, especially those found in a coral reef habitat, are very colorful. The common name of the family is derived from the sounds produced by individuals when they are captured. The grinding of the pharyngeal teeth produces an audible noise, which is amplified by the air bladder.

BLUESTRIPED GRUNT *Haemulon sciurus*   This grunt is rather common in southern Florida and throughout the rest of its range, which extends southward throughout the West Indies and along the coast of Central and South America to Brazil. The average total length of a mature adult is about 10 inches, but larger individuals are sometimes taken. This grunt is distinguished from all others by the color pattern, which consists of continuous blue horizontal stripes over a yellow or brassy-yellow body color. The inside of its mouth is blood-red or carmine in color. The bluestriped grunt has 12 dorsal spines; 16–17 dorsal rays, usually 16; 9 anal rays; 16–17 pectoral rays, usually 16. Pored lateral line scales vary from 48 to 51, gillrakers from 27 to 31, usually 29. Its pectoral fins are naked.

The bluestriped grunt is a bottom feeder. Abundant in relatively shallow water close to the shore, it forms schools along reefs in deeper water.

This species is easy to catch on natural bait such as cut mullet, cut pilchard, or dead shrimp. Bluestriped grunts will also strike flies, jigs, and small plugs. This grunt is excellent eating. A panfish highly appreciated in the Florida Keys, it is a commercial fish of some importance in Florida, the Bahamas, and the West Indies.

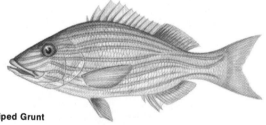

Bluestriped Grunt

CAESAR GRUNT *Haemulon carbonarium*   This grunt occurs in the Florida Keys and the Bahamas southward throughout the West Indies, and along the coast of Central and South America to Brazil. The average total length of mature adults is about 10 inches, but larger individuals are sometimes taken. This species resembles the Spanish

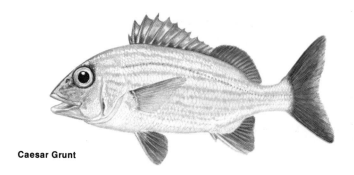

Caesar Grunt

grunt, from which it is distinguished by the number of pectoral rays, anal rays, lateral line scales, and gillrakers. The sides of the body have longitudinal bronze to bright yellow stripes. The mouth is light red. The Caesar grunt has 12 dorsal spines; 15–16 dorsal rays, usually 15; 8 anal rays; and 16–17 pectoral rays, usually 17. Pored lateral line scales vary from 49 to 50; gillrakers from 23 to 250. Its pectoral fins are naked.

The Caesar grunt is a bottom feeder and prefers clearwater. It enters tidal creeks and boat basins along the Florida keys. It fights well on very light tackle. This grunt is taken on dead shrimp, cut mullet, and cut pilchard.

COTTONWICK *Haemulon melanurum* This grunt occurs in the Florida Keys and the Bahamas southward throughout the Caribbean area to Brazil. Mature adults average about 10 inches in total length, but larger individuals are sometimes taken. It is distinguished from all others by the color pattern. The back, the upper half of the caudal peduncle and the caudal fin are black. The inside of the mouth is pale red. The cottonwick has 12 dorsal spines; 15–17 dorsal rays, usually 16; 8 anal rays; and 16–18 pectoral rays, usually 17. Pored lateral line scales vary from 49 to 51; gillrakers from 21 to 23. Its pectoral fins are naked.

Cottonwick

The cottonwick prefers clearwater and avoids murky inshore waters in Florida, where it is usually found about the outer reefs. In the Bahamas, it may be found in the usually clear inshore waters.

This species is good sport on very light tackle. Like other grunts, the cottonwick is taken on cut bait such as mullet, pilchard, and shrimp. This grunt is good eating. A panfish not taken as frequently as other species of grunts.

FRENCH GRUNT *Haemulon flavolineatum* This is one of the most abundant grunts in southern Florida. It also occurs in the Bahamas, West Indies, and along the coast of Central and South America to Brazil. The average total length of mature adults is about 8 inches. The French grunt is distinguished from others by the color pattern. The sides of the body have dark lines and yellow stripes. The mouth is red. The French grunt has 12 dorsal spines. It has 14–15 dorsal rays, 8 anal rays, and 16–17 pectoral rays, but usually 16. Pored lateral line scales vary from 47 to 50, usually 48–49. Gillrakers 22 to 24, usually 23. Pectoral fins are naked.

The French grunt is a bottom feeder occurring in shallow water close to shore and about reefs in deeper water, where it is more abundant. It takes natural bait, such as cut pilchard, cut mullet, and dead shrimp. It is good sport on the lightest of tackle. It is a tasty panfish, but usually too small to be of commercial value.

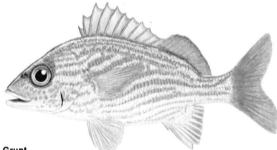

French Grunt

PORKFISH *Anisotremus virginicus* The porkfish is a member of the grunt family. Its genus, *Anisotremus*, is distinctive from other American grunts mainly in the deeper body, blunt snout, and thick lips. *Anisotremus* is well represented in eastern Pacific waters, but there are only 3 species in the western Atlantic, of which only the porkfish and the black margate (*A. surinamensis*) occur in the West Indies and Florida.

The porkfish is easily distinguished by its striking color. The head is yellowish and silvery with a black bar running from the forehead

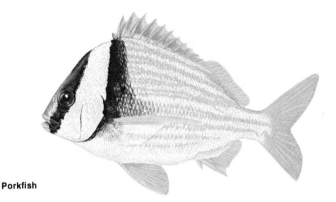

Porkfish

through the eye to the corner of the mouth. Anteriorly on the body is another black bar running vertically from the origin of the dorsal fin to the axil of the pectoral fin. The body is longitudinally striped with light blue and yellow, and the fins are yellow. The young are very differently colored. A young porkfish has a yellow head and a thin horizontal black stripe running posteriorly from the eye to the caudal peduncle, followed by a large round black spot at the base of the tail; there is a second black stripe on the upper part of the body.

The porkfish does not appear to range north of Florida (it has been introduced into Bermuda), but occurs southward to Brazil. It is not a common species in the West Indies, but is often encountered in large schools in Florida.

Adults feed on a great variety of small invertebrate animals, such as crabs, shrimps, mantis shrimps, mollusks (gastropods, pelecypods, and chitons), isopods, amphipods, and brittle stars.

Although not a large species (it attains about 14 inches), the porkfish is an excellent foodfish.

SAILOR'S CHOICE *Haemulon parrai* This grunt is less common than others and occurs in southern Florida, the Bahamas, the West Indies, and along the coast of Central and South America to Brazil. The average total length of mature individuals is about 10 inches. Larger specimens are sometimes taken. This grunt is distinguished from all the others by the color pattern and the scaled pectoral fins. The sides of the body have dark stripes running along the scale rows. The inside of the mouth is red. The sailor's choice has 12 dorsal spines; 16–18 dorsal rays, usually 17–18; 8 anal rays; and 17 pectoral rays. There are 51–52 pored lateral line scales, but usually 52.

This species occurs on or near the bottom in shallow water close to shore and about reefs in deeper water. It is readily taken on dead shrimp, cut mullet, or cut pilchard.

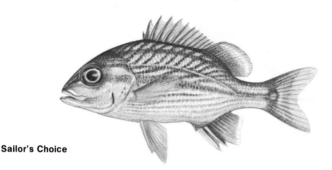

Sailor's Choice

SMALLMOUTH GRUNT *Haemulon chrysargyreum* This small grunt occurs in extreme southern Florida including the keys, southward through the West Indies to Brazil. Mature adults run $7-8^1/_2$ inches in total length. This grunt is distinguished from the others by the color pattern combined with the number of gillrakers. The sides of the body have yellow and bluish-gray stripes. The inside of the mouth is red. The smallmouth grunt has 12 dorsal spines; 13 dorsal rays; 9-10 anal rays, usually 9; and 15-17 pectoral rays, usually 16. Pored lateral line scales number 49-51, usually 50. There are 30-33 gillrakers. The pectoral fins are not scaled.

This species forms large schools about the reefs off Florida. It is also found in shallow water along the shore. It feeds on or near the bottom. It is too small to be considered a gamefish, but is easy to catch with cut bait. The smallmouth grunt is good eating, but it is often too small to be worth cleaning and cooking.

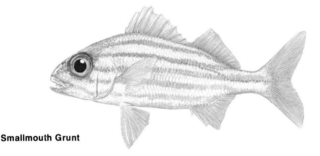

Smallmouth Grunt

SPANISH GRUNT *Haemulon macrostomum* This medium-sized grunt occurs in the Florida Keys and southward throughout the West Indies to Brazil. Mature adults average about 1 foot in total length, and larger individuals are frequently taken. The Spanish grunt is dis-

212

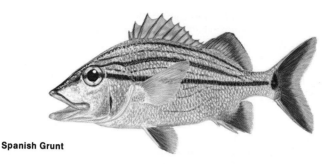

Spanish Grunt

tinguished by the upper sides of the body having longitudinal black stripes converging with a median straight black stripe that extends from eyes to tail. The inside of its mouth is red. This species resembles the Caesar grunt, from which it is distinguished by the number of pectoral rays, anal rays, lateral line scales, and gillrakers. The Spanish grunt has 12 dorsal spines, 15–17 dorsal rays, usually 16; 9 anal rays; 18 pectoral rays, rarely 17. It has 50–52 pored lateral line scales, usually 51; and 26–28 gillrakers. The pectoral fins are unscaled.

The Spanish grunt is a bottom feeder and prefers clearwater about coral reefs. It is caught on cut bait, such as mullet, pilchard, or dead shrimp.

TOMTATE *Haemulon aurolineatum* This is the most widely ranging species of grunt. It is found from Cape Cod to Brazil, including the Bahamas and the West Indies. A mature adult of this rather small species runs 6–8¹/₂ inches in total length. It rarely reaches a much larger size. This grunt is distinguished from the others by the color pattern, which consists of a yellow or brown stripe from the opercle to a black blotch on the caudal fin base. The tomtate has 13 dorsal spines; 14–15 dorsal rays, usually 15; 9 anal rays; and 17–18 pectoral rays, usually 17. Pored lateral line scales number 50–52; gillrakers 24–28. Its pectoral fins are naked.

Tomtate

213

With the exception of the white grunt, this species seems to be more tolerant of colder (extratropical) water than the others. The tomtate is a bottom feeder, abundant in shallow water from the shore to the outer reefs.

This species is too small to be considered a gamefish. It is easy to catch with cut bait. The tomtate is good eating but usually too small to be worth cleaning and cooking.

WHITE MARGATE *Haemulon album*   This is the largest of the grunts. Mature adults average 2 feet in total length, and larger individuals are not uncommon. In addition to the Florida Keys and the Bahamas, the range of this species extends southward throughout the West Indies to Brazil. The margate is distinguished from other grunts by the number of pectoral rays, anal rays, and gillrakers, in addition to its larger size. It is plain-colored or with dark brown stripes. The margate has 12 dorsal spines; 16–17 dorsal rays, rarely 17; 7–8 anal rays, usually 8; and 18–19 pectoral rays. Pored lateral line scales number 49–52. Its pectoral fins are naked.

This grunt is apparently not common in Florida.

White Margate

JACK FAMILY   Carangidae

This large family of marine fishes includes the jacks, scads, pompanos, amberjacks, threadfins, lookdowns, and leatherjackets. This diverse family is represented in all tropical and subtropical marine waters of the world; some species occur in colder, temperate waters. Most of the members of this family are strong, fast swimmers and are excellent gamefishes, especially with light tackle.

AFRICAN POMPANO *Alectis crinitus*   Also called Atlantic threadfin (when young) and Cuban jack, this Atlantic species is not a true pompano.

Its body is deep and thin, but becomes less deep in large specimens. The head profile, in fish larger than about 14 inches long, is blunt and nearly vertical, with the large eyes located anteriorly in the profile.

The first 4–6 softrays of the dorsal fin are elongated in small specimens; the first 2 rays may be 4 times as long as the fish; these rays become shorter with growth and may be shorter than the pectoral fins in very large specimens.

The 7 spines in the first dorsal fin are of nearly equal length in small specimens but are completely covered by skin and molded into the body profile in a fish with a body length of about 4–5 inches. The second dorsal fin has 1 short spine and 18–19 softrays. The 2 separated

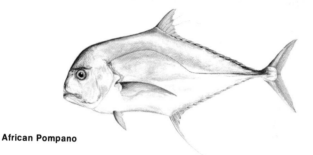

African Pompano

spines of the anal fin disappear in fish of about 4–8 inches long; the remainder of the anal fin consists of 1 spine and 15–16 softrays. The first gill arch has 4–5 gillrakers on the upper limb and 14–16 gillrakers on the lower limb. There are about 24–38 relatively weak scutes in the straight lateral line. Scales on the body are minute, embedded in the skin, and difficult to see. Young specimens have 5–6 bars on the body. Larger specimens are light bluish-green on the back and silvery over most of the remainder of the body.

The African pompano occurs on both sides of the Atlantic Ocean. In the western Atlantic it is recorded from Santos, Brazil, to Massachusetts and the West Indies.

This species probably grows to a length of more than 3 feet; specimens weighing 25–35 pounds have frequently been caught off Florida.

The African pompano is a fairly strong fighting gamefish, usually taken by trolling in tropical waters.

ALMACO JACK *Seriola rivoliana* This Atlantic species has also been called falcate amberjack and, much less appropriately, bonito, and has previously been recorded by the scientific name *S. falcata*.

The nuchal band of the Almaco jack extends from the eyes to the origin of the first dorsal fin. The 5 bars on the body of a young fish are split and irregular and disappear at lengths larger than 8 inches. The body is relatively deep, but the depth decreases proportionally with growth. The greatest body depth goes into the standard length about

215

2.7–2.85 times in specimens up to 16 inches in standard length, about 2.85–3.1 times in specimens 16–24 inches, and about 3.1–3.3 times in larger specimens (standard length is measured from the tip of the snout to the end of the bony plate of the tail). The dorsal fin lobe is relatively long; its length goes about 4.6 times into the standard length, but there is considerable variation in the lobe length. The total number of gillrakers on both limbs of the first arch is relatively high, and this number decreases with growth of the fish; there are about 24–28 gillrakers in fish up to 16 inches in standard length, about 21–25 in fish larger than this size, and sometimes as few as 18 gillrakers in very large individuals.

The first dorsal fin has 7 spines (rarely 8). The second dorsal fin has 1 spine and 27–33 softrays (usually 28–32). The anal fin has 2 detached spines (which may be covered by skin at large sizes), followed by 1 spine and 19–22 softrays. There appear to be several color variations in the adults. The nuchal band is usually olivaceous with golden reflections, but the basic body color may be predominantly dusky or brownish, or more steely-blue, or olivaceous. Frequently the sides also have a lavender tint.

This species occurs on both sides of the Atlantic and in the Mediterranean. In the western Atlantic it extends from Buenos Aires, Argentina, to Cape Hatteras and northward to New Jersey, in the West Indies, and at Bermuda. Fish up to about 32 inches in length and 14 pounds have been recorded.

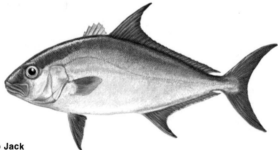

Almaco Jack

ATLANTIC BLUNTNOSE JACK *Hemicaranx amblyrhynchus*
This species occurs only in the western Atlantic. A similar form in the eastern Atlantic off West Africa is considered to be a distinct species, *H. bicolor*.

The second dorsal fin of the Atlantic bluntnose jack has 1 spine and 27–29 softrays. The anal fin has 2 detached spines followed by 1 spine and 22–25 softrays. The first gill arch has 8–10 gillrakers on the upper limb and 19–23 gillrakers on the lower limb. The arch or curved part of the lateral line is relatively short; the straight lateral line is

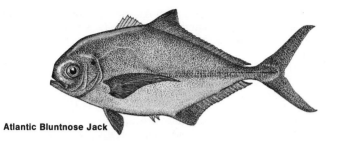

Atlantic Bluntnose Jack

about $2^1/_2$ times as long as the curved lateral line. The straight lateral line has about 45–55 pointed scutes.

The body is moderately deep and thin, the head short and rounded in anterior profile, and the mouth small. The lobes of the dorsal and anal fin are not elongated. At about $1^1/_2$–6 inches in length there are 4 bars on the body and 1 on the nape. Above 6 inches in length the body is usually golden-yellow with a small dark opercular spot.

This species ranges from Santos, Brazil, northward at least to North Carolina. The largest known specimen is 14 inches long.

ATLANTIC BUMPER *Chloroscombrus chrysurus* This Atlantic species is very closely related to the Pacific bumper, *C. orqueta*.

The ventral body contour is much more curved and deeper than the dorsal contour, and the body is very thin. The scutes in the straight lateral line are very weakly developed, only about 7–12 scutes developed out of a total of 61–68 scales in the straight lateral line. The second dorsal fin has 1 spine and 26–28 softrays. The anal fin has 2 detached spines followed by a spine and 25–27 softrays. The first gill arch has 9–11 gillrakers on the upper limb and 31–35 gillrakers on the lower limb. There is a black spot on the upper part of the base of the caudal fin; the body is dark above, light silvery or golden below; a faint black opercular spot is usually present.

In the western Atlantic this species ranges from Massachusetts to Uruguay. It occurs at Bermuda and in the eastern Atlantic from at

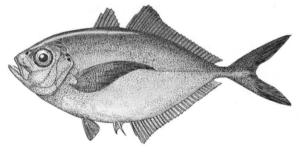

Atlantic Bumper

least Senegal to Angola. In the western Atlantic it reaches a length of 10 inches. In the eastern Atlantic, specimens 12 inches long have been recorded, but the species is reported to grow much larger.

ATLANTIC HORSE-EYE JACK *Caranx latus* Also called goggle-eye jack, this western Atlantic jack crevalle is closely related to the Pacific horse-eye jack, *C. marginatus*, of the eastern Pacific. A species named *C. sexfasciatus*, which ranges in the Indo-Pacific from Hawaii to the eastern coast of South Africa, is very similar to these two, and they constitute a nearly circumtropical species complex.

The chest in front of the pelvic fins of the Atlantic horse-eye jack is completely covered with scales. The second dorsal fin has 1 spine and 19–22 softrays; the anal fin has 2 detached spines followed by 1 spine and 16–18 softrays. Gillrakers on the first arch number 6–7 on the upper limb and 16–18 on the lower limb.

The Atlantic horse-eye jack ranges from Rio de Janeiro, Brazil, to the Manasquan River, New Jersey, throughout the West Indies, and at Bermuda. It is generally dark blue to blue-gray above and silvery-

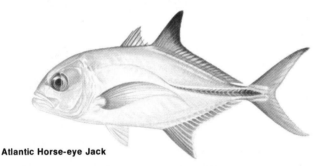

Atlantic Horse-eye Jack

white or sometimes golden on the sides and below, and the tip of the dorsal fin lobe is black in smaller specimens. The caudal fin is yellow. A small black spot may be present on the upper edge of the operculum. Schools of this fish have been seen to change their coloration, as from dark to light, to blend with their immediate surroundings.

The horse-eye is a very strong gamefish especially on light tackle. These jacks occur in blue holes and in the channels adjacent to flats, where they travel in schools. Horse-eyes are taken on a great variety of lures including plugs, jigs, spoons, and flies as well as live bait. They are very common in the Florida Keys and the Bahamas, where fish of 2–6 pounds are average. Maximum size is not really known owing to the horse-eye's similarity to the crevalle and frequent misidentification. Horse-eyes have been authenticated to 12 pounds in weight, however, and it is probable that the fish exceeds that size.

218

ATLANTIC PERMIT *Trachinotus falcatus*   This is also called great pompano and, when young, round pompano. The Pacific permit, *T. kennedyi*, is a very closely related species.

The first dorsal fin of the Atlantic permit has 6 spines; the second dorsal fin has 1 spine and 17–21 softrays; the anal fin has 2 short, detached spines followed by 1 spine and 16–19 softrays. There are no black bars or spots on the sides.

Body and fin proportions change appreciably with growth and are very variable. The body is almost half as deep as the total length in specimens less than 6 inches long; the body depth is progressively less in larger specimens. The dorsal and anal fin lobes are more elongated in smaller specimens; the dorsal fin lobe extends back to the caudal peduncle in specimens about 15 inches long and becomes

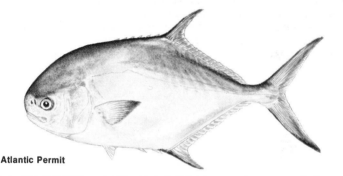

Atlantic Permit

progressively shorter in larger specimens. Coloration is variable. The small, deep-bodied young may be almost entirely black or largely silvery or black and silvery with a dark red tinge; and they can alternate these colors rapidly. Larger fish are usually bluish or grayish on the back, with the remainder of the body silvery, the dorsal fin bluish or black along its anterior margin and lobe, the anterior margin and lobe of the anal fin and the pelvic fins frequently orange, and the caudal fin dusky. Very large permits may have the body almost entirely silvery, with a greenish-blue tinge, and all the fins dark or dusky.

The Atlantic permit ranges from Brazil to Massachusetts, in the West Indies, and presumably at Bermuda. It is supposed to be most abundant and to reach its maximum size off southern Florida. It has been reported to occur in the eastern Atlantic. The maximum size is in excess of 50 pounds, although rod-and-reel catches are ordinarily in the 20- to 30-pound class.

BANDED RUDDERFISH *Seriola zonata*   Also called slender amberjack, this western Atlantic species has previously been confused with *S. lalandi,* a distinct species in the South Atlantic Ocean.

Banded Rudderfish

Fish less than about 11 inches long have a dark nuchal band extending from the eyes to the origin of the first dorsal fin and 6 prominent bars on the body. The anal fin base (excluding the 2 detached spines) is relatively short; the second dorsal fin base is about twice as long as the anal fin base (about $1^1/_2$–$1^2/_3$ times as long as the anal fin base in other Atlantic amberjacks).

The banded rudderfish ranges from Santos, Brazil, to Nova Scotia. Its reported occurrence at Bermuda has been questioned. A specimen slightly less than 25 inches long is the maximum size that has been recorded, and one unsubstantiated account stated that the maximum length was about 3 feet.

This is apparently an inshore species, but the life history has not been investigated. The very young are often found under jellyfish and drifting weeds, and slightly older fish have habits similar to those of the pilotfish in following sharks and other large fish.

This species is sometimes caught by sport fishermen, and occasionally large numbers are taken in traps.

BAR JACK *Caranx ruber*   Also called *cibi mancho* or skipjack, this species is endemic to the western Atlantic.

The gillrakers on the first gill arch of the bar jack number 31–35 on the lower limb (more than in any other jack crevalle in the western Atlantic) and 10–14 on the upper limb. The second dorsal fin has 1 spine and 26–30 softrays. The anal fin has 2 detached spines followed by 1 spine and 23–26 softrays. Specimens larger than about 4 inches in length have a dark band over most of the lower lobe of the caudal fin, contrasting with the relatively unpigmented upper lobe.

The body is moderately deep. The dorsal and anal fin lobes are only slightly produced. There are about 23–29 pointed scutes in the straight lateral line. The straight lateral line is only very slightly longer than the curved part. The body is blue-gray above and lighter or whitish below. In live or fresh fish, a dark blue or black stripe continues forward from the band on the lower caudal lobe along the back to the nape. The color is changeable, depending upon the background. The young up to about 5 inches in length have 6 (rarely 5 or 7) dark bars on the body plus 1 at the nape.

Bar Jack

The bar jack is known to range along the continent from Caledonia Bay, Panama, to Cape Hatteras, North Carolina. It has been taken in the West Indies from as far south as Union Island and northward to the northern Bahamas. The young have been taken well offshore in the Gulf Stream east of New Jersey, and the adults are common at Bermuda. The maximum size and weight attained are not known. Bar jacks of 12–15 pounds have been reported in the Bahamas and Florida.

The bar jack is an active gamefish and will strike a variety of natural baits and artificial lures, including plugs, jigs, streamers, and popping bugs. Unlike most other jacks, it occasionally jumps when hooked. Bar jacks are usually found in large schools in channels, blue holes, and deep flats. This species has firm white flesh and is a highly regarded food in the Bahamas and the Caribbean. It is excellent when smoked.

BIGEYE SCAD *Selar crumenophthalmus* The tropical, worldwide species is also known as the goggle-eye scad, goggle-eye jack, and goggler.

The shoulder girdle of the bigeye scad has 2 papillae on the vertical limb with a furrow, or groove, below the lower. There are no detached finlets at the back of the dorsal and anal fins and no scutes in the curved lateral line. The eyes and the thick adipose eyelids are noticeably large.

The second dorsal fin has 1 spine and 24–26 softrays. The anal fin has 2 detached spines followed by a spine and 21–23 softrays. The first gill arch has 9–12 gillrakers on the upper limb and 27–30 on the lower limb. The anterior curved part of the lateral line has a very

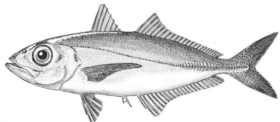
Bigeye Scad

221

shallow arch; there are 30–41 pointed scutes in the straight lateral line. The body and head are silvery or golden, almost uniformly colored, with the upper parts usually darker. A faint elongated opercular spot is usually present.

The bigeye scad occurs in tropical and subtropical waters around the world. In the western Atlantic it is known from Rio de Janeiro, Brazil, to Nova Scotia, in the West Indies, and at Bermuda. In the eastern Pacific it is known from Cabo Blanco, Peru, to Cape San Lucas and Muertos Bay, Baja California, and at the Galápagos Islands. This species has been reported to grow to 2 feet in length in tropical waters.

This species is rarely fished for, but it is an excellent live bait for other fishes.

BLACK JACK *Caranx lugubris* Also called brown jack and *caranx le garbage,* this is primarily an insular species of almost worldwide occurrence in tropical waters.

The body and head of the black jack are very dark brown or black, and the fins and the scutes in the straight lateral line are black. The second dorsal fin has 1 spine and 20–23 softrays; anal fin has 2 detached spines followed by 1 spine and 17–20 softrays. Gillrakers on the first gill arch are 6–9 on the upper limb and 19–22 on the lower limb.

The head and body are deep and moderately compressed. The head is blunt, and the profile is rounded on top with a slight concavity in front of and slightly above the eyes. The dorsal and anal fin lobes are elongated, and the dorsal fin lobe is usually longer than the head, although these lobes are proportionally shorter on very large specimens. A few of the gillrakers on the anterior portions of the upper and lower limbs become rudimentary with growth of the fish. There are about 24–33 pointed scutes in the straight lateral line. The body and head are colored, almost uniformly, dark brown or black, and the fins and the scutes in the straight lateral line are black. The pigmentation of young specimens is unknown.

The black jack has been reported from many tropical waters of the world, principally from around offshore or isolated islands. In the western Atlantic, this species has been recorded from Bermuda, the Bahamas, Cuba, Puerto Rico, Trinidad, well offshore in the Gulf of Mexico, and from Santos, Brazil. All records of its occurrence in inshore continental waters of the United States that have been possible to trace proved to have been some other species. In the eastern Pacific, it has been taken at the Galápagos, Clipperton, and Revilla Gigedo Islands, and at Los Frailes in southern Baja California. Maximum reported sizes are about 39 inches in total length and $15^1/_2$ pounds (length and weight from different fish). One report from Hawaii alleged that this species grew to be 3–4 feet in length.

222

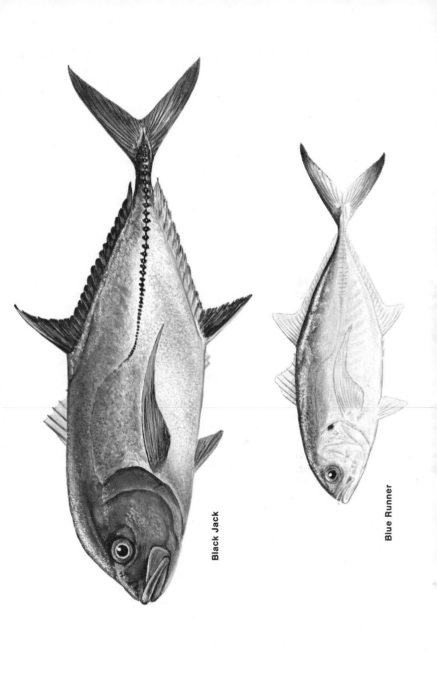

Black Jack

Blue Runner

BLUE RUNNER *Caranx crysos*   Also called hard-tailed jack, this is one of the more common species of jack crevalles in the western Atlantic. A very similar species, the green jack (*C. caballus*) occurs in the eastern Pacific.

The second dorsal fin of the blue runner has 1 spine and 22–25 soft-rays; the anal fin has 2 detached spines followed by a single spine and 19–21 softrays. Gillrakers on the first arch are 10–14 on the upper limb and 23–28 on the lower limb. Pointed scutes in the straight lateral line number about 46–56, and the straight lateral line is about twice as long as the curved portion.

The body shape is more slender in profile and more rounded in cross section than in most other jack crevalles. The dorsal and anal fin lobes are only moderately produced, and the spines of the first dorsal fin are shorter than the length of the dorsal fin lobe. The chest is completely scaled. The coloration is dark black to bluish-green to olive-green on the back, and dark gray to golden to silvery on the belly, with a black opercular spot; the fins are colorless to blackish.

The blue runner ranges from Brazil to Herring Cove, Nova Scotia, in the West Indies, and at Bermuda. The average size is about 1 foot long or less, the maximum recorded length is 28 inches, and the maximum weight recorded is 4 pounds; the fish is believed occasionally to attain 6 pounds.

CALIFORNIA YELLOWTAIL *Seriola dorsalis*   This is a very well known amberjack from the Pacific coast of the United States and northern Mexico, where it is usually known simply as yellowtail—by which undistinguished common name it can be confused with many other kinds of fishes bearing the same name.

The first dorsal fin of the California yellowtail usually has 6–7 short spines, although only as few as 3 spines may be visible in some large fish. The second dorsal fin has 1 spine and 31–37 softrays. The anal fin has 2 detached spines followed by 1 spine and 19–23 softrays. The first gill arch has 4–9 gillrakers on the upper limb and 14–22 on the lower limb, with the anterior gillrakers becoming rudimentary with growth of the fish. A dark or brassy stripe extends horizontally through the eye to the tail in a fish of about 10 inches and longer.

The body is elongate and moderately compressed, tapering to a rather sharp snout. When caught, the yellowtail is bright metallic-blue to green above the stripe and silvery below. The fins are a dusky greenish-yellow except for the bright yellow caudal fin. The young, up to about 7 inches long, have about 9–10 bars on the body, with many of the bars having a median lighter area.

The yellowtail has been taken from Mazatlán, Mexico, into the Gulf of California at Los Angeles Bay on eastern Baja California, and northward to the coast of southern Washington. It is usually common, however, only from Los Angeles County to the tip of Baja California. Yellowtails normally move from central Baja California into southern

California during early spring and south again during late summer and fall. Fish 3–8 years old appear to school with others of similar size and to migrate greater distances than older fish, which seem to be more sedentary and solitary.

The yellowtail is a strong, fast swimmer and provides a very popular sport fishery. This is largely concentrated between Los Angeles and Ensañada and at the Channel Islands, with the Coronado Islands being the most productive. Most fishing is done by casting with live sardines or anchovies for bait. Cast and trolled artificial lures are also used. Most of the fish caught by sport fishermen are eaten fresh or frozen; some are smoked or canned.

The two largest recorded fish were just under 4 feet 10 inches in total length. The larger weighed 80 pounds; the smaller, 63 pounds.

CREVALLE *Caranx hippos* Also called common jack, jack crevalle, cavally, cavalla, horse crevalle, and toro, this species is thought to occur almost around the world in tropical and subtropical waters.

The area between the throat and the pelvic fins of the crevalle has a small circular patch of scales (difficult to see in some very small or very large fish) in a scaleless area that extends up the sides toward the pectoral fins (the only jack crevalle in the western Atlantic and eastern Pacific having this character). The second dorsal fin has 1 spine and 18–21 softrays; the anal fin has 2 detached spines followed by a single spine and 16–17 softrays. The first gill arch has 6–9 gillrakers on the upper limb and 16–19 gillrakers on the lower limb. There is a prominent black opercular spot and a rounded spot on each of the lower rays of the pectoral fins.

The crevalle develops a high, blunt head, with relatively small eyes located near the anterodorsal profile. The posterior 1–4 spines of the first dorsal fin become separated and covered by skin in specimens over 18 inches long. The dorsal fin and anal fin lobes are moderately elongated. The straight part of the lateral line is about $1–1^1/_2$ times as long as the curved part. There are about 26–35 scutes in the straight lateral line in western Atlantic specimens and up to 42 scutes in eastern Pacific specimens. The gillrakers on the anterior ends of the upper and lower limbs become very short or rudimentary with growth (and difficult to distinguish). The crevalle is bluish-black or metallic-green above, silvery and sometimes yellowish below; the dorsal fin is dark and the anal fin may be yellowish. The young, smaller than about 7 inches long, have 5 (rarely 4–6) broad bars on the sides plus 1 on the head.

In the western Atlantic the crevalle has been taken from off Uruguay to Musquodoboit Harbor, Nova Scotia; it is very rare in the West Indies, and reports of its occurrence at Bermuda need to be documented. In the eastern Pacific it ranges from Cape Aguja, Peru, into the northern Gulf of California and up to the outer coast of Baja California at least to San Hipolito Bay.

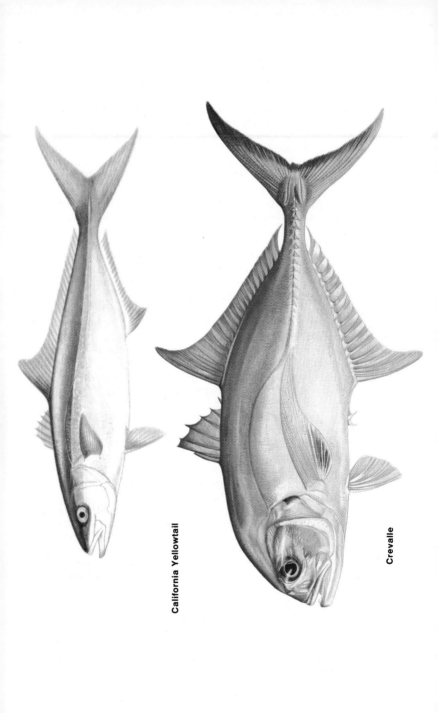

California Yellowtail

Crevalle

In common with the permits, large crevalle always seem to have an extra ounce of energy in reserve. Their tactics are dogged and unrelenting. It is not unusual to play a 20-pounder for an hour or more on light tackle. The maximum size of the crevalle is not known. Specimens of 35–45 pounds are caught every season in Florida waters, and are not uncommon along the state's southeast coast and down through the Keys. One of the largest crevalle taken in recent years was a 55-pound fish from Lake Worth, Florida.

FLORIDA POMPANO *Trachinotus carolinus* This eastern Atlantic species is our most valuable jack. Epicures have proclaimed this to be a foodfish without peer from either fresh- or saltwater. The flesh is firm and rich. The common name was adopted because Florida is the chief commercial source of pompano in the United States.

The first dorsal fin of the common pompano has 5–6 short spines. The second dorsal fin has 1 spine and 22–27 softrays (usually 23–26). The anal fin has 2 spines (that become detached with growth) followed by 1 spine and 20–23 softrays (usually 21–22). There are no dark bars on the sides.

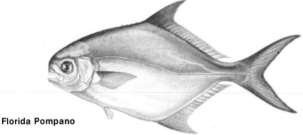

Florida Pompano

The body is relatively shallow, and the body depth decreases proportionally with growth. The dorsal and anal fin lobes are relatively short at all body sizes, but the proportional length changes with the growth of the fish; in fish about 12 inches long and larger, the length of the dorsal fin lobe is about equal to or less than the length of the head. The back and upper sides are grayish-silvery-blue or bluish-green, the sides silvery, and the ventral surfaces flecked with yellow. The dorsal fin is dusky or bluish, the anal fin yellowish or light orange, and the caudal fin dusky or yellowish.

The Florida pompano ranges from Santos, Brazil, to Massachusetts, in the West Indies, and at Bermuda. The largest known specimen is 25 inches in total length (obtained from the New York market, the location of capture unknown). Maximum weight is 8 pounds. Spawning probably occurs in offshore waters. The two smallest known specimens of this species, $3/_8$ and $1/_2$ inch long, were taken 60 and 30 miles off the coast of South Carolina in August and September. Spawning off the southeastern United States probably extends at least from March into September. The developing young move inshore and northward along the eastern states from about May to December and then move out. Young and adults appear to be influenced greatly by water temperature changes. They run in schools, are abundant around inlets and along sandy beaches, and at times move in and out with the tide. Young fish eat a variety of pelagic and benthic invertebrates and sometimes smaller fishes. Larger pompano are thought to prefer bivalve mollusks and small crustaceans, and have been described as rooting in the sand and mud for these.

This is an excellent gamefish on light tackle. It strikes fast and runs fast. Fishing success is definitely improved with skill and know-how. Beach-casting with live sandbugs is a popular method, but small artificial lures, such as jigs and flies, are successful also.

GAFFTOPSAIL POMPANO *Trachinotus rhodopus* Also called pompanito, this eastern Pacific species is closely related to *T. glaucus,* the palometa from the Atlantic.

The body of the gafftopsail pompano has 4–5 narrow black bars high on the sides. Dorsal and anal fin lobes are long and falcate; the dorsal lobe extends to or beyond the fork of the caudal fin when the lobe is depressed. The first dorsal fin has 6 short spines. The second dorsal fin has a spine and 19–21 softrays. The anal fin has 2 anterior spines (which become detached in large fish) followed by a spine and 18–20 softrays.

The range of this species is from Cabo Blanco in northern Peru, into the Gulf of California, and northward to Zumi Beach, California, and at the Galápagos and Tres Marías islands. A specimen 14 inches long appears to be the largest reported.

GREATER AMBERJACK *Seriola dumerili* This is the largest and most important of the Atlantic amberjacks.

The nuchal band of the greater amberjack extends from the eyes to the origin of the dorsal fin. The 5 body bars on young fish are not present in specimens over about 8 inches long. The body is relatively slender, and the depth decreases proportionally with growth. The greatest body depth goes into the standard length about 3.0–3.3 times in specimens up to 16 inches in standard length, about 3.3–3.7 times in 16- to 24-inch specimens, and about 3.7–4.5 times in larger specimens (standard length is measured from the tip of the snout to the end of the bony plate of the tail).

The first dorsal fin usually has 7 spines. The second dorsal fin has 1 spine and 29–35 softrays (usually 31–33). The anal fin has 2 detached spines (possibly covered by skin in the large individuals), followed by a spine and by 19–22 softrays. In larger fish the nuchal band is olivaceous, the body is dark above, lighter along the sides with laven-

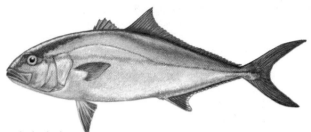

Greater Amberjack

der and golden tints but sometimes with an amber band from eyes to tail, and silvery-white ventrally; the dark area may be brownish, olivaceous, or a dark steely-blue.

The true range of the greater amberjack has been obscured by confusion of this fish with other, closely related species. Its known range is in the eastern Atlantic from the western coast of Africa to the Mediterranean, and in the western Atlantic from Brazil to Cape Cod, Massachusetts, in the West Indies, and at Bermuda. A maximum weight of 177 pounds was reported for a fish from Trinidad.

This species is the most important to sport fishermen of all the Atlantic amberjacks and is particularly sought by charter boat fisheries of Florida and the Carolinas. It is edible. It is usually caught trolling near the surface, but has been taken fishing with cut bait on the bottom in 30 fathoms.

GREEN JACK *Caranx caballus* This eastern Pacific species is very closely related to the western Atlantic *C. crysos,* the blue runner.

The second dorsal fin of the green jack has 1 spine and 22–24 softrays; the anal fin has 2 detached spines followed by 1 spine and 19–20 softrays. Gillrakers on the first arch are 13–16 on the upper limb and 28–32 on the lower limb. The vent is located near the first spine of the anal fin and behind the tips of the pelvic fins.

The body is more slender and rounded than in any other eastern Pacific jack crevalle. The straight part of the lateral line is about twice as long as the curved part. There are 40–51 pointed scutes in the straight lateral line. The dorsal and anal fin lobes are only moderately elongated. The green jack is generally greenish above and silvery to white below with a small black opercular spot that is sometimes indis-

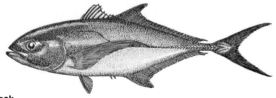

Green Jack

tinct. Specimens nearing spawning condition tend to become melanistic, males more so than females. The young, up to about 6–7 inches long, have 7–8 broad bars on the body plus 1 on the head; these bars frequently occur in larger living fish but fade out rapidly after capture.

The green jack has been taken from Lobos de Tierra, Peru, to Los Angeles County, California, into the northern Gulf of California.

LEATHERJACKETS *Oligoplites* spp.   Also called leathercoats and leathernecks, these interesting fishes are superficially more like the scombrids (tunas and mackerels) than the Carangidae.

They are distinguished by the semidetached finlets of the posterior 6–9 rays of the dorsal and anal fins; the flattened, spinelike, embedded scales on the body; the 4–5 short dorsal spines (rarely 3–6), the anterior 2–3 spines inclined forward; and the long, thin jaws (the premaxillaries are not protractile).

There are 3 Atlantic species (*O. saurus, O. saliens,* and *O. palometa*) and 4 Pacific species (*O. altus, O. inornatus, O. mundus,* and *O. refulgens*). One of the Pacific species (*O. inornatus*) is so similar to one of the Atlantic species (*O. saurus*) that it has abeen classed as a subspecies of the latter. Because these fish are generally similar in appearance and infrequently caught, their common names are less meaningful than their scientific names.

The relatively deep-bodied *O. mundus* apparently attains the largest size of any of the leatherjackets, reaching 15 inches in total length.

The leatherjackets generally are not listed as gamefish, but the larger ones can be exceptionally strong and stubborn on light tackle.

Leatherjacket

LESSER AMBERJACK *Seriola fasciata*   This is a small and rare species of the western Atlantic.

The dark nuchal band of the lesser amberjack extends obliquely backward from the eye to the nape, ending well in front of the first dorsal fin. The body at all known sizes has 8 (rarely 7) split and wavy bars. The body is relatively deep; the greatest body depth goes about 2.6 times into the standard length (standard length is measured from the tip of the snout to the end of the bony plate of the tail).

The first dorsal fin has 8 spines. The second dorsal fin has 1 spine and 30–32 softrays. The anal fin has 2 detached spines followed by a single spine and 19–20 softrays. The length of the dorsal fin lobe goes about 6.7 times into the standard length. The first gill arch has a total of about 22–28 gillrakers, about 6–8 on the upper limb and 17–20 on the lower limb. The back is olive brown, the sides and belly silver-gray. and the bars brown.

This species has been reported from Cuba to Massachusetts, in the northeastern and southwestern Gulf of Mexico, in the Bahamas, and from well offshore in the Florida Current and the Gulf Stream. Records of its occurrence in the eastern Atlantic are not substantiated and are doubtful. The largest specimen caught was $10^1/_4$ inches in total length.

LOOKDOWNS Genera: *Selene* (lookdowns) and *Vomer* (moonfish). These 2 genera have blunt head profiles, deep and very thin bodies, and minute scales that may be difficult to locate.

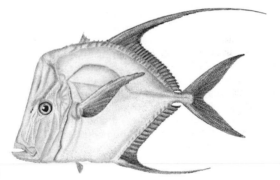

Lookdown

The true lookdowns (*Selene*) have a very high and steep anterior profile, with the head almost $1^1/_2$ times as deep as long. The dorsal and anal fin lobes are elongated, extending to the ends of the fins when depressed. The Atlantic lookdown, *S. vomer,* occurs on both sides of the Atlantic; in the western Atlantic it is known to range from Uruguay to Massachusetts and at Bermuda. The 2 eastern Pacific species can be distinguished as follows. The blackfin lookdown, *S. brevoortii,* has 21–22 dorsal softrays and 17–19 anal softrays. The Pacific lookdown, *S. oerstedii,* very closely related to the Atlantic lookdown, has 16–18 dorsal softrays and 15–16 anal softrays.

The moonfishes (*Vomer*) have a head profile that is only moderately high, with the head only slightly deeper than long. The dorsal and anal fin lobes are very short (except in specimens smaller than 1 inch in length). The Atlantic moonfish, *V. setapinnis,* occurs on both sides of the Atlantic; in the western Atlantic it ranges from Uruguay to Nova Scotia. The Pacific moonfish, *V. declivifrons,* ranges from near Chimbote in Peru to Long Beach, California. The 2 species are very similar.

231

Both the lookdowns and the moonfishes grow to about 10–12 inches. They are caught by casting artificial lures, such as small ($^{1}/_{8}$–$^{1}/_{4}$ ounce) jigs and streamer flies in open bays, and also around docks at night in Florida.

MAZATLAN JACK *Caranx vinctus*   This species is endemic to the eastern Pacific. It has been called striped jack (in reference to the persistent vertical markings on the body), but this name is not appropriate because in the most usually accepted terminology, a vertical marking is a *bar* and a horizontal marking is a *stripe* (and an oblique marking is termed either of these or a *band*).

The Mazatlán jack has 8 dark bars on the body (rarely 7–9) plus 1 on the nape, which persist to the largest known sizes in live fish and preserved specimens. The second dorsal fin has 1 spine and 22–24 softrays; the anal fin has 2 detached spines followed by 1 spine and 19–21 softrays. Gillrakers on the first gill arch number 10–13 on the upper limb and 27–30 on the lower limb. The vent is about midway between the anal fin spines and the insertion of the pelvic fins, and the tips of the pelvic fins extend past the position of the vent.

The body is only moderately deep, but is thinner and more laterally compressed than in any other eastern Pacific jack crevalle. The dorsal and anal fin lobes are short and not pronounced. The straight lateral line has about 44–52 pointed scutes, and is about 2–3 times as long as the curved part. The back is darkened, and most of the sides and the belly are light. All fins remain unpigmented. There is a small elongated opercular spot.

This species has been reported from Manta and La Libertad, Ecuador, to Topolobampo, Mexico, and from Concepción Bay on the east coast of Baja California. The largest known specimen is 13$^{1}/_{2}$ inches long.

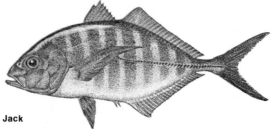

Mazatlán Jack

MEXICAN SCAD *Decapterus hypodus*   This very inadequately known eastern Pacific species has a detached, single-rayed finlet behind the dorsal and the anal fins. There are pointed scutes in the straight lateral line, but no scutes in the curved lateral line. The vertical edge of the shoulder girdle has a moderate-sized papillalike

232

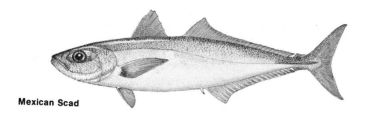

Mexican Scad

projection at its upper and lower extremities, but no furrow below the lower projection.

The second dorsal fin has 1 spine, about 32–33 softrays, and the detached finlet. The anal fin has 2 detached spines followed by about 26–28 softrays and the detached finlet. The straight lateral line has about 34–41 pointed scutes.

The Mexican scad is believed to range from the Galápagos Islands to Monterey Bay, California, and to grow to more than 1 foot in length.

MILKYMOUTH CREVALLE *Uraspis secunda*   The tongue and central portions of the mouth are a milky-white, surrounded by dark violet on the sides of the mouth. There are more gillrakers on the medial side of the fourth gill arch than on the lateral side of the first gill arch. In specimens up to about 8–10 inches in length, most of the points of the scutes in the straight lateral line are turned outward and forward. There is a scaleless area on the chest and lower sides in front of the pelvic fins (similar to that of the crevalle, *Caranx hippos,* but lacking the small, central patch of scales that distinguishes the crevalle).

The second dorsal fin has 1 spine and 27–30 softrays. The anal fin has 2 detached spines (which become covered by skin in medium-sized fish), followed by 1 spine and 21–22 softrays. The first gill arch has 5–7 gillrakers on the upper limb and 14–16 on the lower limb. There are about 32–38 scutes in the straight lateral line. Maximum size is unknown, but 6- to 7-pound fish have been caught in Florida and the Bahamas.

This is a very unusual and rare species and is found primarily in offshore waters and around oceanic islands in tropical and subtropical

Milkymouth Crevalle

waters around the world. Less than 200 specimens are known to have been taken. In the western Atlantic it is known from Brazil, Puerto Rico, and Cuba, in the Gulf of Mexico, and from off Florida, North Carolina, New Jersey, and Massachusetts. In the eastern Pacific it has been taken only at the Revilla Gigedo Islands.

The closely related cottonmouth jack, *U. helvola,* has not been taken in the western Atlantic and is known in the eastern Pacific only from the Revilla Gigedo Islands.

PACIFIC AMBERJACK *Seriola colburni* This species is endemic to the eastern Pacific.

The Pacific amberjack has a dark nuchal band extending diagonally from the front of the first dorsal fin through the eye. The dorsal and anal fin lobes become more elongated with growth; the dorsal lobe is greater than one-fourth to less than one-seventh as long as the head and body (without the tail) in specimens 12 inches and longer. First dorsal fin has about 7 spines; second dorsal fin has 1 spine and about 28–31 softrays; anal fin has 2 detached spines followed by 1 spine and about 21 softrays. First gill arch has about 14–19 gillrakers on the lower limb, the rakers becoming shorter and rudimentary with growth.

The body is elongate, moderately compressed, and fairly deep for an amberjack. The head profile is not as pointed as in the California yellowtail, and the body and fins are darker than in that species.

The range extends from the Gulf of Guayaquil, Ecuador, through the Gulf of California, to Oceanside, California, and at the Galápagos and Tres Marías islands.

The first specimen identified as this species was 49 inches long. A specimen from Cape San Lucas was reported to weigh about 112 pounds.

PACIFIC JACK MACKEREL *Trachurus symmetricus* This species is also known as California horse mackerel. It has enlarged scutes along the entire portion of both the curved and the straight lateral lines. There are no detached finlets behind the dorsal and anal fins, although the last ray of each fin is slightly more separated than the other rays; and there are no papillae or furrow on the shoulder girdle.

The second dorsal fin has 1 spine and 30–35 softrays. The anal fin has 2 detached spines followed by 1 spine and 28–31 softrays. The first gill arch has about 13–16 gillrakers on the upper limb and about 39–42 on the lower limb. The curved lateral line has about 48–51 scutes, and the straight lateral line has about 43–48 scutes. There is an iridescent green color above, sometimes with a bluish luster, often mottled with lighter and darker shades, and the sides and belly are silvery.

The Pacific jack mackerel ranges from Cape San Lucas, Baja California, to southern Alaska. It occurs from inshore waters up to

600 miles offshore. The largest recorded specimen was 32 inches long and weighed 5 pounds. These are important light-tackle gamefish in California, where they occur in local abundance and where they are usually caught using live anchovies for bait.

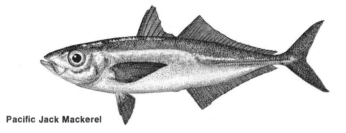

Pacific Jack Mackerel

PACIFIC PERMIT *Trachinotus kennedyi* This eastern Pacific species has also been called the palometa and is the same species as *T. culveri,* Culver's pompano, under which name it has sometimes been described. It is very similar to the Atlantic permit.

The first dorsal fin of the Pacific permit has 6 short spines. The second dorsal fin has 1 spine and 17–18 softrays. The anal fin has 2 detached spines, followed by 1 spine and 16–17 softrays. The body is moderately to very deep, but variable, and the body depth decreases with growth of the fish. The dorsal and anal fin lobes are relatively short; the length of the lobes is shorter than the length of the head. There are no dark bars on the body.

The Pacific permit ranges from San Pablo, Ecuador, into the Gulf of California, and north on the western coast of Baja California at least to Abreojos Point. It possibly extends to southern California. It has been reported to attain a length of 3 feet, but there are no recognized records of fish this large.

PALOMA POMPANO *Trachinotus paitensis* This eastern Pacific species is very closely related to the Florida pompano, *T. carolinus,* of the western Atlantic.

The first dorsal fin of the paloma pompano has 6 short spines. The second dorsal fin has 1 spine and 24–27 softrays (usually 25–26). Its anal fin has 2 spines (which become detached in large fish) followed by 1 spine and 20–25 softrays (usually 22–24). The dorsal and anal fin lobes are moderately short, and there are no black bars on the body.

The range is from Independencia Bay, Peru, to the northern Gulf of California, and northward to Redondo Beach, California. An unsubstantiated report lists it from as far south as Valparaiso, Chile. A specimen from Peru of about 15 inches in total length may be near the maximum size attained. The life history is not known.

Presumably, this is a good light-tackle gamefish and equal in palatability to the common pompano of the Atlantic. It has been reported to be one of the best foodfishes of Peru, entering the commercial catches in fair quantities; it is usually found there on fairly rough sand beaches and is caught in seines, gillnets, and trammel nets. It is also sold in markets in Panama and Mexico.

PALOMETA *Trachinotus goodei*   Also called the gafftopsail pompano and the longfin pompano, this species is endemic to the western Atlantic and is very closely related to the gafftopsail pompano, *T. rhodopus*, in the eastern Pacific.

The palometa has a first dorsal fin with 6 short spines. The second dorsal fin has 1 spine and 19−20 softrays. Its anal fin has 2 anterior spines (which become detached in larger fish), followed by 1 spine and 16−18 softrays. The body has 4 narrow bars high on the sides with a trace of a fifth bar in back of the fourth. The dorsal and anal fin lobes are greatly elongated (especially in specimens of 6 inches and longer); the dorsal fin lobe may extend beyond the fork of the tail when the lobe is depressed.

The body is moderately deep. The coloration of the palometa is dark silvery above with silvery or golden sides, a yellowish belly, and a bright orange breast. The lobes of the dorsal and anal fins are almost black, the remainder of these fins dusky or pale with bluish edges. The caudal fin is dusky or bluish, the pectoral fins golden and bluish, and the pelvic fins whitish. The narrow dark body bars and the dark falcate lobes of the dorsal, anal, and caudal fins make this a beautiful and striking fish.

An excellent panfish, it strikes live baits and artificial lures. It may attain 3 pounds, but is usually less than 1 pound in size.

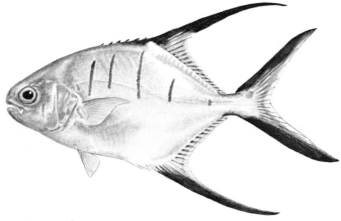

Palometa

RAINBOW RUNNER *Elagatis bipinnulatus* Also called rainbow yellowtail, runner, skipjack, and shoemaker, this species, of world-wide occurrence in tropical marine waters, is structurally similar to the amberjack genus *Seriola*.

The rainbow runner has a detached finlet behind the dorsal and the anal fins, composed of the last 2, closely spaced rays of each of these fins.

The body is slender and spindle-shaped, with a relatively sharp-pointed head profile. The first dorsal fin has 6 spines. The second dorsal fin has 1 spine and 25−27 connected softrays followed by the 2-rayed finlet. The single detached spine at the origin of the anal fin is covered by skin in most specimens more than 1 foot long; the remainder of the fin consists of 1 spine and 16−18 connected softrays followed by a 2-rayed finlet. The dorsal and anal fin lobes are relatively very short. There are 10−11 gillrakers on the upper limb and 25−28 on the lower limb of the first arch.

The color pattern is unique. The back is greenish-blue; high on the sides is a broad, dark blue stripe, followed in succession down the sides by a narrow light blue stripe, a broader cadmium-yellow stripe, frequently another narrow light blue stripe; the remaining third of the sides and the belly are white or yellowish-silver. The fins are greenish-yellow.

The rainbow runner occurs in tropical waters around the world. In the western Atlantic it has been reported from Colombia to Massachusetts and in the West Indies. In the eastern Pacific it has been recorded from northern Peru and the Galápagos Islands and Cocos Island to Cape San Lucas, Baja California.

The largest known specimen was $3^{1}/_{2}$ feet long and weighed 23 pounds, from Hawaii.

Rainbow Runner

ROUGH SCAD *Trachurus lathami* Also known as saurel, this is a species of the western North Atlantic.

Enlarged scutes cover the entire portion of both the curved and the straight lateral line. There is no detached finlet behind the dorsal or anal fin, and there are no papillae and no furrow on the shoulder girdle.

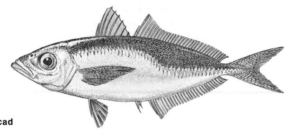

Rough Scad

The second dorsal fin has 1 spine and 28–33 softrays. The anal fin has 2 detached spines, followed by 1 spine and 26–30 softrays. The first gill arch has 12–14 gillrakers on the upper limb and 34–37 on the lower limb. The curved lateral line has 30–37 scutes, and the straight lateral line has 31–41 pointed scutes. Color is bluish-green above and silvery below, with a small, sometimes indistinct, opercular spot.

This species is known from Maine to Florida and throughout the Gulf of Mexico. It grows to about 8–10 inches, possibly larger.

ROUND SCAD *Decapterus punctatus* This is the more common of the 2 species of this genus occurring in the western Atlantic.

The round scad has a detached, single-rayed finlet behind the dorsal and the anal fins, pointed scutes in the straight lateral line, and no scutes in the curved lateral line. The vertical edge of the shoulder girdle has a moderate-sized papillalike projection at its upper and lower extremities, but no groove below the lower projection.

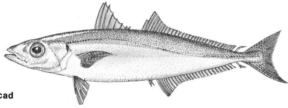

Round Scad

The second dorsal fin has 1 spine and 28–32 softrays and the detached finlet. The anal fin has 2 detached spines, followed by 1 spine and 25–27 softrays and the detached finlet. The first gill arch has 12–15 gillrakers on the upper limb and 34–40 gillrakers on the lower limb. There are 36–44 pointed scutes in the straight lateral line. There are usually 20 rays in each pectoral fin. The color is dark above and silvery below with a golden tinge. A row of small dark spots occurs along the anterior part of the lateral line, and there is usually a small opercular spot.

238

This species ranges in the western Atlantic from Rio de Janeiro, Brazil, to Nova Scotia, and at Bermuda. A very similar form from the eastern Atlantic has been reported under this name. The maximum size is not known; it may be less than 12 inches.

SPOTTED JACK *Caranx melampygus*   Also called blue jack and blue crevalle, this species ranges into the Indo-Pacific. In the eastern Pacific it has also been erroneously designated as *C. stellatus* and *C. medusicola*.

The chest in front of the pelvic fins of the spotted jack is completely scaled. The second dorsal fin has 1 spine and 20–23 softrays. The anal fin has 2 detached spines, followed by 1 spine and 17–20 softrays. The first gill arch has 7–9 gillrakers on the upper limb and 17–21 on the lower limb.

The scutes in the straight lateral line number about 30–42. Specimens up to about 4 inches long have 5–6 bars on the body and 1 on the nape, and specimens of this size and slightly larger have dark dorsal and anal fin lobes. When the fish is about 9 inches long, small spots begin to form on the body and head, and the number of these spots increases rapidly with growth. The dorsal and anal fins become very dark, frequently with dark blue at their bases. The back of larger specimens is dark blue or bluish-green that fades into lighter sides and belly. The body is never entirely black or dark brown.

The spotted jack occurs in most areas of the tropical Indo-Pacific westward to South Africa. In the eastern Pacific it is known from Mazatlán, Chacala, and Cape San Lucas, Mexico, and at the Revilla Gigedo, Tres Marías, Clipperton, and Cocos islands. It has been reported from Panama and the Galápagos Islands. This is a large jack and may exceed 100 pounds.

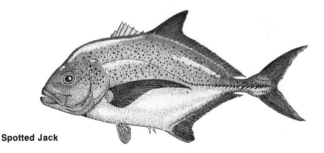

Spotted Jack

YELLOW JACK *Caranx bartholomaei*   This species is endemic to the western Atlantic.

The second dorsal fin has 1 spine and 25–28 softrays. The anal fin has 2 detached spines, followed by 1 spine and 21–24 softrays. On the first gill arch there are 18–21 gillrakers on the lower limb and 6–9 on the upper limb.

The body is moderately deep. The dorsal and anal fin lobes are only slightly produced. The scutes in the straight lateral line number about 22–28. The straight lateral line is as long as, or only slightly longer than, the curved part. The coloration is light bluish-green on the back; sides are silvery with a golden yellow tint. The fins are chiefly yellow. Particularly after death this fish has a yellowish cast, to which it owes its name. The pigmentation changes in small juveniles are unique. Like most jack crevalles, the yellow jack develops vertical body bars, usually 5 (rarely 4–6), plus 1 on the nape and a prominent nuchal band through the eye. These develop at a length of about $^3/_4$ inch. Then in a very compressed length interval, several changes occur. At about 1 inch long the upper and lower parts of the posterior 3–4 bars bend backward; by $1^1/_8$ inches all the bars have become distorted or wavy; and by $1^3/_8$ inches all the bars have broken into a mottled or spotted pattern that persists to about $4^1/_2$ inches in length or larger.

The yellow jack has been recorded from Maceió, Brazil, to Woods Hole, Massachusetts, and in the West Indies. It seems to be fairly common in the Bahamas and around Cuba. A maximum size of about 39 inches has been recorded. A specimen from Puerto Rico was $35^1/_4$ inches long and weighed 16 pounds 11 ounces.

Yellow Jack

BILLFISH FAMILY Istiophoridae

The billfish family comprises the spearfishes, sailfishes, and marlins. These are marine species of moderate to extremely large size. Characteristically, the adults of all the members of this family have the upper jaw more or less prolonged into a spear or bill, which is fairly round in cross section and is covered with small prickles.

BLACK MARLIN *Makaira indica* This marine species is found from Mexico to Peru, with unverified rumors of occasional occurrences as far north as southern California. It is well known from the central Pacific, although apparently rather scarce around Hawaii. In the western Pacific, the range extends from Japan in the north to Australia and New Zealand in the south. It is reported to be the most numerous marlin around Taiwan. In the Indian Ocean, it has been recorded all the way from Sumatra to Africa, north to the Muscat coast and south to Mauritius and South Africa.

The outstanding identifying feature of the black marlin is the rigid nature of the pectoral fins. In contrast to all other istiophorids, the pectoral fins of this species are held out rigidly, at right angles to the body, and cannot be folded flat without breaking the joint. This characteristic holds, even in the smallest specimens known.

The body of the black marlin is a little deeper than in other species, though closely rivaled in this respect by the blue marlin. The black, however, seems to have a more prominent shoulder hump so that it looks deeper. The sides of the body are quite flat, and this feature is emphasized in the really big individuals. The lateral line is an inconspicuous double row of pores and is generally not visible in any but the smallest fish. Its vent is just in front of the anal fin. The spear of the black marlin gives the appearance of being heavier and more robust than that of other species.

In color, the black marlin is highly variable. Most specimens are dark slate-blue above, changing more or less abruptly to silvery-white below the lateral line. Occasionally, pale blue stripes may be seen on the sides when the fish are alive, but these seldom if ever persist after death. Sometimes the fish are milky-white, hence the Japanese name, *shirokajiki* (white marlin), and the Chinese *pu-pi* (white skin). But the white color seldom persists long after the fish is out of the water. Sometimes a black marlin will turn an almost uniform bronze color as it comes out of the water, but this seldom lasts long. All the fins are dark.

The pelvic fins of the black marlin are shorter than in other marlins, almost always less than 1 foot long, regardless of the size of the fish. In all other marlins, a mature fish with unbroken pelvic fins only a foot long is a rarity.

The black marlin rivals the blue in size, being reported by commercial fishermen up to about 2,000 pounds. Most of the large (over 1,000 pounds) black marlins taken by sport fishermen are caught off the Australian coast.

BLUE MARLIN *Makaira nigricans* This is a marine species of worldwide distribution in warm and temperate seas. Highly valued by sport fishermen because of its size and the spectacular fight it puts up when hooked, it is sought in many parts of the world by commercial fishermen also because of the fine quality of its meat. It is reported to be the largest of the istiophorid fishes. The distinguishing characters of the blue marlin are the relatively low dorsal fin and relatively high anal fin, the latter averaging about 86 percent of the height of the former, which in turn averages about 79 percent of the body depth in adults; the round, rather than flat, sides; and the nearly cylindrical form of the anterior part of the body before the first anal fin.

In general, the blue marlin is colored like the striped marlin; dark steely-blue on the dorsal areas, fading to silvery-white on the ventral side. The sides of the body are usually marked with a series of lighter-colored vertical bars, but these are never as prominent as they are in the striped marlin, and they tend to fade out rather quickly after the fish is boated.

The blue marlin is reported by Japanese long-liners to be the largest of the marlins, reaching weights of over 2,000 pounds. This has not been the experience of anglers, however; a blue of 1,805 pounds was caught in 1972 by rod and reel, although it was disqualified for record because more than one angler handled the tackle. This fish came from Hawaii. The giants of the blue marlin species appear to be mainly creatures of the high seas, for the long-liners claim they get these big ones only far offshore. This suggests that the really large blue marlins are probably not common in the areas accessible to sport fishermen. The biggest blue marlins are always females. The males seldom get much heavier than 300 pounds, and any blue much over this weight is almost certainly a female. In the Pacific, the males are reported to be 200–255 pounds. Parenthetically, this is the region from which come the biggest females.

Off the Atlantic coast of the Americas, the marlin has been found commonly as far north as Cape Cod, even straying occasionally into the Gulf of Maine and to Georges Bank. The principal center of abundance is much further south, however, apparently off North Carolina in the summer and even further south in winter.

The blue marlin appears to undertake regular north-south migrations according to the season of the year, moving away from the equator in the warmer times and back again in the cooler months. This holds true in both the Atlantic and the Pacific oceans. A blue marlin tagged off the Virgin Islands in 1976 was recaptured in 1977 off the Ivory Coast of Africa, suggesting some transatlantic migration.

All reports indicate that the blue marlin is broadly carnivorous on fishes and cephalopods, with fishes perhaps favored over the squids and octopuses in most areas. Particularly among the larger blues, tunas and bonitos are favored foods. And some blues have been found with young broadbill swordfish in their stomachs.

HATCHET MARLIN *Tetrapturus* sp. This uncommon Atlantic marlin has only recently been recognized as a new species. Its most distinctive characteristics are a truncate lobe on the dorsal fin; large dark spots along the base of the dorsal; and pointed tips on the pectorals. This species has been reported from North Carolina to the coast of Venezuela.

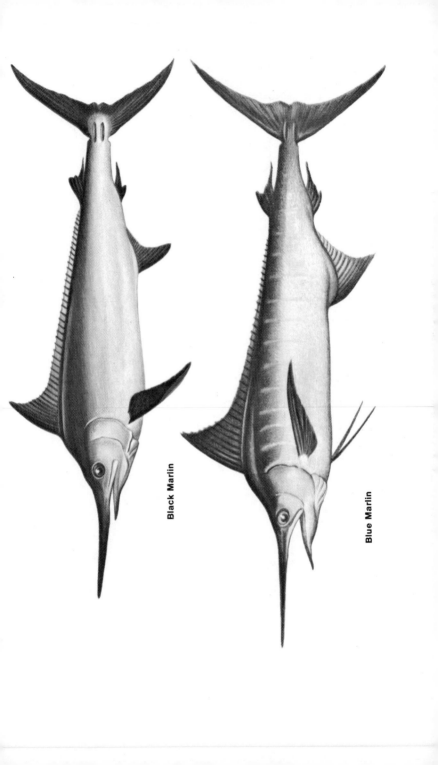

Black Marlin

Blue Marlin

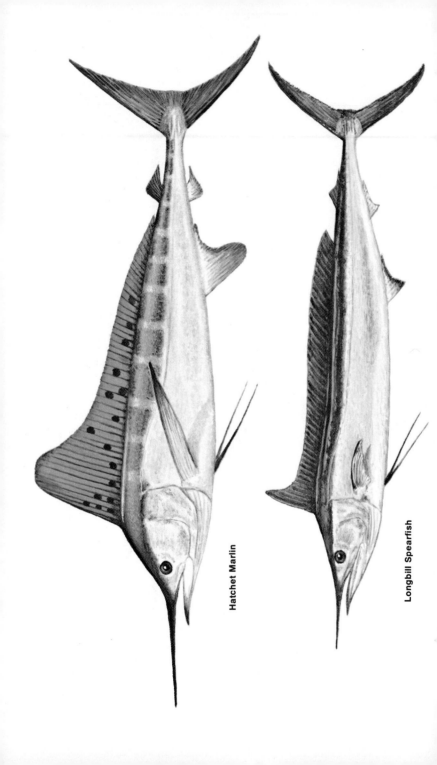

Hatchet Marlin

Longbill Spearfish

LONGBILL SPEARFISH *Tetrapturus pfluegeri* This Atlantic marine species, of rather small size for this family, is occasionally taken off the southeastern and Gulf coasts of the United States. It is generally found more or less offshore, in waters of 50 fathoms or deeper.

The longbill spearfish is elongate and slender, with fairly long pectoral fins, a crescent-shaped anal fin, and a long, relatively high dorsal fin. The anterior part of the dorsal fin forms a sharp peak, and behind this peak the rest of the fin maintains a fairly even height about equal to or greater than the depth of the body. The vent is located some distance in front of the anal fin. In young individuals the snout is considerably longer than the lower jaw, but in older specimens the snout and lower jaw tend to become more nearly equal, although the snout is always the longer. The body is long and slim, the sides flat, the lateral line single and quite prominent. Color is dark metallic blue, or sometimes greenish, above, fading through silver-gray to white or silvery on the belly. A few hours after death the dorsal colors fade to a dark slaty blue-gray. The fins are all dark, and there are no spots or bars on the body.

The longbill spearfish is the smallest member of the group, seldom exceeding 40–50 pounds in weight.

This fish is not at all common; hence practically nothing is known of its life history. Presumably, its food, like that of the shortbill spearfish, includes smaller fishes and squids. It is primarily a fish of the open waters, occurring most commonly some distance offshore.

SAILFISH *Istiophorus platypterus* This marine species is highly prized by anglers because of its outstanding sporting characteristics. Although present taxonomy suggests that the Atlantic and Pacific sailfishes are the same species, it is probable that there are at least three, including an Indo-Pacific form.

The outstanding characteristic of the sailfish is the enormous dorsal fin, which is much higher than the greatest depth of the body. This height is maintained for almost the entire length of the fin. The longest ray is usually about the twentieth, counting from the anterior end, and the length of this ray is usually about 150 percent or more of the greatest depth of the body. In addition, the pelvic fins of the sailfish are much longer than those of other istiophorids, reaching nearly to the anal fin. These fins also have a wide membrane attached to them, missing in other forms, which is quite noticeable in the freshly caught fish. If allowed to dry, however, the membrane sticks tightly to the fin rays and is not at all obvious.

The body of the sailfish is long, slender, and compressed, resulting in a slab-sided appearance. The lateral line is single and quite prominent. The vent is just in front of the anal fin. The spear is long and slender, often slightly curved, with the upper jaw generally a little more than twice as long as the lower. In color, the sailfish is dark steely-blue dorsally, fading to white or silvery on the ventrum. On the sides of the body, a number of pale vertical bars, often made up of rows of pale spots, may be present and may or may not persist after death. The vertical fins are bright cobalt-blue in life, and the dorsal fin, especially in its posterior part, may be more or less liberally sprinkled with round or oval black spots. Sometimes the fish are a deep bronze color when brought into the boat, but this color does not persist after death.

The pectoral fins are moderately long, and the pelvics are the longest of any istiophorid and are provided with a broad membrane.

The average weight of angler-caught fish in Florida waters is somewhere around 40 pounds, although the largest on record weighed 141 pounds. The length averages about 7 feet. In the Pacific, sailfish are considerably larger, with the present record at 221 pounds.

The list of the foods of the sailfish is a long one. This does not mean that the sailfish has a more varied diet than other istiophorids, merely that it has been better investigated. Squids and octopuses, especially the paper nautilus, form about 17 percent of the total diet in the Florida area, with various fishes making up the remaining 83 percent. Among the fishes, the mackerels and tunas seem to be the most important, followed by jacks, halfbeaks, and needlefishes.

In the Atlantic, the sailfish has been taken regularly from Cape Hatteras to Venezuela, including such spots as Bermuda, Puerto Rico, the Windward Islands, and the Gulf of Mexico. It may stray as far north as Cape Cod, perhaps even into the Gulf of Maine (unconfirmed reports), in warm summers, and a few have been recorded from as far south as Brazil. The Pacific sailfish is found all the way from southern California to Ecuador.

SHORTBILL SPEARFISH *Tetrapturus angustirostris* This is a marine fish of the Pacific Ocean, known from Hawaii and, very rarely, from off southern California in the United States and off the western coast of South America. It occurs more frequently in the central Pacific and in Oriental waters, where it is fairly common in the longline fisheries. It is of relatively small size and is generally found well offshore.

The shortbill spearfish is elongate and slender, the sides of the body flat, with a single rather prominent lateral line. The pectoral fins are short, the anal fin crescent-shaped, and the dorsal fin long and relatively high. The anterior part of the dorsal fin forms a sharp peak, behind which the fin maintains a fairly even height about equal to the greatest depth of the body. The vent is located anterior to the anal fin by a distance nearly equal to the length of the anal fin base. The shortbill spearfish is metallic-blue or greenish above, fading rather abruptly to silvery or white on the lower sides and belly. The fins are all dark, and there are no spots or bars on the body. The snout, at least in adults, is scarcely longer than the lower jaw.

The shortbill spearfish reaches a maximum weight of over 100 pounds. The largest recorded in the literature is a specimen of 114 pounds, but the average weight of those taken by commercial longlines seems to be somewhat under 40 pounds.

STRIPED MARLIN *Tetrapturus audax* An extremely valuable sport and commercial fish from the Pacific and Indian oceans, the striped marlin occurs in eastern Pacific waters from southern California to Chile. These fish are ordinarily caught fairly close inshore by sport fishermen, but commercial fisheries take them all the way across the Pacific.

The striped marlin is most easily distinguished by its high, pointed dorsal fin. The sickle-shaped anterior part of this fin is higher than the greatest depth of the body; the posterior portion is long and low. Rarely, in a large individual the dorsal fin height may be less than the body depth, leading to possible confusion with the blue marlin. In a young specimen, up to about 40–50 pounds, the posterior part of the fin is relatively high, and this has sometimes led to confusion with the shortbill spearfish. However, the large striped marlin has flatter sides and a more uniform taper to the body than does the blue, as well as generally more prominent stripes; the young striped marlin is short and chunky, and the spearfish of the same weight is long and slender.

In a fish of average size, the body is slightly slab-sided, and the depth decreases gradually from the shoulder hump to the anal fin. The anus is close in front of the anal fin. The spear is long, as are the pectoral fins.

The color of the striped marlin is typically dark steely-blue above and on the snout, fading to white on the belly. The sides of the body are marked with a varying number of prominent, pale bluish, lavender, or whitish vertical stripes. The fins are dark, except for the first dorsal and first anal, which are, in life, brilliant cobalt-blue with dark tips. The intensity of the colors, particularly of the stripes on the sides, varies widely in different individuals and in fish from different regions. In some, the stripes are prominent and brilliant; in others they may be scarcely visible. In all, the stripes tend to fade out after death, and the whole fish slowly assumes a dull, dark blue-gray color.

The usual weight of a fish caught by angling is in the neighborhood of 200–250 pounds. The present record for rod and reel is 415 pounds, and a fish over 300 pounds is something to brag about. The maximum size seems to vary from one area to another. The 415-pounder was from New Zealand. At La Jolla, California, a fish of 406$^{1}/_{2}$ pounds was taken in 1955. In the Honolulu fish market, the maximum seems to be a little over 300 pounds, but in New Zealand waters striped marlin approach 400 pounds. These weights may reflect real differences in the maximum size reached by fish in the several areas, but they may equally well express angling intensity.

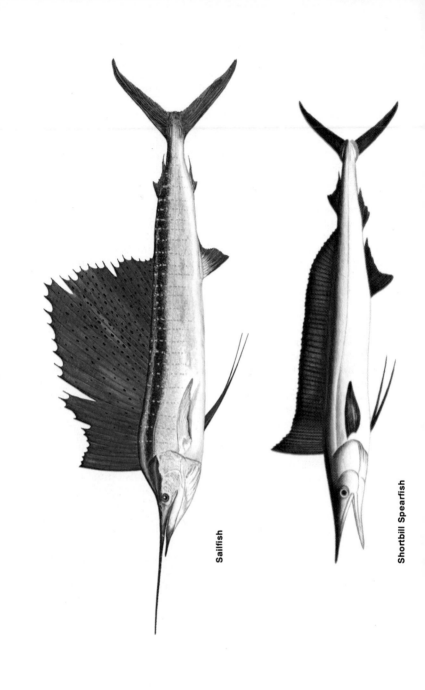

Sailfish

Shortbill Spearfish

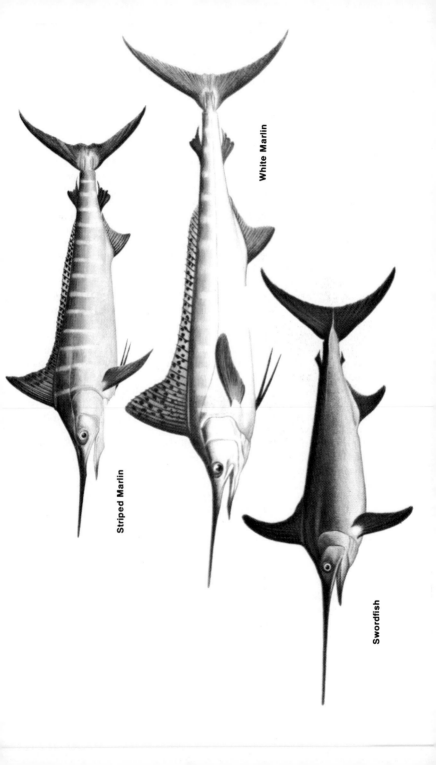

Striped Marlin

White Marlin

Swordfish

WHITE MARLIN *Tetrapturus albidus* A marine species confined to the Atlantic Ocean, this gamefish is very popular with American anglers. The white marlin differs from all other members of the family in that the tips of the dorsal and anal fins are rounded, rather than sharply pointed. The pectoral fin is long and rounded at its tip. The body is slender, the sides rather flat, and the lateral line single and fairly prominent. The vent is placed close to the base of the anal fin. The spear is moderately long, the upper jaw being noticeably longer than (about twice as long as) the lower jaw. The anterior peak of the dorsal fin is as high as or higher than the greatest depth of the body, while the posterior part of the dorsal fin is much lower.

This species commonly shows more green than do other marlins. The upper part of the body is a brilliant greenish-blue, which changes abruptly to silvery-white at about the lateral line. The belly is white. Along the sides of the body are varying numbers of light blue or lavender vertical bars, which usually fade out and disappear soon after death. The dorsal fin is bright blue, usually spotted or blotched with black or purple, and with white marks on the basal part of the fin. The anal fin may be similarly marked. All fin rays are dark. The pectoral fins are long, about one-fifth the length of the body, and their tips are rounded.

The white marlin does not reach great size, although it is larger than the spearfishes. The maximum recorded weight for a white marlin taken on rod and reel is 161 pounds, but the usual weight for a fish taken in this manner runs 50–60 pounds.

Like all the other istiophorids, the white marlin is mainly piscivorous in its diet. Its favorite foods along the Middle Atlantic coast are herrings and squids, but it will also eat anything it can capture, such as anchovies and jacks.

The white marlin has been found all the way from Nova Scotia in the north to Brazil in the south. The normal northward limit to the range, however, seems to be south of Cape Cod, and the Nova Scotian records probably represent strays that wandered further north in unusually warm summers. However, the times at which concentrations of fish occur in places like Ocean City, Maryland, and Montauk Point, New York, suggest that white marlins make coastwise migrations each year, moving north in the spring and south in the fall.

SWORDFISH FAMILY Xiphiidae

SWORDFISH *Xiphias gladius* A marine species of considerable importance to sport and commercial fishermen alike, it is also called broadbill or broadbill swordfish. Of worldwide distribution in temperate and tropical seas, the swordfish is readily identified by the long, flat sword, which is much longer than the rest of the head behind it; the absence of pelvic fins; the presence of but a single keel on each side of the caudal peduncle; and the absence of scales in adults.

The body of the swordfish is deepest just behind the head, beneath the dorsal fin, whence it tapers posteriorly to the tail; the sides of the body are rounded rather than flat. The dorsal fin is high and sickle-shaped and lacks the low posterior portion characteristic of the related istiophorids. The anal fin is likewise sickle-shaped, and the second dorsal and anal fins are quite small. The spear, or sword, is long and flat, much longer than the rest of the head, and lacks prickles. There is only a single keel on each side of the caudal peduncle. The pectoral fins are moderately long, and pelvic fins are missing entirely.

The color of the swordfish is quite variable, ranging from dark brown or bronzy to grayish-blue or black above, and whitish below. The extent of the dark color also varies. In some individuals, it extends no more than halfway down the sides; in others almost the whole body may be colored, with only a little dirty-white on the underside. The lower parts of the sides of the head are generally whitish, and all the fins are dark.

The usual size of swordfish taken commercially in the United States is probably not over 200–250 pounds, but some huge ones have been caught, weighing over 1,000 pounds. One specimen boated at Iquique, Chile, was 1,182 pounds.

Along the Atlantic coast of North America, in the north central part of the Pacific Ocean, and doubtless in other parts of the world also, swordfish carry out seasonal north-south migrations. They appear off New England and further north in late June and early July, remaining in that area through the summer. After that, they disappear, moving south and offshore into deepwater with the onset of winter. Until very recently, their winter habitat was unknown, but in the fall and winter of 1962 good catches of swordfish were taken by long-lining in deepwater along the edge of the continental shelf south of Block Island and Long Island. The most productive angling area today is Florida's southeast coast; an after-dark (9 P.M. to 5 A.M.) fishery discovered in 1976.

ROOSTERFISH FAMILY Nematisiidae

ROOSTERFISH *Nematistius pectoralis* Also called *papagallo, gallo,* and *pez de gallo,* this unique species lives only along the western coast of the Americas in the eastern Pacific. This fish is classed in a distinct family, but is very closely related to the Carangidae.

The roosterfish has 7 elongated rays in the first dorsal fin, the longest about half as long as the total length of the fish.

The body shape tapers like that of an amberjack. There are 8 spines in the first dorsal fin, the last 7 greatly elongated; the second dorsal fin has 1 spine and about 25 softrays; the anal fin has 3 spines and about 15 softrays; the anal fin is much shorter than the second dorsal fin, and the lobes of both fins are short; the pectoral fins are elongated. Color is green to black on the back and white or golden below; there are 2 black stripes curving downward and backward from under the

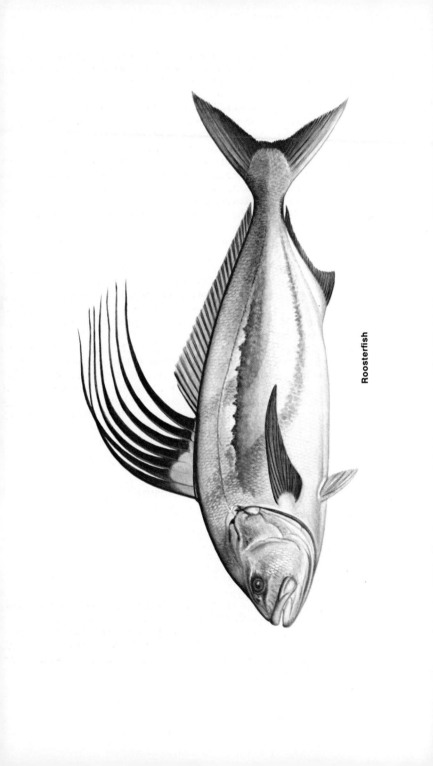

Roosterfish

first dorsal fin, a black nuchal band, and a black spot on the pectoral fin base; the dorsal spines are striped with alternate blue-black and white.

The roosterfish is known from Cabo Blanco, Peru, into the Gulf of California and up the outer coast of Baja California to Turtle Bay, and at the Galápagos Islands; there is a sight record for this species from San Clemente Island off southern California. It is most common over sandy beaches from the surf zone to moderate depths and has been said to be most abundant off Ecuador. The maximum recorded size and total length are 111 pounds and 5 feet 2 inches.

Essentially nothing is known of its life history. Ripe specimens have not been reported, and some specimens examined in December to June were reported to be sexually immature. The smallest specimen known, $^3/_8$ inch in total length, was taken in July off Costa Rica. Specimens under 1 foot long may travel in close schools; larger fish seem to move in looser groups. They are known to feed on small fishes in the surf.

Roosterfish are excellent and exciting gamefish. When chasing prey, they may leap 3–6 times in dolphin fashion. When swimming at the surface they often "flash the comb" by erecting the long spines of the first dorsal fin out of the water.

SURGEONFISH FAMILY Acanthuridae

In Spanish-speaking countries, the tangs are known as *medico* and *barbero*, or doctor and barber, because of their razor-sharp caudal peduncle spines. When tangs are disturbed, the spines are erected and used in a slashing attack. These fish are characterized by their ovoid shape, which makes them look the same in front and rear.

BLUE TANG *Acanthurus coeruleus* The blue tang is known from the entire Caribbean area south to Brazil. It is found occasionally

Blue Tang

along the eastern seaboard of the United States as far north as New York and is common in Bermuda. The blue tang is one of four surgeonfishes from the western Atlantic. All are species of *Acanthurus*. As implied by the name, *A. coeruleus* is blue as an adult and is most easily distinguished by color. It is not a uniform blue, however, but has numerous lengthwise, irregular dark lines on the body. The young are bright yellow.

The teeth of species of *Acanthurus* are close-set and denticulate on the edges, thus ideally adapted for feeding on filamentous algae, which form the main part of the diet. The word *tang* means seaweed in German, and the use of this name for various of the surgeonfishes is probably based on knowledge of their plant-eating habits. Tangs are sometimes caught on various natural baits.

TRIGGERFISH FAMILY   Balistidae

The triggerfishes are a distinctive group of fishes named for the interlocking arrangement of the bases of the first 3 dorsal spines such that the enlarged first spine can be fixed in the erect position. If the second spine is depressed, the first spine is no longer locked in the vertical position.

QUEEN TRIGGERFISH *Balistes vetula*   The queen triggerfish is easily separated from other Atlantic species by the long filaments from the tail and front of the soft dorsal fin and by its color. It is olive

Queen Triggerfish

with 2 broad, curved blue bands from the snout to the pectoral bases. Chin and lower cheek are yellow-orange; yellow-edged dark lines radiate from the eyes. There are blue submarginal bands in the dorsal, anal, and caudal fins.

The queen triggerfish is broadly distributed in the Atlantic from Brazil to Florida, straying north to Massachusetts. It is common in the West Indies and is recorded from Bermuda, the Azores, and Ascension Island.

Where abundant or when chummed for, the queen triggerfish will strike almost any small artificial lure, including jigs and plugs. A strong gamefish, it makes determined runs to the bottom using its broad body to advantage. Despite its coarse skin and odd appearance, it is a fine foodfish. The flesh is firm and white and is often likened to frogs' legs in texture. But the tough skin must be removed.

PARROTFISH FAMILY   Scaridae

Parrotfishes are well named for their beaklike jaws and gaudy colors. The queen parrotfish is one of the most common of the 13 species known from the western Atlantic, most of which fall into the genera *Scarus* and *Sparisoma*. These genera are readily distinguished from one another by the position of the upper jaw relative to the lower. In *Scarus* the beak of the lower jaw fits inside the upper when the mouth is closed; in *Sparisoma* the upper fits inside the lower. *S. vetula* differs from all other Atlantic species by having 4, not 3, rows of scales on the cheek.

Like most parrotfishes, the queen parrotfish displays one color pattern for the female and small male and a more colorful phase for the large male.

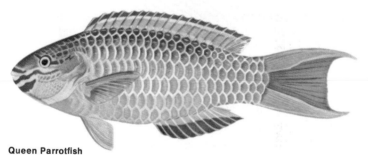

Queen Parrotfish

BUTTERFLYFISH AND ANGELFISH
FAMILY   Chaetodontidae

The chaetodontids are among the most beautifully colored fishes of the sea. They are high-bodied and compressed. Their mouths are small and their teeth brushlike. Two subfamilies are grouped in the family: the butterflyfishes (Chaetodontidae) and the angelfishes (Pomacanthinae).

The angelfishes are moderately large, deep-bodied, and compressed, and differ from the butterflyfishes principally in possessing a stout spine at the angle of the preopercle. The genus *Holacanthus* is distinctive in having, in addition, smaller spines on the rest of the preopercular margin, 50 or fewer scales in longitudinal series on the body, and a truncate caudal fin. There are 3 species of *Holacanthus* in the tropical western Atlantic: the queen angelfish (*H. ciliaris*), the blue angelfish (*H. bermudensis*), and the yellow-and-black rock beauty (*H. tricolor*).

The queen angelfish is found on coral reefs in the West Indies and Florida. Although reported to reach a length of nearly 2 feet, it probably does not exceed 18 inches. The blue angelfish, which attains about the same size, occurs in Florida, the western Bahamas, and Bermuda.

Chaetodon is the largest butterflyfish genus. In the tropical western Atlantic there are 6 species. Most are small, rarely exceeding 7 inches in length. Usually there is at least some yellow coloration. Perhaps the best known is the foureye butterflyfish (*C. capistratus*), the most common species of the family on West Indian reefs.

Foureye Butterflyfish

Queen Angelfish

256

BARRACUDA FAMILY   Sphyraenidae

GREAT BARRACUDA *Sphyraena barracuda* This is one of the largest of the barracudas. It is known to reach a weight of 106 pounds and a probable length of 6 feet. Large specimens are rare, and most of those caught by anglers do not reach 50 pounds. The species is common in the American Atlantic from Florida to Brazil.

The great barracuda is long, slim-bodied, and has a pointed head. In shape it somewhat resembles the pikes. The body coloration is dull to bright silver with a whitish belly, although sooty-black areas occur on many individuals with varying degrees of intensity. There are usually a few irregular black blotches scattered on the sides of the body, particularly toward the tail. The pectoral fins reach beyond a vertical from insertion of the pelvic fin. The anterior rays of the second dorsal and anal fins reach to, or beyond, the tip of the last ray when the fin is depressed. The jaws are studded with large, pointed teeth. The posterior teeth of the mandible are not slanted backward. The great barracuda has 5 dorsal spines, 10 dorsal rays, and 10 anal rays. Its 78–82 scales along the lateral line separate it from other Atlantic species.

Young individuals up to about 3 pounds usually occur close to shore in the shallow water and may be found in harbors and coastal lagoons. Large adults may occur farther offshore in deeper water, occasionally far out to sea. This aggressive, carnivorous fish frequently attacks flashing objects and other disturbances that presumably appear as prospective prey. Such behavior may account for attacks on humans. Although barracuda display an extreme curiosity toward persons wading or swimming, and will approach quite closely, the known records of attack are comparatively rare. However, the species must be considered potentially dangerous.

An underrated gamefish, small individuals are taken from shore, bridge, and boat with spinning, plug, and fly tackle. Larger barracuda are most commonly caught trolling offshore on fairly heavy tackle. However, when specifically sought on the inshore flats or channel edges with light gear, the great barracuda can be a spectacular gamefish. When hooked in the shallows, the fish makes an incredibly swift run and frequently jumps. Despite its aggressive reputation, the barracuda is often lure-shy and can be difficult to hook on artificials. Its flesh is frequently toxic and is not recommended as food.

GUAGUANCHE *Sphyraena guachancho* This species is much smaller than the great barracuda, but reaches a somewhat larger size (at least 20 inches) than the sennet. It is most abundant in the tropical Atlantic from Florida southward to Brazil, but may occur farther north.

The body coloration of the guaguanche is an olive-gray on the back and silvery below. There are no black blotches scattered on the sides, as on the great barracuda. The maxillary reaches beyond a vertical

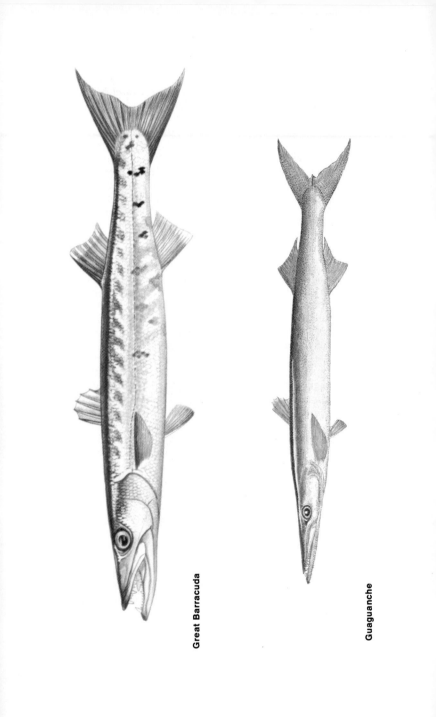

Great Barracuda

Guaguanche

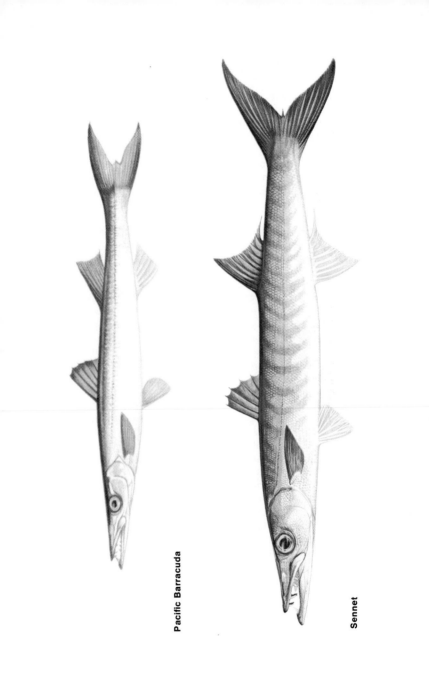

Pacific Barracuda

Sennet

from the posterior nostril. The pectoral fins reach beyond a vertical line from the insertion of the pelvic fin. The anterior rays of the second dorsal and anal fins do not reach the tip of the last ray when the fin is depressed. The posterior teeth of the mandible are slanted backward. The guaguanche has 5 dorsal spines, 10 dorsal rays, 10 anal rays, and 100–120 scales along the lateral line.

The guaguanche is a schooling fish, usually occurring along the shore in relatively shallow water. It may be found in clear bays and harbors close to the bottom, where it may be taken by still-fishing with live or cut bait. This fish also strikes artificial lures and provides good sport on light spinning and fly tackle. It is frequently taken in southern Florida, but is more abundant in the Bahamas and the West Indies.

It is the best foodfish of Atlantic barracudas, has never been known to be poisonous, and is considered a delicacy in the West Indies. It is an important commercial fish in the Greater Antilles.

PACIFIC BARRACUDAS *Sphyraena* spp. There are 4 described species of barracudas occurring in the eastern Pacific. Of these, the Pacific barracuda, *S. argentea*, is the best known. Also called California barracuda, barrie, snake, scoots, and scooter, this species occurs along the Pacific coast of North America from Alaska southward to Magdalena Bay, Baja California. Its common range, however, is between Point Conception, California, and Magdalena Bay. This species reaches a length of 44 inches and a weight of about 12 pounds, but most of the individuals captured by anglers are much smaller. Weights of 14–18 pounds have been reported, but are unverified.

The Pacific barracuda is brownish with a blue tinge, metallic-black or gray on the back, shading to silvery-white on the sides and ventral surface, with the tail yellowish. It lacks black blotches scattered on the sides of the body, as does the great barracuda. It has 5 dorsal spines and 10 dorsal rays; the anal elements consist of 2 spines followed typically by 9 rays. There are more than 150 scales along the lateral line. Its maxillary does not reach beyond a vertical from the posterior nostril, and the pectoral fin does not reach to a vertical from the insertion of the pelvic fin. The anterior rays of the second dorsal and anal fins do not reach the tip of the last ray when the fin is depressed. The posterior teeth of the mandible are not slanted backward.

There are at least 3 other species of barracudas in the eastern Pacific: *S. lucasana*, commonly called the Gulf barracuda, is distributed from Cedros Island to Cape San Lucas and throughout the Gulf of California (usually not north of San Juanico Bay on the outer coast). The exact north-south range of 2 other species, *S. ensis* and *S. idiastes*, is not known, but for the former may be given as Mazatlán to Panama, and for the latter as Panama to Peru and the Galápagos Islands. These 3 barracudas are not as large as *S. argentea;* none has ever been measured at over 30 inches or in excess of 4 pounds.

The Pacific barracuda is an excellent foodfish of some commercial importance.

SENNET *Sphyraena borealis*   This close relative of the Pacific barracuda rarely reaches a length of more than 15 inches. It occurs along the coast of New England and intergrades southward with the form called southern sennet (*S. picudilla*), with which it appears to be conspecific. The southern sennet occurs from Florida southward to Brazil.

The sennet has 5 dorsal spines, 10 dorsal rays, 11 anal rays, and 115–130 scales along the lateral line. The maxillary does not reach beyond a vertical from the posterior nostril. The pectoral fins do not reach to a vertical from the insertion of the pelvic fin. The anterior rays of the second dorsal and anal fins do not reach to the tip of the last ray when the fin is depressed. The posterior teeth of the mandible are not slanted backward. There are no black blotches scattered on the sides of the body.

Similar in habits to the Pacific barracuda, it is a schooling fish usually occurring not too far from shore. It is usually too small to be considered a gamefish except when taken by anglers on very light tackle with small spoons, plugs, and jigs.

It is excellent eating, and the flesh is never known to be poisonous. Especially in the American tropics, it is a commercial fish of some importance.

DORY FAMILY   Zeidae

AMERICAN JOHN DORY *Zenopsis ocellata*   This species occurs in the upper continental slope at depths of about 100–500 fathoms. It is a compressed, deep-bodied fish with a large mouth and projecting

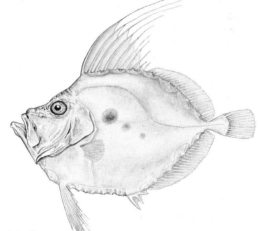

American John Dory

lower jaw. The species is restricted to the western North Atlantic and is found from Nova Scotia to Cape Hatteras. It has been taken up to a length of 24 inches and a weight of 7 pounds. A similar species occurs in the Pacific, the mirror dory (*Z. mebulosa*).

Its color is silvery all over. The young up to about 10 inches are marked on each side with about 12–24 vaguely outlined dark spots, irregularly arranged. Most of these spots disappear with growth, for specimens more than 16 inches in length have only one spot on each side a short distance behind the gill opening.

The body of the American John Dory is deep and flattened. Other distinguishing characteristics include: first dorsal fin with 9–10 spines, the first 3 prolonged, their length about equal to body depth, remainder progressively shorter; second dorsal fin with 25–27 softrays, low, extending almost to caudal peduncle; anal fin with 3 spines and 24–26 softrays, spines stout; pectorals small, inserted below and behind eye, tips of rays free; pelvics larger than pectorals, ventral to and in front of pectorals; caudal small, brush-shaped.

The head has a lower jaw projecting, large mouth set very obliquely, dorsal profile of head concave. The body is scaleless but with bony bucklers, each with one or more hooked thorns, arranged near dorsal and ventral edges; 2–3 along base of spiny dorsal, 4 along base of soft dorsal, 2 in midline in front of pelvic fins, 1 in midline behind pelvics, 6 pairs along belly to the anal fin, and 5 along base of anal fin.

GREENLING FAMILY   Hexagrammidae

KELP GREENLING *Hexagrammos decagrammus* One of the more important greenlings, this genus (4 species) is unique in having 5 lateral lines on each side of the body. The kelp greenling is a handsome fish of striking colors and considerable gameness. A bony support extends from each eye across the cheek just under the skin. The dorsal fin is long and has about 21 spines. There is a single anal fin spine. The fish has no canine teeth. There are 2 pairs of fleshy flaps on top of the head.

The kelp greenling is colored gray or brown in varying shades. An ocellus is situated at the posterior end of the rayed portion of the dorsal fin in both sexes; in the male it has a blue or copper tinge; in the female it often has a brown or bluish ground color. The forepart of the male has blue spots in an aureole of reddish-brown; in the female it is covered with small reddish-brown spots except ventrally.

The fish grows to a length of about 20 inches and a weight of 2–3 pounds.

It is distributed from Alaska to Point Conception, California. It frequents shallow water over rocky bottoms near shore, where it feeds on marine worms, crustaceans, and fishes.

Kelp Greenling

Lingcod

LINGCOD *Ophiodon elongatus* A Pacific marine species of some value both as a sport and commercial fish, the lingcod is known in many areas as the cultus cod. It occurs in North American waters from California to Alaska. As a rule these fish run at a wide range of depths from 2 to more than 70 fathoms.

The lingcod has a large mouth, large pectoral fins, a smooth body, and a long, continuous dorsal fin divided by a notch into spiny and soft parts. A young individual is slender throughout, but an older fish is moderately robust with a large head and jaws. The color is variable, usually mottled against a dark gray or brown body. Fish taken from the same reef are frequently colored alike, and as a result experienced anglers claim they distinguish the locale of capture by the fish's appearance.

Lingcod reach large size. The largest specimen recorded is 70 pounds, but the rather frequent occurrence of 50- to 60-pounders in commercial catches makes it probable that the 70-pound weight is occasionally exceeded. Maximum length runs $4-4^1/_2$ feet. Males are much smaller than females, and it is doubtful that they exceed 3 feet in length or a weight of 25 pounds. Female lingcod grow about $2^3/_4$ pounds per year, and males $1^3/_4$ pounds. The rate of growth is not constant throughout life, so that at 8 years of age a male lingcod weighs about $9^3/_4$ pounds and a female $14^3/_4$ pounds.

COBIA FAMILY Rachycentridae

COBIA *Rachycentron canadum* Also called the crabeater or ling, this species has a worldwide distribution in tropical and warm temperate waters. In the western Atlantic it is found from Bermuda and Massachusetts to Argentina (35° S) and is widespread in the Gulf of Mexico. This species has no close relatives and is placed in a family by itself.

The cobia is distinguished as follows: 8−10 dorsal spines; 28−33 dorsal rays; anal fin with 1 spine and 23−26 rays; body elongate, fusiform; head very long, much depressed; snout broad; mouth moderate, the lower jaw projecting; maxillary reaching anterior margin of eye; teeth small, in bands on both jaws, vomer, palatines, and tongue; 7−9 short gillrakers on lower limb of first arch.

Color is dark brown above, a paler brown on sides and below. A black lateral band, wider than the eye, extends from snout to base of caudal fin. The ventral surface of the head is pale; fins are mostly black. The black lateral band is very conspicuous in the young, but tends to become obscured in the adult.

The cobia feeds on crabs, shrimps, and small fishes of all kinds. The young are frequently caught in bays and inlets, but the adults prefer the shallow parts of the open ocean. They are attracted to floating objects of any kind, being found close to buoys, anchored vessels, and floating debris. Small live fish are very attractive bait. The largest cobia ever caught with hook and line was taken off Cape Charles,

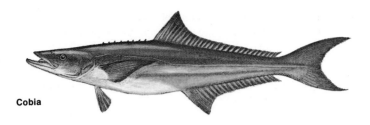

Cobia

Virginia, on July 3, 1938. It weighed 102 pounds and was 5 feet 10 inches in length.

The cobia is an exceptionally good foodfish. It is occasionally found in the market, but the commercial catch is very small. Adults of 30–50 pounds are commonly seen.

In the summer, this species migrates north as far as Chesapeake Bay and Cape Cod. In the fall, it apparently moves south to tropical waters.

MULLET FAMILY Mugilidae

Most mullets are tropical. Only 2 species frequent the mid-Atlantic coast, and 2 others occur mainly in Florida. Mullets are commonly found in brackish water and to a considerable extent in freshwater. Only the striped mullet is known on both Atlantic and Pacific coasts.

STRIPED MULLET *Mugil cephalus* The striped or black mullet has a spiny first dorsal fin with 4 spines and a soft dorsal fin with 1 spine and 8 softrays, the two well separated. The ventral fins are on the abdomen behind the point of insertion of the pectorals; the anal fin usually consists of 3 spines and 8 softrays, with only 2 spines in very small fish; the caudal fin is forked moderately deep. The soft dorsal and anal fins are almost naked (scaled in most other American mullets), but the body and head are clothed with large, rounded scales. Adults are bluish-gray or greenish above, silvery on the lower part of the sides and below; the scales on the sides have dark centers that form longitudinal lines. The lining of the body cavity is black. The striped mullet grows to 30 inches or more and over 15 pounds in warmer waters.

Along the east coast the striped mullet reaches northward to Cape Cod occasionally and southward to Brazil. It schools most densely off the southeastern United States and the Gulf of Mexico.

WHITE MULLET *Mugil curema* The white or silver mullet is known on the Atlantic coast from Cape Cod to Brazil. Two other mullets occur in portions of this range, *M. trichodon* (fantail mullet)

265

and *M. gaimardiana* (redeye mullet), but these are of very limited distribution.

The silvery sides of the white mullet lack the conspicuous dark stripes of the striped mullet. The small scales on the second dorsal and anal fins, except on the edges, also separate it from *M. cephalus*.

The white mullet averages about 5 inches. It seldom exceeds 1 foot in length and 2 pounds in weight.

In contrast with the striped mullet, which spawns during late fall or winter when water temperatures are falling, the white mullet begins spawning in early spring when water temperatures are rising over the continental shelf. The young spend the first several weeks of their lives in the open ocean. At a length of about $^3/_4$–1 inch, the larvae move inshore, where they thrive in estuarine habitats until they have reached lengths of up to 5 inches. These juveniles apparently move from the estuary areas to the outer beaches.

TRIPLETAIL FAMILY Lobotidae

TRIPLETAIL *Lobotes surinamensis* Also called the buoy fish, buoy bass, blackfish, and chobie, this species has a broad distribution in the Atlantic, Indian, and western Pacific oceans. In the western Atlantic it is found from Bermuda and Massachusetts to Argentina (38° S) and throughout the Gulf of Mexico. It has only one close relative, *L. pacificus*, found on the Pacific coast from Petacalco Bay, Mexico, to Panama.

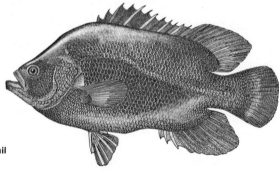

Tripletail

The tripletail is distinguished as follows: dorsal spines 12, rays 16; anal spines 3, rays 11; lateral scales 45; body deep, compressed; anterior profile concave; head small; mouth moderate, oblique; the lower jaw projecting; maxillary barely reaching middle of eye, 2.6–3.0 in head; teeth small, pointed, with an irregular outer series and a band of minute teeth behind it; dorsal spines strong, the median ones very slightly longer than the posterior ones, the soft part of fin much higher; ventral fins long, pointed, exceeding length of head to preopercular margin; pectoral fins very short.

The color varies widely, but most specimens seen have been black, brown, or yellow. Sometimes the yellow and brown of a large autumn leaf are perfectly imitated.

Although the adults seem to prefer a pelagic existence, the young are found close to shore, often in bays and estuaries. In such places, they are usually found floating on their sides at the surface. Both the movement and coloration of a dead leaf are imitated. This fish offers one of the best examples of protective mimicry in marine fishes.

The tripletail attains a length of 3 feet and a weight of 30–50 pounds. It is a good foodfish and puts up a strong fight when hooked. Tripletails are usually sought around wrecks, buoys, and floating or sunken debris. Live bait, such as shrimps, clams, and mullets, are preferred, but jigs and spinning lures are successful at times.

SNOOK FAMILY Centrompidae

FAT SNOOK *Centropomus parallelus* This is the second largest of the West Indian snooks. It occurs in Florida as far north as Lake Okeechobee and throughout the American Atlantic tropics. The fat snook occasionally reaches a total length of about 20 inches, but larger individuals are rare. The largest known specimen measured 28 inches in total length. The robust body is heavier than in the other species at the same length.

The fat snook has 79–92 lateral scales. Gillrakers 10–13, usually 11–12 on lower limb of first arch, not including rudiments. Anal rays 6. Pectoral rays 14–16, usually 15. Second anal spine not reaching beyond vertical from caudal base. Pectoral fins not reaching to a vertical from tip of pelvic. Pelvic fin reaching to or beyond anus. Maxillary reaching to or beyond a vertical from center of eye.

The greater number of lateral scales and the more robust body distinguish this snook from the others. A closely related species from Brazil, *C. constantinus*, has fewer lateral scales (68–79). Another relative, *C. poeyi*, from the vicinity of Veracruz, Mexico, usually has 9 dorsal rays instead of 10.

SNOOK *Centropomus undecimalis* An important marine gamefish. In the United States, this species occurs in most of Florida and in southwestern Texas. As a stray, it has been reported from as far north as Delaware. The snook is found throughout the American tropics on the Atlantic and Pacific sides. This is, by far, the largest and most common species of snooks. One of the heaviest specimens on record measured 4 feet 7 inches in total length and weighed 50 pounds 8 ounces. A related species, the black snook, occurs on the Pacific side of tropical America.

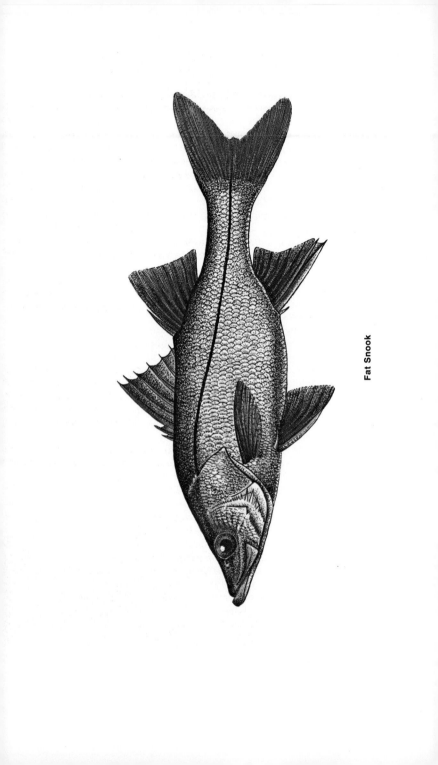

Fat Snook

Snook

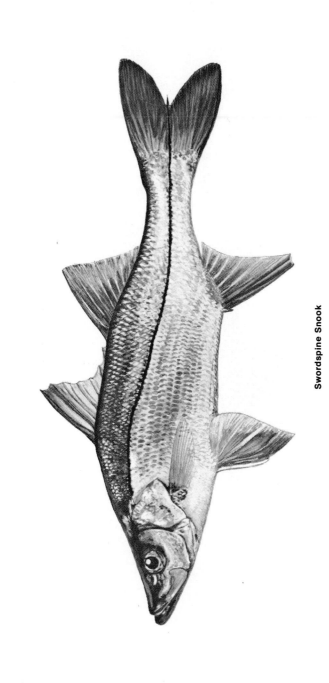

Swordspine Snook

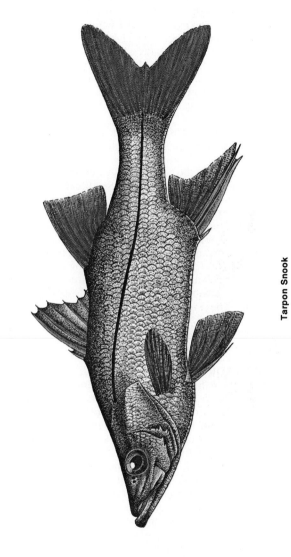

Tarpon Snook

The snook is long-bodied but thick through the middle, with the upper snout depressed and a protruding lower jaw. The color is variable according to habitat, but is usually a brownish or brown-gold on the back shading to a lighter color on the belly; it has a pronounced black lateral stripe along the sides, which extends to the tail. Lateral scales 67–78. Gillrakers 7–10, usually 8–9 on lower limb of first arch, not including rudiments. Anal rays 6. Pectoral rays 14–16, usually 15. Second anal spine not reaching to vertical from caudal base. Pectoral fin not reaching to vertical from tip of pelvic. Pelvic fin not reaching to anus. Maxillary reaching to or beyond vertical from center of eye.

This species is distinguished from the other Atlantic snooks by the fewer gillrakers, the shorter second anal spine, and the pelvic fins not reaching to the anus.

This snook occurs along the coast in saltwater, in addition to bays, estuaries, canals, and freshwater streams. Small, immature individuals, less than a year old, usually occur in the marginal areas of coastal lagoons and estuaries. Adults occur well inland, being caught in Florida's Lake Okeechobee with some frequency.

The common snook feeds primarily on fishes, but crustaceans are also an important food item. The spawning season extends from June to November. This species may reach the age of at least 7 years, and nearly all specimens are mature by their third year of life. The common snook, and probably the other species of snooks also, is very sensitive to cold. The minimum temperature tolerated is about 60° F.

The common snook is presently being considered for more widespread introduction into freshwater areas of Florida.

SWORDSPINE SNOOK *Centropomus ensiferus* This is the smallest and rarest of the snooks. It occurs in extreme southern Florida and southward throughout the American Atlantic tropics. Full-grown adults probably do not attain a total length of much more than 12 inches. The common and scientific names refer to the long second anal spine. Two related species, *C. armatus* and *C. robalito*, occur on the Pacific side of tropical America.

The swordspine occurs in estuaries and in the lower course of streams and canals. It has 49–59 lateral line scales. Gillrakers 12–16 on lower limb of first arch, not including rudiments. Anal rays 6. Pectoral rays 14–16, usually 15. Second anal spine reaching beyond vertical from caudal base. Pectoral fins reaching to vertical from tip of pelvic. Pelvic fin reaching to or beyond anus. Maxillary not reaching beyond vertical from center of eye.

In addition to its smaller size, this snook is distinguished from the other Atlantic species by the longer second anal spine and the fewer lateral line scales.

TARPON SNOOK *Centropomus pectinatus*   In the United States, this species is confined to Florida, from the Caloosahatchee River southward. It occurs throughout the American Atlantic tropics. Although larger than the swordspine snook, the maximum known size attained is about 16 inches in total length. The common name refers to the upturned snout, reminiscent of the tarpon. A very close, nearly identical relative, *C. grandoculatus*, occurs on the Pacific side of tropical America.

The tarpon snook occurs in bays, estuaries, and the lower course of freshwater streams and canals.

The tarpon snook has 62–72 lateral scales. Gillrakers 15–18 on lower limb of first arch, not including rudiments. Anal rays 7. Pectoral rays 13–15, usually 14. Second anal spine not reaching beyond vertical from caudal base. Pectoral fin not reaching to vertical from tip of pelvic. Pelvic fin reaching beyond anus. Maxillary not reaching to vertical from center of eye.

The greater number of anal rays, fewer pectoral rays, and more upturned snout distinguish this species from the other Atlantic snooks. Also, the body is much more compressed.

INDEX OF FISHES

Page numbers set in *italics* indicate the main entry of a fish, and page numbers in **boldface** indicate illustrations. Page numbers for passing references to fishes are set in roman type.

277

280